Christian Character in the
Gospel of Luke

1980.

Christian Character
in the
Gospel of Luke

Brian E. Beck

EPWORTH PRESS

Fernley-Hartley lecture
1978.
Published 1989.

For Margaret

*

British Library Cataloguing in Publication Data

Beck, Brian E.
    Christian character in the Gospel of Luke.
    1. Bible.   N. T. Luke – Critical studies
    I. Title
    226'.406

    ISBN 0-7162-0463-0

First published 1989
by Epworth Press
Room 195, 1 Central Buildings, Westminster
London SW1H 9NR

Phototypeset by J&L Composition Ltd,
Filey, North Yorkshire
and printed in Great Britain by
Billing & Sons Ltd, Worcester

Contents

	Abbreviations	vi
	Foreword	vii
1	Introduction	1
2	Love	16
3	Wealth – I	28
4	Wealth – II	46
5	A Sense of God	55
6	Faith	71
7	Discipleship	93
8	Imitation?	105
9	The Pharisaic Mind	127
10	Luke's Structure	145
11	Conclusions	170
	Notes	187
	Bibliographical Details	211
	Index of authors cited in the notes	213
	Scripture Index	215
	Subject Index	229

Abbreviations

AG	W.F. Arndt, F.W. Gingrich, *A Greek-English Lexicon of the NT and Other Early Christian Literature*, Cambridge and Chicago 1957
A&P	R.H. Charles, *Apocrypha & Pseudepigrapha of the Old Testament*, Oxford 1913
BC	F.J. Foakes Jackson, K. Lake, *The Beginnings of Christianity, pt I The Acts of the Apostles*, London 1920–1933
BD	F. Blass, A. Debrunner, R.W. Funk, *A Greek Grammar of the NT and Other Early Christian Literature*, Cambridge and Chicago 1961
ChQ	*The Church Quarterly*, London 1968–
ET	*The Expository Times*, Edinburgh 1889–
JB	*The Jerusalem Bible*, London 1966
JBL	*The Journal of Biblical Literature*, Philadelphia 1882–
JTS	*The Journal of Theological Studies*, Oxford 1899–, new series 1950–
LXX	The Septuagint
MH	J.H. Moulton, W.F. Howard, N. Turner, *A Grammar of NT Greek*, Edinburgh 1906–1976
MNT	R.E. Brown, K.P. Donfried, J.A. Fitzmyer, J. Reumann, *Mary in the New Testament*, Philadelphia and New York 1978
NEB	*New English Bible*, Oxford and Cambridge 1961, 1970
NT	*Novum Testamentum*, Leiden 1956–
NTS	*New Testament Studies*, Cambridge 1954–
PNT	R.E. Brown, K.P. Donfried, J. Reumann, *Peter in the New Testament*, London 1974
RSV	*Revised Standard Version*, London 1952
SJT	*Scottish Journal of Theology*, Edinburgh 1948–
TDNT	G. Kittel, G. Friedrich, *Theological Dictionary of the New Testament*, Grand Rapids 1964–76
VT	*Vetus Testamentum*, Leiden 1951–

The Dead Sea Scrolls, the Mishnah and the Talmud are cited by the standard abbreviations.

Foreword

The chapters that follow develop ideas originally put
forward in the Fernley-Hartley Lecture delivered at the
Methodist Conference of 1978. That they have taken so
long to appear in this form is due in part to the pressure
of other duties which left far too little time for reading and
research. The bulk of the writing was done during five
months of sabbatical leave in 1983. Such time as has been
available since then has had to be devoted to completion and
revision, and, as the discerning student will immediately
notice, it has not been possible to take account of more recent
work on Luke. I hope nevertheless that the reader will catch
some of the excitement I have felt in trying to pay close
attention to the text of Luke's gospel and reflecting on its
meaning.

The heart of this work is close textual study. I have done
my best to make it readable, but it depends for what validity
it may have upon frequent reference to the text and the
implications of small details. Large numbers of biblical
quotations are inevitable, and the strength of the argument
will only be appreciated if they are looked up. Reluctantly I
have transliterated the Greek and Hebrew, avoiding the
unsightliness which comes from trying to distinguish long
and short vowels or iota subscript. Those who cannot read
the original are not much helped by such detail, and those
who can do not need it. Reference to the original languages if
often essential to the argument, but I have always assumed
that some readers will not be familiar with them, and have
tried not to put them at a disadvantage. For the same reason I

have usually referred to scholarly works in their English editions where available.

I gladly pay tribute to those who have especially made this work possible: to the Leverhulme Trust for a research grant to cover my sabbatical leave in 1983; to the members of the ecumenical community at Hengrave Hall who gave me a home during that period and at intervals since, and kept me going by their loving enthusiasm and encouragement; and to the Fernley-Hartley Trustees for their initial invitation to give the Lecture and the editorial committee of the Epworth Press for their willingness to publish the final text. Particular acknowledgment must be made of the help I have received from scholars with whom I was able to discuss the project in its early stages: Professor Kingsley Barrett, the late Professor G.W.H. Lampe, and especially Professor C.F.D. Moule, whose encouragement has always been far more generous than I could deserve. My thanks must also go to Mrs Alison Woodgate for her help in typing part of the work and to John and Vivienne Vickers who have very generously prepared the indexes. Lastly, none of this would have been possible without the patience and support of my wife, whose contribution, in allowing me the freedom to pursue this project, is to be found on every page.

London
August 1989

1

Introduction

In 1944 F. B. Clogg produced a study entitled *The Christian Character in the Early Church* in which he argued that the New Testament sets forth an ideal of Christian character which was formed, not as an abstraction by combining ideal virtues but as a reflection of the life of Jesus as he actually lived it. Today the limitations of his study are obvious. He adopted a standpoint common to many British scholars of the time which was dismissive both of the form-critical method associated with R. Bultmann and others, and of the eschatological emphasis associated with Johannes Weiss and Albert Schweitzer. His work antedated the development of redaction criticism and the publication of the Dead Sea Scrolls. He generalized too much, his title '*The* Christian Character', betraying his assumption that the New Testament speaks with one voice. Furthermore he treated the gospels indiscriminately as sources for a portrait of Jesus, created by harmonization from all four. The question to which he addressed himself, however, remains an interesting one to which little attention has been given since.

'Character' is defined by the *Oxford English Dictionary* as among other things, 'the aggregate of the distinctive features of any thing ... the sum of the moral and mental qualities which distinguish an individual or a race, viewed as a homogeneous whole.'[1] The two aspects of wholeness and distinctiveness are alike important and underlie the question which we intend to put to Luke's gospel: what sort of person does Luke expect a Christian to be? In part this is a study of Christian ethics, although we shall be more concerned with typical responses than with specific moral problems. But it also includes spiritual attitudes and practices. In other words, what is the configuration of personality and style of life which in Luke's view should identify the disciple of Jesus?

Few of the details in the pages that follow have any claim to originality. All the topics we shall deal with have been thoroughly examined by others in separate studies. In this book, however, we are concerned with the overall picture, the 'aggregate of features', to which the definition refers. We are also concerned with their distinctiveness. In part this means the distinctiveness of Luke's view as contrasted with that of other New Testament writers and in particular the other synoptic evangelists whose material he partly shares. This will occupy us throughout our study as we try to specify what Luke's view is, by referring to differences between Luke and parallel passages, and by relating particular instances to the overall impact of the gospel and Acts. But the wider question is also raised: in what ways does Luke expect the Christian disciple to be distinguishable from the best representatives of Jewish or pagan piety? To this we shall return at the end.

It is evident that Luke's gospel is not a straightforward treatise on Christian character. It has been traditionally regarded as a gospel, and whatever the precise definition of that class of literature, it is clear that Luke himself regards the central theme of his work as the activity and teaching of Jesus, the events which have now come to fulfilment (cf. Luke 1.1; Acts 1.1). To a large extent therefore we are exploring the assumptions Luke makes in his writing, the profile he holds at the back of his mind of the ideal Christian, which is revealed in his choice of material for his gospel and the emphasis he gives to certain aspects of it, but is never explicitly set forth in one place. Nevertheless the result of our examination will be to discover that the question of Christian character is more important to him than is sometimes recognized. While not the chief purpose of his work, it is one of his main concerns and to some extent explains the contents and arrangement of the gospel.

This procedure involves some assumptions of my own, and I owe it to the reader to state them clearly at the outset. They are assumptions only in the sense that they have to be

taken for granted in this book. They have been adequately
defended by others and do not need to be restated in detail.
The first is that the two-document theory is still the most
adequate explanation of the relationship between the first
three gospels.[2] This identifies Mark as the earliest gospel and
a source for the other two, and postulates an additional source
for Matthew and Luke, conventionally referred to as 'Q'. In
spite of recent attacks on this theory, it remains difficult to
say why the shorter Mark should have been written, if either
Matthew or Luke (which incorporate almost all its contents)
already existed, or why its author, who lays proportionately
greater stress on Jesus as a teacher than any other gospel
writer, should have omitted so much of the teaching which
both the other gospels contain if he knew them. It is hard also
to believe that Luke was dependent on Matthew, both
because of details in the text (why should Luke, who is
so concerned with the right use of wealth, have omitted
Matthew's description of Joseph of Arimathea as a rich man,
Matt. 27.57?) and because of the overall peculiarity that
Luke follows Mark's outline but systematically allocates the
additional material he is supposed to have derived from
Matthew to new Marcan contexts. We are therefore obliged
to work with the view, still adopted by the majority of contemporary scholars, that Luke used Mark, but not Matthew,
and that in common with the latter he employed the source
known as 'Q'. Whether the original order of 'Q' can now be
recovered, and whether it was a single document or a series of
documents, or even, as is more probable, represents several
oral and written sources, are questions which need not now
concern us. Nor need we go into the question whether Luke
proceeded by incorporating Mark into a previously compiled
gospel of his own (the so-called 'Proto-Luke'), although the
evidence is against it.[3]

Our second assumption is that before being written down
the material in the gospels was transmitted in oral form and
in the process underwent various modifications as it was
adapted to new contexts in the life of the church. The work of
the gospel writers is but the last stage in this process, carried
out more systematically and on a larger scale. This view
combines the insights of form criticism and redaction criticism.[4]
At all stages a tension can be observed between adaptation

and innovation on the one hand and fidelity to tradition on the other. Gospel writers along with their predecessors in the oral tradition felt free to present the deeds and sayings of Jesus in new ways that would communicate the truth as they perceived it, yet to some extent they felt bound by the forms and content of the traditions as they had received them. The widely differing forms of the nativity stories in Matthew and Luke illustrate one side of the tension, some of the more obscure gospel sayings, which can only be accounted for as unassimilated tradition, illustrate the other; both are apparent in the passion narratives. Whether the evangelists or the oral teachers reflected upon the process in which they were engaged as we have just done is doubtful; what they did probably seemed the natural thing to do.

Two consequences follow from all this. One is that the recovery of a proper historical statement of the words and deeds of Jesus 'as they actually happened' is a difficult and technical task which in the nature of the case can have only limited success. In the final analysis there can be no definitive objective statement of events so long ago for which we have only much later accounts and no primary source material; even for contemporary events an 'objective' account is only relatively so, for everything must be narrated from the standpoint of some observer. The point to be underlined, however, is that we are concerned in our study with Luke's presentation of the activity and teaching of Jesus, and not with the historical truth that lies behind it. We shall ask what Luke betrays of his own understanding of Jesus and discipleship by writing as he does, not what we may understand of Jesus himself as a figure in history. If the reader is sometimes tempted to think we are analysing Luke as though he were a novelist entirely free to dispose of his narrative as he chose, our reply is that while historical questions about Jesus are important, they are not relevant to the study we are conducting here. Whether Luke disposed of his narrative freely or under constraint from the traditions he inherited, he will have understood them in a certain way, and we are trying to recover that understanding.

The second consequence, however, is that Luke did not work with an entirely free hand. Recently some interpreters have sought to show that the gospel was more or less a free composition, developing themes found in Matthew, Mark and the Old Testament. The Jewish term 'midrash' has been used to describe this, although the appropriateness of the term has been disputed.[5] But while it can be shown that, for example, the vocabulary of the Lucan parables is distinctively his, and that the good Samaritan and the prodigal son in their present form owe much to his artistry, it has not been shown that they are entirely his creations. Certain passages, such as the sayings in the middle of chapter 16 and the beginning of 17 remain obstinately difficult to account for except as Luke's adaptation of traditional material which he has only partially made subservient to his purpose. Attempts to explain them by reference to Old Testament models remain unconvincing.[6] We are obliged to work with the assumption that for most of his gospel Luke was, with varying degrees of freedom, an adaptor.

This does not require us, however, to follow a procedure of identifying at every place the form in which Luke received his material before asserting the use he has made of it. Where we have Mark's text before us, the agreements and disagreements help us to see more clearly what is distinctive about Luke. Without Mark the re-creation of sources is more speculative, and may in the end be circular. Even where there is a parallel in Matthew it is of only limited help, for there is no infallible method for determining which represents the original 'Q' version. At best it sets Luke's version in relief. Vocabulary in this regard is also of only limited help. We do not have a definitive list of the words Luke knew and used. In some instances the presence of a word commonly found in Luke and rare elsewhere may suggest an editorial touch; it cannot, however, be proved.[7] Conversely, the presence of words which are uncommon in Luke cannot be used as evidence that in such passages he is reproducing a source untouched. Luke is too varied a writer to be tied to a limited vocabulary. It is impossible on purely linguistic grounds to distinguish tradition and redaction. For this reason we shall not engage in exhaustive linguistic analyses of the passages we examine, and for this the reader will no doubt be grateful.

There are in fact three criteria which can be safely used to reach an understanding of Luke's view. Underlying them is the assumption that the gospel as a whole and in its parts represents what Luke wanted to say (or if the more cautious expression is preferred, what he felt bound to say). If he could not identify himself with an item of tradition he had the option of omitting it, and Mark shows that on occasions he exercised that option. The three criteria are, (*a*) in the case of parallels with Mark, a detailed study of omissions, additions, amendments and rearrangements, both within individual pericopae or sections, and in the plan of the gospel overall; and elsewhere, (*b*) detailed editorial evidence, such as the recurrence of particular themes, words or phrases, and sometimes signs of editorial arrangement such as the 'flagging' in advance of topics which are then dealt with in sequence,[8] and, (*c*) on a larger scale, the overall thrust of the book, the balance of its emphases, and the stage at which topics are introduced. As with any other narrative book whose sources are now inaccessible to us, these are the tools which have to be used to ascertain what the author is wanting to say.

Throughout our study we shall refer to the author as 'Luke'. For the sake of convenience all the evangelists are referred to by their traditional names without intending commitment to any particular theory of their identity. In the case of the third gospel and Acts a strong case can be made for holding one writer to be responsible for both; and there are good arguments, although less strong, in favour of identifying him as Luke, a companion of Paul. In the nature of the case they cannot be conclusive. The strongest ground is that the identification is traditional and ancient, although this could simply be the outcome of the use in ancient times of the kind of reasoning we now use to support it. The differences between the narrative of Acts and the evidence of Paul's letters suggest that any association between Paul and our author lay well in the past. On these and other grounds a relatively late date, towards the end of the first century but not into the second, is likely. Acts may have been planned from the outset as a sequel to the gospel; it was certainly written with the gospel in mind, though perhaps after an interval.[9] It is probable that the readers Luke had in mind were Gentiles. They were not unfamiliar with the Old Testament but relatively ignorant of contemporary Jewish thought and practice, as we shall see.

If the gospel and Acts are a pair from one hand it may be

asked why we are confining our study to the gospel. Would it not be more reasonable to range over the whole double work? From time to time we shall in fact look at evidence from Acts, especially where this is helpful in confirming or illustrating conclusions we draw from the gospel, but the nature of the two books justifies confining our exploration to the first. While it is true that the gospel is not a formal treatise on Christian character, it is a didactic book in a way that Acts is not. Both, as we shall see later, can present narrative with an exemplary purpose, but the words and deeds of Jesus are determinative for Luke in a way that is not true of apostolic figures. The speeches and sermons of Acts present samples of Christian preaching but their content differs from much of the teaching in the gospels. In Acts, Christians are regularly referred to as disciples, but the meaning of this term is governed by what is said of discipleship in the gospel. In short, the gospel invites our study in a way that Acts does not, and extending it systematically to Acts would not materially add to it.

How important is the question we have raised? Earlier generations were more evidently interested than ours in specifying the character which the Christian believer was expected to display and cultivate, as is shown by the neglect of our question by recent scholarship. It is a concern more appropriate to a settled age with more clearly defined and unified expectations of behaviour in society. It tends also to be individualistic in emphasis and views discipleship in a static way, unrelated to growth or responses to changing circumstances. In recent times the social framework has changed and fragmented. In Christian theology and ethics the emphasis is more upon the problems of society and Christians' collective response to them, and this encourages a more dynamic view of discipleship in terms of evils to be attacked and causes to be supported. But one cannot wholly divorce what a Christian believer is expected to do from the sort of person he is supposed to be. Debates about the involvement of Christians in radical and revolutionary movements for social change and their association with violence illustrate the fundamental association of the two. Life is not only about response to special needs, but about habitual responses, the choice of priorities which govern day-to-day living and the expectations others come to have of one, built up by observation over years and dependable in a crisis.

Moreover, Christian character is a subject with which, we shall submit, Luke is in fact concerned. This study took its origin from reflection on the text of Luke. Certain passages, notably 16.14, suggested the question; it was not imposed from outside. If recent scholarship has not attended to it, this may be because modern scholars have been distracted by their own preoccupations. It is at least worth exloring whether we are hearing what Luke is trying to say.

For this reason much of the following pages will be exegetical in character. From time to time it will be necessary to summarize and synthesize, with references for the reader to look up, but much of our work will rely on the attempt to discern what particular passages are saying. The force of our argument will become apparent only if readers study the passages alongside the synoptic parallels for themselves, preferably in the original.

Before we can properly begin, however, it will be necessary to close off two lines of inquiry which turn out to be dead ends. They might have been more fruitful. The fact that they are not must at least be recorded. The first of these is to investigate Luke's ethical vocabulary. It might have been thought that if Luke was interested in questions of character, the fact would be revealed in his use of language. Common Christian terms, or, if his sympathies lay elsewhere, the terminology of other groups would be in frequent use. This turns out not to be the case.

To deal with common Christian vocabulary first, in his chapter on 'The Christian character as a concrete conception', Clogg offered an outline of the Pauline ideal. Beside referring to the newness of the Christian life and its relation to Christ himself, he listed nine chief characteristics: love (*agape*), longsuffering or patience (*makrothymia*), endurance or fortitude (*hypomone*), humility (*tapeinophrosyne*), meekness (*praytes*), gentleness (*epieikeia*), self-control (*enkrateia*), and the avoidance of covetousness and fornication (*pleonexia, porneia*). He did not confine himself to the occurrences of the actual words, but included other passages expressing the same ideas, but he clearly considered these concepts to sum up the Pauline ideal. How far his analysis is correct we need not consider here, although if we turn to a passage in which Paul himself might be thought to be setting out his ideal, the 'fruits of the Spirit' in Gal. 5.22f. we find a list which only partly overlaps with Clogg's: 'love, joy, peace, patience, kindness, goodness, faithfulness, gentleness, self-control'. The point of interest for us, however, is that only a few of these words are common in Luke or Acts: joy, faith, peace, the adjective good and the verb to love. Most occur occasionally in either Luke or Acts but rarely in both; meekness does not occur at all.[10] Of course analyses of vocabulary have limited value. Of Paul's own list in Galatians 5 'self-control' does not occur anywhere else in his letters, 'goodness' only three more times and the adjective 'good' as applied to persons only once.[11] A writer's ideas are not necessarily expressed consistently in a fixed vocabulary. Nevertheless, most of the words we have been reviewing have some wider currency in the New Testament, and Luke's sparing use of them marks him off not only from Paul but to some extent from other contemporary Christian writers. This point becomes more evident still if we look at the list of the 'works of the flesh' in Gal. 5.19–21. Only six of the fifteen terms in that passage occur in either of Luke's two volumes.[12]

A similar end is reached if we consider other vocabulary upon which Luke might have drawn. Both in the pagan and the Jewish worlds there were available rich stocks of terms for moral and religious characteristics, some of them extremely common. It is striking how rarely some of them occur in the New Testament generally, and it is perhaps especially surprising in the case of Luke, if one recalls his general indebtedness to the Old Testament and the evidence of his acquaintance with the culture of the non-Jewish world. If with the aid of a concordance one takes a random selection of Old Testament terms, especially righteousness (*tsedaqah*), 'holy' (*qadosh*), 'lovingkindness' (*chesed*), 'truth' (*'emeth*), 'blameless' (*tamim*), 'upright' (*yashar*), and looks for their common LXX Greek equivalents in the New Testament (*dikaiosyne, hagios, eleos, aletheia, amomos, amemptos, euthys*), including verbs, nouns and adjectives in each case, one finds that only the first two are strongly represented both in the Lucan writings and in the New Testament as a whole. The next two, lovingkindess and truth, while common in the

New Testament, are much less common in Luke. The remaining words occur only seven or eight times each in the New Testament, and only once or twice in Luke. A similar random list of common Greek ethical terms might produce virtue (*arete*), self-sufficiency (*autarkeia*), freedom from emotion (*apatheia*), piety (*eusebeia, eulabeia*), conscience (*syneidesis*), wisdom (*phronesis*), moderation (*sophrosyne*), desire (*epithymia*), pleasure (*hedone*), emotion (*pathos*). All of these occur in the New Testament except the distinctively Stoic *apatheia*, although only *eusebeia, epithymia* and *syneidesis*, with more than ten occurrences each, can be called common. In Acts there are between one and three examples each of desire (the verb), piety (both words), conscience and moderation. Luke's gospel offers one example each of piety (*eulabeia*), pleasure, wisdom, and the verb *sophronein* in the sense of 'be of sound mind'. There are five occurrences of the noun and verb 'desire'.

Of course such a cursory survey, which has made no attempt to distinguish different shades of meaning, can be used only with caution, but it underlines the fact that if we are to get at Luke's understanding of Christian character it will not be by a simple analysis of dominant ethical terms. By this criterion we might think he had no interest in the subject. It certainly reinforces the point that his gospel is not primarily an ethical treatise. But three points need to be borne in mind, for they illustrate the limitations of this kind of approach. The first is that within the New Testament generally, although we encounter lists of virtues and vices from time to time, particularly in the epistles, the vocabulary employed is surprisingly varied, and it is clear that no standard terminology for Christian character had developed. Secondly, there is a difference between Jewish and Greek traditions in this area. The Hellenistic philosophical schools were accustomed to discussing morality in abstract terms. The Old Testament tradition is more concrete. It employs verbs and metaphors more frequently than abstract nouns. So central a concept as obedience for example is expressed, not by a noun but by such expressions as 'hear' or 'walk in the way of' God's commandments. So a list of Old Testament ethical terms would very likely omit altogether such central duties as care for parents and observance of the sabbath. Further, while the

New Testament writers, like the Greek translators of the Old Testament before them, did employ Greek ethical vocabulary, one reason why some terms (such as *apatheia*) are not common is because they express ideals foreign to their thought, while other, un-Greek, concepts, (such as humility, *tapeinophrosyne*) come to the fore, or like *agape*, love, are given new depth of meaning. In our study therefore, while word studies will play their part, and in some cases we shall find evidence of words and concepts which Luke likes to employ, we shall have to range more widely and look at the content of the teaching of Jesus and the narratives which Luke presents.

A second line of inquiry is to follow up Luke's understanding of repentance, for the call to repentance is an important theme in the Lucan writings. He uses the noun and verb 'repentance' and 'repent' fourteen times in the gospel and eleven times in Acts, accounting for nearly half the occurrences in the New Testament. For Luke 'repentance and forgiveness' together sum up the Christian good news.[13]

Whether Luke considered the need for repentance to be universal is at first sight uncertain. The summons to all to repent (Acts 17.30) is counterbalanced by his description of righteous Israelites (Luke 1.5f., 26ff.; 2.25, 37). But this need not mean that they do not need to repent. Cornelius' godliness is twice favourably described in Acts 10.4, 31, but the conclusion to be drawn from his receiving the Spirit is nevertheless that God has granted Gentiles repentance (11.18). Certainly the contrast between righteous and sinners in Luke 5.32, 7.47, 15.7 should not be pressed to mean that Luke believed that there was a category of persons not needing salvation – 11.39ff., 16.15, 18.9ff., 20.20, 46f. show that he had serious reservations about such people. Whatever their virtues in other respects, in some of their attitudes and particularly in their attitude to Jesus they still needed to repent.

Discipleship at all events presupposes repentance. If there were any doubt of this it would be dispelled by 5.32 where to Mark's 'I came not to call the righteous, but sinners' (Mark 2.17) Luke adds the words 'to repentance'. He wants to remove any doubt that may linger around the phrase 'a friend of sinners' (7.34). Jesus welcomed sinners and assured them of forgiveness only on the ground of their repentance.

The importance of this for our study is obvious. If we could deduce from the sayings on repentance and forgiveness any information about Luke's understanding of sin it would help to give form to his idea of Christian character. What is the disciple to avoid? What is the fruit which is fitting evidence of repentance (3.8), the good fruit to be expected of the good tree (6.43ff.)? For the most part, however, Luke's language is very general. While forgiveness of sins is frequently stressed, both in the ministry of Jesus and in the preaching of the church, there is little detail about what he has in mind.[14] Of course the advantage of such general language is that it permits a wider range of application, but it does not help us to get at Luke's ideas. His vocabulary is a little more limited than the other gospels, for he avoids 'trespass' (*paraptoma*), as also the Pauline word 'transgression' (*parabasis*), and is sparing with the concepts of debt (*opheilein*, especially 13.4, and cf. 11.4 with Matt. 6.12) and law-breaking (*anomos, anomia*, 22.37, Acts 2.23 only). This suggests that he does not particularly understand sin in terms of breaking the commandments of the law, but there is not a wide vocabulary for sin in the New Testament anyway.[15] On the other hand he regularly uses *hamartia* ('sin') in both singular and plural, and, as 7.47 shows, thinks of sin in terms of individual acts which can be numbered rather than as a condition of sinfulness. This is evidence against the view that 'sinners' is just a description of a social class, those who were ostracised by the Pharisees for failure to adopt and observe Pharisaic interpretations of the law.[16] Such a view is unlikely for Luke anyway, as announcing 'forgiveness' for such would imply endorsement of the Pharisaic view of them, and Luke is not sympathetic to Pharisaic views, as we shall see. But beyond this we have to glean clues as to the content of sinful acts mostly from incidental remarks. The one passage which refers to 'this sin' is Acts 7.60, but it is not clear how far Luke is thinking of the stoning of Stephen simply as the sin of murder or as the rebellious rejection of God through his spokesman (cf. 7.51–53). The same uncertainty attaches to the prayer of Jesus (Luke 23.34, cf. Acts 3.14f.) and the deceit practised by Ananias and Sapphira which is against the Holy Spirit (Acts

5.3, 9). In both cases the predominant idea may be the act committed against God in the person of his representative, Jesus in the one case and Peter in the other, rather than cruelty or deception against a human being.

We probably see some reflection of Luke's own attitude in the behaviour condemned by the Pharisee in the parable at 18.11; the tax-collector is admittedly a sinner (v. 13), so there is no reason to think that Luke intends us to dissent from the Pharisee's judgment on the other items in his list, extortion (or rapacity), injustice and adultery. These terms recur. Rapacity is found again in 11.39 in conjunction with the general term wickedness, and greed at 12.15.[17] It is the key to what must be avoided in the advice of the Baptist in 3.10–14. Injustice is a broad term, as is justice (11.42), and we are given no guidance as to how Luke understands either. Adultery is prohibited again in the quotation of the commandments in 18.20, and reflected also in 16.18. The tax-collector in the parable is not specifically accused of these faults and the nature of his sinfulness is not made clear. Elsewhere in Luke as in Matthew and Mark tax-collectors are bracketed with sinners (5.30; 7.34; 15.1) in what has clearly become a conventional phrase. The original reason may have been that they were regarded as belonging to an unclean profession, or as traitors, or simply as too dishonest to be trusted.[18] Luke probably thought of them as dishonest, as 3.12 and the words of Zacchaeus in 19.8 suggest, but there is no reason to think that he believed this to be their only fault, or that he was interested in more precise reasons why they should be classed as sinners.

Luke mentions other vices elsewhere. Gluttony and drunkenness are accusations made against Jesus (7.34), and Luke is likely to have felt that they carried as much of a sting as the accusation that John the Baptist suffered from demon possession (7.33). Such conduct is reflected in the description of the untrustworthy servant in 12.45, where bullying is also referred to, in the behaviour of those who are unready at the last day (21.34), and presumably in the reference to the prodigal's 'loose living' (15.13). In this connection prostitutes are also mentioned (15.30).[19] Whether loose living was the prodigal's only sin is not clear. He admits that he has offended against his father (15.18, 21), but whether this includes his claiming the property and leaving home as well as his subsequent behaviour depends on the legal background which is uncertain.[20] Highway robbers are mentioned in 10.30, 22.52, although the criminals at the crucifixion are not called this in Luke, but simply felons (*kakourgoi*) who are deservedly punished (23.32, 39–41). Barabbas is convicted of revolution and murder, and Luke shows by repetition of the phrase his abhorrence of the release of one guilty of such acts in exchange for Jesus (23.19, 25).

Luke knows that the Gentile Christians of his day have been released from circumcision and the law of Moses by the decision of the Jerusalem Council in Acts 15; hence perhaps his sparing use of words like 'trespass'. All that is required of them is now summed up in the so-called 'apostolic decrees' (Acts 15.20, 29; 21.29). It is often held that these represent provisions for enabling Jewish and Gentile Christians to share meals, since food offered to idols, meat slaughtered without drawing the blood, blood as an element of diet, and (less certainly) marriage within forbidden degrees of consanguinity, are all prohibitions laid on Gentiles as well as Jews in Lev. 17 and 18.[21] Luke does not allude to this purpose, however, and it is not certain how far he was aware of their precise force; he may for example have interpreted unchastity (*porneia*) more widely. At all events, because the law is no longer binding on Gentile Christians we should be cautious in our estimate of the way Luke depicts Paul in Acts or the families of John and Jesus in the first two chapters of the gospel as law-abiding. His primary aim was to show the continuity between Christianity and the faith of Israel; it was not through renegades that the two were linked.[22] This tells us little about Luke's expectations of behaviour for his Gentile contemporaries, any more than the fact that Jesus tells the Pharisees that they ought to continue their tithing (Luke 11.42) indicates Gentile Christian obligation. Some at least of the commandments, however, do seem to have force for Luke. This is particularly true of the two love commands in 10.26ff., which we shall discuss in the next chapter, and some of the ten commandments. He depicts Jesus endorsing the prohibition of adultery, murder, theft and false witness and the injunction to honour parents, and perhaps by implication the whole decalogue, in his response to the ruler in 18.20.[23] Others of the ten commandments are alluded to elsewhere. Covetousness may be reflected in Acts 20.33 and idolatry as such is repudiated in Acts 14.14ff., 17.22ff. (cf. 10.26). The main exception in this context concerns Jesus' attitude to the sabbath, but on this the issue is how rather than whether it should be observed.

All this is very ordinary. In 12.10 Luke refers to blasphemy against the Holy Spirit as the one unforgivable sin.[24] With this exception, which has a specifically religious reference, all the items in the above list of sins represent a very conventional inventory of moral values with which few in the ancient world would have quarrelled. It is also superficial. We do not see here the sensitivity of a Paul or an Augustine, or even the inward emphasis of Matt. 5.21ff.[25] But the list is important in trying to determine what Luke understood by repentance. The Christian disciple will at least have repudiated all this. It is important in another way. It throws into relief the areas in which we encounter Luke's chief concerns, only hinted at so far, to which he devotes much more space. Passages we have yet to examine will show that the sins against which he most wants to urge Christians to be on their guard are those connected with wealth on the one hand and the Pharisees on the other.

Attempts to obtain a clear impression of Luke's under-standing of Christian character by concentrating upon his ethical vocabulary or his ideas of sin thus fail to produce the evidence we need. They illustrate the fact that Luke's Gospel is not in the formal sense a treatise on character (in the sense that, say, Theophrastus' *Characters* discusses systematically different character types or the books of Proverbs and the Wisdom of ben-Sira concentrate on moral advice), and he does not primarily express himself by means of abstract nouns and adjectives. We shall get further if we look at particular passages and themes in the gospel, and at the often slight changes he makes in the material he reproduces from his sources. These will reveal to a surprising degree the interest Luke has in our question.

2

Love

We turn in our search for Luke's understanding of Christian character to the sermon on the plain in Luke 6.20–49. It is an appropriate starting-point because it is the first sustained example of Jesus' teaching in Luke since the opening sermon at Nazareth in chapter 4, and the first teaching addressed to disciples. The setting of the sermon in 6.12–19 indicates its importance. Luke has rearranged the order of Mark's paragraphs so as to show the selection and appointment of the twelve apostles, preceded by prayer and followed by the gathering of a much larger band of disciples and of crowds from a wide area to hear Jesus' teaching and be healed from illness and demon possession. The apostles are a key group for Luke, the witnesses and guarantors of the memory of Jesus' ministry, death and resurrection from Galilee onwards (Acts 1.21f.; 13.31). The sermon is the first utterance of which they formally constitute part of the audience, and its importance in the overall plan of Luke's gospel is thereby underlined. They are only part of the audience, however, and it is clear that Luke understands this teaching as having a much wider application.

As the commentaries indicate, there are several critical problems.[1] A relationship with Matthew's sermon on the mount is indicated by the similarity of beginning and ending, and the close verbal similarity of certain passages. Yet it is unsatisfactory to regard either simply as a version of the other, and more probable that both are edited versions of an earlier form of sermon, some of the editing perhaps having taken place in oral tradition. Linguistic evidence suggests that

Luke has made his own amendments. There are good reasons
for thinking that the woes in 6.24–26 have been composed by
him to balance his version of the beatitudes,[2] and that 6.27–36
represents a conflation of material originally more clearly
arranged and linked to antitheses, as in Matt. 5.38–48. Some
of Luke's material is parallelled in other contexts in Matthew.
While therefore we cannot affirm that the Lucan sermon
owes its form entirely to Luke, we can be sure that he was
satisfied that it said what he believed ought to be said at this
stage of his portrayal of Jesus' ministry.

A second critical problem concerns the analysis of the
sermon's structure. The divisions are not clear and different
analyses have been proposed. It is important not to be
distracted by the way the material is divided in the Matthean
parallels. Matthew 5.48 clearly ends a section, but Luke 6.36
looks forward at least as much as it looks back. The question
of structure is bound up with a third problem, that of the
audience, or more strictly, the addressees, since it is clear
from 7.1 that the crowds have been hearing the sermon,
whether or not all its contents are meant to be applicable to
them. 6.20a suggests that the disciples (not just the twelve)
are being referred to in what follows. Are they the poor of
6.20b? Who then are the rich of 6.24? Who are the hearers
addressed in 6.27? Whom again does Luke have in mind at
6.39f., and where do the crowds of 6.17, 19, 7.1 come in? In
answering such questions it is important to pay attention not
only to the content of the sayings but also to the scant
grammatical clues Luke gives.[3] The view taken here is that
the sermon divides into the following sections: vv. 20–23
addressed to disciples, 24–26 to bystanders in the crowd, 27–
38 to disciples, 39–45 to disciples but with a change of topic,
and 46–49 to all listeners including the crowds.[4] What Luke
believes that these groups represent in terms of his own day is
a question to be considered further in a later chapter.

When we compare Luke's sermon with Matthew's we are
immediately struck by the concentration upon a very few
topics. Its shortness overall is achieved not by compression
and precis but by omission. The consequence is that love
stands out as the central theme of the whole. The core is
in 6.27–38, in which material parallel to two sections of
Matthew's sermon, 5.38–42 on not returning evil for evil,

and 5.43–48 on loving enemies, has been conflated, as the
following list shows:

Luke vv. 27f.	= Matt. v. 44
vv. 29f.	= vv. 39–42a
vv. 32f.	= vv. 46f.
v. 34	= cf. v. 42b
v. 35	= v. 45
v. 36	= v. 48

Luke v. 31 is parallelled in Matt. 7.12. It is hard to see why
Matthew should have shifted it from a Lucan position, and
we must consider its Lucan setting as part of Luke's design.
Verses 37f., partly parallelled in Matt. 7.1f., also belong to
this section, and continue the thought of mercy suggested by
v. 36, which as we noted looks forward as well as back. The
next subject division does not occur until v. 39. So twelve out
of the thirty verses of the sermon are concerned with the
theme of love.

This is a surprising fact when one remembers that love is
not a widely distributed word in Luke or Acts. The noun
(*agape*) only occurs at Luke 11.42 and the verb (*agapan*) only
six times outside the sermon (7.5, 42, 47; 10.27; 11.43; 16.13).
Neither occurs in Acts. The related word 'mercy' (*eleos*), used
in the LXX of God's love, occurs five times in the canticles of
Luke 1 (vv. 50, 54, 58, 72, 78) and at 10.37, and the verb
(*eleein*) at 16.24, 17.13, 18.38f.; neither occurs in Acts. But
the prominence not only of the word but of the material it
introduces and binds together in the sermon (vv. 27, 32, 35)
guarantees its importance for Luke.

In a manner common to the synoptic gospels (as elsewhere
in the Bible) the sayings in 6.27–38 reinforce one another in
synonymous parallellism, re-stating a point two or more
times in similar terms. The use of such synonyms enables us
to see what the idea of love holds for Luke. At the same time,
there is some progression of thought, roughly from loving
enemies, through loving without expectation of return, to
generous and uncensorious attitudes. The main points can be
summarized as follows.

1. Love is expressed in action. While generous attitudes,
forgiving and not censorious, are important (v. 37), the main
expressions of love are, doing good (*kalos poiein* v. 27,

agathopoiein vv. 33, 35), blessing and praying (v. 28), giving and lending (vv. 29f, 34f, 38), doing to others as you would have them do to you (v. 31).

2. It is non-reciprocal. The 'golden rule' is cited (v. 31) but its force is not to limit the scope of our actions to those who would benefit us in return, but to suggest a standard by which we may measure what we do for anyone (*kathos* ... *homoios*, as ... similarly). The emphasis is on going beyond a balance of payments. Thus resistance is not to be shown to enemies (v. 29), they are to be blessed, prayed for and have good done to them (vv. 27f.). Loans, good deeds, love are not to be restricted to those who can show the same favour in return (vv. 32–35).[5] So love is neither a return for love received nor a gift in expectation of such return. Verses 37f. are of course no exception to this, for what is in mind in these verses is not how people repay each other but how God responds to our behaviour. The passive verbs ('be judged ... be condemned ... be given') are the 'reverential passives' which refer obliquely to what God does.[6]

3. This generosity has its model in God. He is kind to the ungrateful and the wicked (*ponerous*, 'selfish' RSV v. 35). He is merciful (v. 36) and this is the reason why we should be merciful in our attitudes to others (vv. 37f.). Above all he is generous, filling the measure, pressing it down and heaping it up till it overflows before pouring it into our lap (v. 38). If we wish to be his sons we must show similar love (v. 35).

4. It is worth noting how prominent is the use of possessions in all this: clothing (v. 29), loans (vv. 34f.), gifts (vv. 30,38). In Matthew the expressions of love are chiefly prayer and social greetings (5.44, 47).

5. It is important to consider who is in mind in the reference to enemies. Matthew 5.39–41 cites three situations: a blow to the right cheek (with the back of the hand and thus a deliberate insult), a lawsuit in which an adversary claims the undergarment (perhaps in repayment for a loan), and the enlistment of civilians by the military to carry baggage for the regulation distance of one mile. The instruction is to offer the left cheek also, to surrender even the outer garment, needed as a blanket at night and exempted from being given as a pledge by the law (Ex. 22.25–27; Deut. 24.10–13) and doubling of the distance. The conditions of occupied Palestine and

Jewish customs and legal procedures are obviously in mind. Luke (v. 29) lacks the last of these (perhaps because it was irrelevant to his readers), represents the blow on the cheek as a general case of assault (by omitting 'right') and envisages robbery of the clothing in which the outer garment is taken and the undergarment offered with it. We are not in a Jewish setting, it would seem, but one which Gentiles might experience. Yet Jews apparently remain in the background. While Luke avoids Matthew's word 'persecute' (*diokein*) in the sermon, this is clearly what he has in mind. The word 'hate' (*misein*) in v. 27 echoes v. 22, where exclusion (from the synagogue?) by the descendants of those who persecuted the prophets and rejection 'on account of the son of man' are referred to; and in v. 28 'curse' (*kataromenous*) suggests a Jewish reaction to Christians.[7] This reference to Jewish-Christian relationships, combined with less specific detail than in Matthew is a phenomenon to which we shall have to return. For the moment the important point is the primary (though not exclusive) reference to enemies as persecutors.

6. Luke includes the concept of reward. Of the word itself he is more sparing than Matthew. Apart from 6.23, 35 he uses it only twice, in the everyday sense of 'wages' at 10.7, Acts 1.18. His preferred term is *charis* (vv. 33–35), which should probably be translated 'thanks',[8] but it is clear that God's approval is intended. The summary in v. 35 uses 'reward' (*misthos*) without Matthean parallel in a phrase which echoes the beatitude in 6.23 (= Matt. 5.12), and as we have seen, vv. 37f. speak of God's response to our attitudes, judgment for judgment, gift for gift, but with an overwhelming generosity. What Luke understands by this reward we shall investigate later.

Before we leave the sermon on the plain we should briefly take note of some of its other features. The opening beatitudes and woes (vv. 20–26) are more direct than the beatitudes in Matthew, and less susceptible of being interpreted as a profile of the ideal disciple.[9] Apart from the reference to persecution on account of the son of man, Luke concentrates on the basic experiences of poverty, hunger and grief, proclaiming to those who now experience them the assurance of a share in the coming kingdom of God, its abundance and joy, and to those who are already wealthy, well-fed and joyful the warning of hard times to come. It introduces sharply and in a prominent way the themes of wealth and the reversal of fortunes which will occupy us in the next chapter. The sermon ends with the parable of the two houses which emphasizes strongly the importance not only of hearing but of putting into practice what Jesus teaches (vv. 46–49). This theme we shall take up again in a moment.

This discussion of the sermon on the plain has introduced a number of themes to which we shall return in later pages: the use of possessions, generosity, persecution, the treatment of enemies, reward, doing as well as hearing. We might also note for future reference, the mention of joy in 6.23 (*charete . . . kai skirtesate*, both favourite words with Luke), and the reference to the heart as the treasury from which good words come (6.45). But the most important point is the primacy given to the idea of love in this first, programmatic exposition of Jesus' teaching for his followers. With that observation it is natural to turn next to the other major exposition of the same theme in 10.25–37.

The various difficulties of the parable of the good Samaritan and its introductory dialogue need not detain us here.[10] We merely note in passing that it is unclear whether the conversation with the lawyer is based on Mark 12.28–34, omitted in Luke 20, or on some other source; that the form of the quotation from Deut. 6.4f. in 10.27 differs not only from Mark but from Matthew and the LXX; and that, as with a number of parables peculiar to Luke, it is not clear how much of the story of the good Samaritan is due to Luke's own narrative skill. Whatever the sources there is good evidence that Luke has shaped this material to his own purpose.

The lawyer asks what he should do to inherit eternal life. The question anticipates 18.18, where Luke adapts Mark 10.17 to produce an identical form of words (*didaskale . . . ti poiesas zoen aionion kleronomeso*). It is a question about the action which will lead to life, and this is kept in focus throughout (v. 28 '*do* this and you will live', v. 37 'go and *do* likewise'). The answer is to be found in obedience to the law which the questioner already knows. It is uncertain to what extent the two commands of Deut. 6.4f. and Lev. 19.18 had already been joined in Jewish thought before the time of Jesus as an epitome of all the law required, but in Luke it is the

lawyer who quotes the commandments which in Mark
12.30f. are proclaimed by Jesus to be the greatest and the next
greatest. When asked to define who the neighbour is, Jesus
tells the story of the man who fell victim to robbers,
was ignored by priest and Levite, but was helped by the
Samaritan, who proved himself to be his neighbour by
showing mercy to him.

The emphasis on love in action is obvious. 'Mercy' (*eleos*)
in v. 37 carries the suggestion both of compassion for the
unfortunate and of God's love for Israel.[11] The risks taken by
the Samaritan on the dangerous road and his generosity are in
stark contrast to the indifference of the two previous passers-
by. Note, however, how Luke presents the quotation of the
law in v. 27. In Mark 12.30f. (cf. Matt. 22.37–39) two
commands are given, reflecting the fact that different Old
Testament passages are being cited. They are ranked as 'first'
(in answer to the scribe's request) and 'second'. In Luke there
is no such hierarchy. Deut. 6.4f. and Lev. 19.18 are quoted
together in a single sentence as one command. Love is
indivisible. Though it may have different objects, and to that
extent love to God and to neighbour may be intellectually
distinguished, they cannot be kept apart in practice. There is
no 'first' commandment which can be fulfilled independently
of the second (or vice versa). It is in keeping with this that
Jesus says, 'do *this* and you will live' (v. 28 *touto*; compare
Mark 12.31; Matt. 22.40, 'these').

It is important to note that in answering the lawyer Jesus
directs him back to the law of which he is an expert. The way
to inherit life is to be found in the Old Testament scriptures.
There is other evidence in Luke and Acts of an emphasis on
the continuity between Christianity and its Jewish past, and it
is perhaps for this reason that there are no antitheses between
the teaching of Jesus and 'what was said to the men of old' in
Luke's sermon on the plain such as we find in Matthew's
sermon on the mount. There is no new teaching here.[12] What
is important, apart from conjoining love for God and neighbour, is the stress on obedience. 'Doing' (*poiein*) binds the
passage together (vv. 25, 28, 37).

There is therefore a special sting in the selection of the three
characters in the story, in Jewish eyes two members of the
religious establishment and one religious heretic: the first two

fail to observe the law, the third keeps it. In the light of what has been said in v. 28 and the command to 'do likewise' in v. 37 we have to conclude that in passing by on the other side the priest and Levite did not love God, and on this test would not inherit eternal life, while the Samaritan in showing compassion did love God and would inherit. So the whole passage shows that the Jewish community whom the lawyer represents have before them all the instruction they need for eternal life, but that it is possible for those outside that community to share the inheritance.[13]

What is of interest is the way in which this section echoes the emphases of the sermon on the plain. It is common for commentators to draw attention to the animosity Jews felt towards Samaritans. For the readers of the gospel however the point which has been made so far is the animosity of Samaritans toward Jews (9.52f.), to which James' and John's angry remark in 9.54 is a reaction. The Samaritan's action is therefore an example of love for enemies and doing good to those who cannot repay (6.35). It takes tangible form in caring for the man's wounds and paying two *denarii* for his keep, probably the equivalent of two days' wages for a labourer. We might note too that, as in 6.35 such generosity is promised a heavenly reward, so here the Samaritan becomes an heir of eternal life.

Is there also an echo of the 'golden rule'? Interpreters puzzle over the difference between the question, 'who is my neighbour?' and the reply, 'who proved to be a neighbour?'. The focus shifts from recipient to giver. There is no need to think of a conflation of different sources or a misunderstanding by Luke; the point of the parable lies precisely in the shift. In identifying the neighbour we are asked to consider how others would find us to be. In 6.31 there is a similar point; in deciding what to do for others we are to put ourselves in their shoes, imagining ourselves to be the recipients. Is Luke hinting at this similarity in the repeated phrase 'do likewise' (6.31; 10.37)?

Before leaving this passage we must ask about Luke's attitude to the lawyer. It is easy to form the impression that relations between Jesus and his questioner are cordial. The lawyer produces the right answer to his own question and is commended for it; he feels foolish for asking about the obvious and goes on to put a supplementary. But we should beware of transferring the warm commendation of Mark 12.34 to this passage. Apart from one occurrence at Matt. 22.36, Luke is the only evangelist to use the word 'lawyer' and all other references show them in a hostile light as adversaries of Jesus sharply criticized by him (7.30; 11.45f., 52; 14.3).[14] So 'put him to the test' (10.25 *ekpeirazon*) should be allowed its full force. The intention is to trap Jesus, and Jesus' reply is not benign; he confounds the questioner out of his own mouth, driving home the essential point, 'do this!' It is no light matter to know the law but not obey it. We shall see further examples of this point in the parable of the rich man and Lazarus and elsewhere.[15]

In view of this strong emphasis on the practice of love toward the neighbour it is remarkable that Luke follows the parable of the Samaritan with the episode of Mary and Martha (10.38–41). We have no means of knowing how far Luke was guided by source material in this arrangement, if at all, but the contrast is striking, for of the two sisters, Martha, much distracted by the preparations for entertaining Jesus and his companions (which Luke refers to explicitly as service, *diakonia*, v. 40), and Mary, who sits at Jesus' feet (in the position of a disciple, v. 39, cf. Acts 22.3) listening to his word (*logon*, RSV 'teaching'), it is Mary who is declared to have chosen the better option, of which Jesus refuses to deprive her.[16] The modern reader tends to have sympathy for the hard-pressed Martha, but it is quite clear that for Luke listening to the word of Jesus takes priority over service, much as it does in Acts 6.1–6, where the apostles will not allow themselves to be deflected from prayer and the ministry (*diakonia*) of the word by the need to serve at tables (*diakonein trapezais*). It is an important corrective to the impression which might otherwise be gained from the parable of the Samaritan. The two commandments of love are one, but neither component can be reduced to the other. Obedience, important as it is, can only follow from a hearing of the word of Jesus.

We may now briefly review the other occurrences of the word 'love' in Luke's gospel. As has already been pointed out, it is not a common word in the gospel and does not occur in Acts. Two instances can be swiftly dealt with. 11.43, in the Lucan section of 'woes', refers to the Pharisees' delight in prominent seats in the synagogue and public greetings which acknowledge their self-esteem. It has a parallel in Matt. 23.6, although Matthew uses a different verb (*philousin* as against *agapate*). While this saying will be important later for our discussion of the Pharisees, 'love' is apparently used in an everyday sense, and would add nothing to our understanding of Christian character at this point. It is possible, however, that there is a play on words with the reference to the love of God in the previous verse.[17] In both places the use of the word is peculiar to Luke (*agapen, agapate*), and while the presence of a catchword device to aid memory in oral tradition cannot be ruled out, there is no reason why Matthew should have changed it, and he did not keep the two sayings together (23.6f., 23), so that it is more likely Luke introduced the word here. If there is a play on words it is to contrast the love of God with the love of public acclaim, with the suggestion that one excludes the other. This is certainly the point of 16.13, 'no servant can serve two masters; for either he will hate the one and love the other, or he will be devoted to one and despise the other', a saying identical with Matt. 6.24 with the addition of 'servant'. The point is made at the end, 'you cannot serve God and mammon' and the rest of the saying illustrates it. There is no special force in 'love' or 'hate' here. They are very general descriptions of two incompatible attitudes a household slave will have. Feelings rather than actions are in mind, for the slave will be compelled to obey both masters whatever he feels about them, but this is governed by the terms of the illustration and should not be pressed. The point is that the claims of the service of God are absolute.

7.5 refers to the regard the centurion of Capernaum feels for the Jewish people. Here we are given a brief sketch of a kind and generous Gentile, who is attracted to the Jewish faith and does not exploit his position in the occupying army to oppress the Jews. We notice again the link between love and generosity, and the suggestion (not made explicit) that love transcends boundaries which enmity might lay down. It is part of the generally warm picture we are given of this man, whose faith Jesus praises; we shall return to him at a later stage in our discussion.

11.42, another of the Lucan 'woes', presents several difficulties, especially when compared with Matt. 23.23. Luke's list of items tithed is not only more general ('every herb') but includes items which were either not listed for tithing in Jewish tradition (mint), or were specifically excluded (rue).[18] If our information is correct, we must assume either that Luke was ignorant of actual practice, or that he is criticizing excessive zeal which went beyond legal requirements. In view of the end of the verse, 'these you ought to have done without neglecting the others', the last solution seems unlikely. This ending to the verse is itself surprising. There is no suggestion here that tithing should be dropped, only that one obligation should not be passed over for another. We shall have to come back later to these questions. What must occupy us now is the statement of what the Pharisees have omitted and should include, 'justice and the love of God'. Justice is certainly the right translation for *krisis*; 'judgment' would be incongruous with 6.37, which forbids judging.[19] But what is the love of God? Not God's love for us, which is alien to a context that stresses what we are to do; but is it our love for God or the love for others which God requires of us? The former interpretation has suggested to some commentators an echo of the two commandments in 10.27 (love for God and justice for neighbour) but the echo is faint.[20] Nevertheless 'love such as God requires' would suggest an antithesis to Pharisaic traditions not required by God which is not present in the text. Love of God then must mean our love for him. The possibility referred to earlier of a play on words with v. 43, if accepted, would confirm this. The difference is slight, for we have already shown that for Luke love for others and for God are inseparable, but precision is worth striving for here because apart from 10.27 we have not found any other explicit references in Luke to loving God.

The only other passage using the word 'love' is 7.36–50. Here the word is employed both in the parable of the two debtors, vv. 41f., and in its application to the woman's lavish devotion to Jesus at v. 47. A discussion of this passage, however, will be more appropriate in a later chapter, because it involves a number of other important Lucan ideas as well.

This survey of residual passages has added little to our discussion of *agape* in Luke's gospel.[21] There is no question of its central importance for Luke, because of the place it occupies in the sermon on the plain, and his handling of the commandments in 10.25ff. But we have to ask why, since that is so, the idea plays so little part elsewhere in the gospel and none in Acts. Is the prominence we have seen the accidental result of the traditions Luke uses, or is the reason that he prefers to state the case in more particular terms and by concrete examples, just as in 6.27ff. he spells out the meaning of love by synonymous expressions which give it more concrete form? Our study of wealth will help with the answer.

3

Wealth – I

In the last chapter we noted at various points that love
involved the use of possessions. Our next step is to explore
Luke's views on wealth in more detail.[1] His interest in this
topic is extensive, although it is not easy to reconcile the
emphases of different passages. We begin by surveying the
main body of gospel evidence, starting with four blocks of
material where wealth receives extended treatment, and
concentrating on the teaching of Jesus. A later chapter will
take note of examples provided by the narrative.

1. Chapter 16 contains two parables linked in vv. 14–18 by
the reaction of the Pharisees and Jesus' reply.

(a)The parable of the unjust steward, 16.1–13, is notorious
for its difficulties.[2] What was the steward doing when he told
his master's debtors to alter the amounts they owed? How
could he be praised for it (v. 8)? Why is he nevertheless called
'unrighteous' ('dishonest', RSV, *ho oikonomos tes adikias*)?
Where does the parable end and comment on it begin? What
is the sequence of thought in vv. 8–13? If they represent
different comments added to the parable,[3] what did it mean
without them? For our purpose, however, it is necessary to
inquire only into Luke's understanding of the passage, and
we must keep firm grasp of the clues he puts in our hands.
First, the parable is closely linked in the narrative to chapter
15, which deals with the contrast between the righteous and
sinners and with repentance (15.7, 10, 17, 18, 21, 24, 29, 32).
There is also a parallel between the descriptions of the
behaviour of the prodigal son (15.13, 'squandered') and of the
steward (16.1, 'wasting'; *diaskorpizein* in each case). We are

encouraged therefore to look for signs of a change of attitude
in the steward's behaviour. Secondly, the steward's action
with the debtors was intended to win friends, perhaps so that
he could obtain further employment.[4] It would hardly then
have been the sort to undermine their trust. His employer in
any case approves of it; so it can hardly have been dishonest.
It has been suggested that he was cancelling interest which,
though strictly illegal in Jewish law, had nevertheless been
charged by means of the technicality of expressing the debts
in kind. He would thus have won for his master a reputation
for piety in conforming to the spirit of the law against usury
as well as securing gratitude from the debtors.[5] It is doubtful
whether Luke's readers, who do not appear to have had close
familiarity with Jewish law, would have understood so much
but there is evidence that they would have recognized the
reduced amounts as cancelling interest due and perhaps have
concluded that the steward was waiving his own commission
or paying off the interest himself, although 'another's' (v. 12)
suggests that the master's money was involved.

This conclusion in turn affects our understanding of *adikia*
and *adikos* in the passage, which the RSV translates variously
as 'unrighteous' and 'dishonest'. The Greek words do not
have an entirely consistent meaning. In vv. 9 and 11 they
appear to characterize wealth in a general and morally neutral
way as belonging to this world where unrighteousness pre-
vails (and could perhaps be translated 'worldly'), rather than
expressing a moral judgment on specific instances, as though
wealth was sometimes evil and sometimes good.[6] In v. 10 on
the other hand, as commonly in Luke, we have an expression
of disapproval. If *adikia* in v. 8 is a general description of the
steward it will have to be in the broader and weaker sense of
v. 9; he was a 'man of the world'. But it is more likely that
Luke is contrasting the steward's irresponsible behaviour at
the beginning with his later actions and using 'unrighteous' in
the specific and stronger sense. In his response to the threat of
unemployment the steward shows a change of heart comparable to the repentance of the sinners of chapter 15. He moves
from unrighteousness to 'prudence'.

Thirdly, the most important feature of the passage is the
parallel, even closer in Greek than in the RSV, between the
steward's intention in v. 4 and the application of the parable

in v. 9 (note *hina . . . hotan . . . dexontai . . . eis . . .*). What the steward did brought benefit to his master's debtors and made friends of them, securing a future for himself in return. His 'prudence' (v. 8) lay in his choosing and achieving that aim. It is not clear whether the debtors were needy tenants who had been compelled to borrow and would offer a home to a fellow destitute when he was sacked, or business partners, who might subsequently employ him, but it was a generous action. If he was waiving his own commission or paying the interest for them, it involved him also in personal loss, but the main point is the benefit brought to others. So too Jesus' disciples (cf. v. 1) are to use the wealth of this world in such a way as to gain friends and secure an eternal dwelling.[7] If we understand vv. 1–9 in this way, vv. 10–12 now make more sense. By his conduct under one employer the steward showed himself fit for employment elsewhere. So disciples are to demonstrate by their use of worldly wealth, a small thing in comparison, their fitness to handle heavenly treasure. Verse 10 states the general principle, vv. 11f. spell it out.[8] But v. 13 adds a warning: wealth is to be used, but it is not to become our master. There is a danger of idolatry if it is not kept in its proper place. For its use we must answer to God.

The point of the parable for Luke thus lies in vv. 8–13. People in everyday life show a common sense which disciples lack in the religious sphere.[9] They are ready to change their attitude in a crisis and secure their future by responsible activity in the present. Disciples for their part must learn to handle the world's transient wealth responsibly if they are to have an entry to God's eternal dwelling and there be entrusted with real treasure. What responsible handling might mean is not explicitly stated, although generosity and personal cost may be implied. It is made more clear later in the chapter by the second parable, of the rich man and Lazarus.[10]

(*b*) This parable (16.19–31) was probably originally adapted from a popular folk tale.[11] In its Lucan version it has two main points. The second will come before us in a later chapter: what Jesus is calling for is not new but a reiteration of the demand of the Old Testament, and if the rich are too stubborn to hear it, not even someone rising from the dead (Luke's Christian readers will think of Jesus) will make them change their ways. The other point in the story concerns wealth. The rich man enjoys his luxury in utter disregard for the poor man who lies starving and degraded in full view of his table. But with death comes a reversal. Lazarus is taken to Abraham's bosom (presumably to sit next to him at the heavenly banquet)[12] while it is the rich man's turn to experience hunger and thirst. There is no relief for him for he has already had (*apelabes*, v. 25) his full enjoyment of good things. We are reminded of the woe in 6.24: the rich have had (*apechete*) their comfort (*paraklesin*). Now Lazarus is comforted (*parakaleitai*). If he had only shared his wealth with Lazarus the rich man would now be sharing his blessedness. But it is too late to make changes; as he denied Lazarus the crumbs from his table so now he is denied the drop of water. In effect, he failed to make friends by means of the unrighteous mammon and was not received into the eternal dwellings. What may have been hinted at in the parable of the steward is now spelled out explicitly. Right use of wealth means giving to the poor.

2. Earlier in Luke, 12.13–34 constitutes a section on possessions, in which sayings are addressed partly to disciples, partly to the public. Some of the material is parallelled in Matthew 6.

It begins with the refusal of Jesus to arbitrate between two brothers in the division of their inheritance (vv. 13f.). The reason for their request is not stated. As the basic principles for the division of inheritance were laid down in the Old Testament (Deut. 21.17) and not in dispute, the problem must have been either failure to agree on the arithmetic, or a claim by one brother to exclusive use of his share of a joint holding.[13] Verse 15 draws the moral. It was originally a separate saying, as the opening shows, and is addressed to the crowd.[14] Care is needed, however, in the translation. The brother's problem is not 'covetousness' (RSV), for the brother had a right to his inheritance, but 'greed'. Neither brother would give way for fear of loss. But RSV is right to continue, 'a man's life does not consist in the abundance of his possessions', for it is the better translation and more in line with the wider context. It is the accumulation of riches, not just inner attachment to them, which is discouraged. The alternative, 'even when they are abundant a man's life does not consist in his possessions' (cf. NEB, JB), is more tolerant of wealth.[15]

The parable of the rich fool follows (vv. 16–20). Confronted with a bumper harvest a rich man decides to build bigger barns, live at ease (no more farming!) and enjoy his wealth 'for many years'. But that night God requires him to return the life he has held in trust[16] and the loaded storehouses are left ownerless and unenjoyed. But more is involved, as the application in v. 21 shows. Not only was he unprepared for the imminence of death but he lacked the wealth he needed to face God. He suffered a reversal of fortunes, wealth to poverty, which he could have avoided. What alternative had he? The fault lay, not in the wealth itself, for a good harvest must be regarded as a gift of God (cf. Acts 14.17), but in his selfish enjoyment of it and his arrogant assumption that he could count on the future. He was a fool, who gave no thought to the ways of God, to his own loss.[17]

In vv. 22–34 Jesus turns to the disciples. They are not to be anxious about food or clothing; the body and life itself are more important. God supplies the needs of the crows and makes the flowers more resplendent than Solomon though they last only a day; why should he not take even greater care of disciples, for he knows their needs? Instead of devoting anxiety and effort to food and drink, as the nations of the world generally do, they should seek God's kingdom and they will find that they have these necessities as well. The passage speaks for itself and requires detailed comment only at v. 31. The parallel in Matt. 6.33, 'seek first his kingdom and his righteousness and all these things shall be yours as well', not only spells out the meaning of seeking the kingdom in terms of Matthew's characteristic concern for righteousness, but is also capable of giving the impression that what matters is the order of priorities. It is natural to seek food and clothing and they will be supplied provided the kingdom is put first. Luke is more uncompromising. The disciples are not to seek these things at all (v. 29, cf. Matt. 6.31). 'All' is omitted in vv. 30 and 31 (Matt. vv. 32f.), surprisingly for Luke, for whom it is a favourite word, and 'first' is absent from v. 31 (Matt. v. 33). The kingdom for Luke is not first priority but the only goal, and v. 31 is set in direct contrast to v. 29. Only when a choice has been made, for the kingdom against food and clothing, will 'these things' be provided. The starkness of this is underlined by the fact that we are discussing not luxuries but the necessities of human survival. To adopt such an attitude is a profound act of faith. To relinquish the fundamental drive to provide for our own survival is to let go of our last hold on life; what is there left between us and extinction? Verse 32 supplies the necessary reassurance. Disciples can rely on God. He intends to give them the kingdom, the greatest gift of all; so (we are to infer) he will surely add food and clothing meanwhile; there is no need to fear. But still promise and condition go together.

Verse 33 reiterates the demand to seek the kingdom, not now in terms of the necessities we lack but of what we already have. 'Sell your possessions and give alms; (in that way) provide yourselves with purses that do not grow old, with a treasure in the heavens that does not fail, where no thief approaches and no moth destroys.' We are moving back to the situation of the rich man of the parable, and we now see what it means to be 'rich towards God' (v. 21). The new element here is almsgiving. The rich man's folly lay not merely in ignoring the possibility of death but in storing up his good fortune for his own use (v. 21). He should have shared it with the poor. Heavenly treasure does not depreciate in value nor do we lose possession of it once it is ours. It is secured by selling off our possessions and giving to the poor. So we have a parallel to the interpretation we gave of making friends of the unrighteous mammon in 16.9, which is reinforced by a verbal echo in the reference to the failure of worldly wealth. Indeed there are other points of contact with chapter 16. The story of the rich man and Lazarus in 16.19ff. spells out more fully the plight of the rich fool at 12.16f. Both enjoy their wealth in this life, without regard for the poor, but at death, when the tables are turned, find themselves empty-handed before God.[18]

There is therefore a straight alternative: possessions or the kingdom. The point is made in the final verse of the section, 12.34, 'where your treasure is, there will your heart be also.' It is futile to think that, with worldly wealth or even anxiety for necessities, we can have our heart set on the kingdom. As in 16.13, service of God and mammon are incompatible. Chapter 12 is thus sharper in tone than chapter 16. There is something of the same emphasis on the right use of wealth, but the dominant note is the opposition between wealth and the kingdom which received only minor emphasis in chapter 16.

3. The next group of passages to be considered occurs in chapter 14, in which vv. 1–24 form a unit by being set at a meal in a Pharisee's house (14.1). In this discussion we concentrate on vv. 12–14 which form the second of two short paragraphs, one addressed to other guests, the other to the host, and on vv. 15–24 which serve as a reply to a remark by one of the guests.

Verses 12–14 read at first sight as simple moral advice about hospitality, but by now we should be alert to the possibility of overtones. First, there is the emphasis on showing hospitality not to one's friends but to the poor. 'The poor, the maimed, the lame and the blind' (v. 13) are those like Lazarus. We are again dealing with the right use of wealth. Secondly, it is explicitly said that such guests cannot repay (v. 14). So there is no danger that we shall be hospitable in hope of something in return; with wealthy guests a return favour is virtually guaranteed (v. 12). Thirdly, there is the assurance of heavenly reward, expressed this time in terms of repayment (v. 14). All this repeats in fresh terms the argument of the sermon on the plain (6.31–35). In fact the parallel goes further. The reward in 6.35 is spelled out as, 'you will be sons of the Most High'. Some interpreters take this to mean that in showing love disciples resemble God now, as children resemble their father.[19] But 20.36 shows that the reference is to the future: those who attain to the age to come and the resurrection of the dead 'are sons of God, being sons of the resurrection'; sonship comes when we are raised from the dead. So here in 14.14 repayment comes at the resurrection of the just for those who have renounced the hope of repayment in this life. 6.35, however, took the discussion a step further, for it rooted the appeal for generosity in the character of God who is kind to those who do not reciprocate (cf. 6.36). 14.14 does not state this, but remarkably the thought does occur in the next paragraph.

It is generally agreed that the parable of the great feast (vv. 15–24) is another version of the parable in Matt. 22.1–14, and that Matthew's version has undergone extensive elaboration to serve his particular interests. But it would be unwise to conclude that Luke preserves the original form intact. Indeed the double sending of the servant in vv. 21, 23 is widely but mistakenly regarded as an embellishment representing stages in Christian mission.[20]

The opening remark in v. 15, on which the parable hangs, 'blessed is he who shall eat bread in the kingdom of God', is closely connected to the preceding paragraph, picking up the word 'blessed' from v. 14 and continuing the idea of the resurrection of the just in terms of the banquet of the kingdom. The parable which forms Jesus' reply does not deny what the guest says but challenges the assumptions behind it. There may be surprises when the guest list is revealed (and the seating plan too, vv. 7–11 might suggest!). The point of the parable lies in the closing remarks of the host, vv. 23c, 24. Those who had been invited have insultingly excused themselves at the last moment. Hence the host's anger and his determination that they will not now share the feast. But it has been prepared for many guests and he is equally determined that his house shall be full.[21] What attracts attention is the description given of the two kinds of guest. The first group are characterized by the reasons they give for their refusal, which are spelt out more fully than in Matt. 22.5. They are wealthy (five yoke of oxen indicates a considerable estate), but they are preoccupied by their every-day business and domestic affairs.[22] Those who are invited in their place are poor (v. 21). They are to be found, naturally enough, begging in the streets of the town and sheltering under the hedgerows in the open country. What is striking is that they are described in precisely the same terms as in v. 13. This cannot be accidental and justifies our concentrating on the economic condition of the guests. Those who refuse are rich; those who accept are the poor who cannot repay.[23]

The parable is about the banquet of God's kingdom, and the host must represent God.[24] The effect of its position here is therefore to give a foundation for the advice of vv. 12–14. God too shows generosity to the poor. But there is a warning also. In the kingdom the seats will be filled by the poor who come empty handed, depending on the generosity of the host, while the rich, preoccupied with their day-to-day concerns, are left out. When the parable is viewed in that light

How can the poor be fed if they are not rich?

it becomes doubtful whether we should attempt to see different phases of mission in vv. 21, 23. Attractive as the theory is when the parable is studied in isolation, it becomes a distraction in the context of chapter 14. Its advocates do not in any case agree on what the phases are. When Luke wants to allude to the church's mission in 19.11–27 he is more explicit. Rather the stress is on filling the house (cf. v. 22, 'still there is room'). No effort is spared for this, and the different locations where the guests are found emphasize their poverty and the host's determination to fill every place.[25]

At 14.25 the scene changes: Jesus is on the move with the crowds. But 14.33 brings us back to the theme we have been discussing. The intervening verses, 26–32, deal with the cost of discipleship, which must be counted before committing oneself. The cost is stated primarily in terms of family ties and taking up the cross rather than wealth, but v. 33, which is clearly intended as a summary, renews the reference to possessions. 'Whoever does not renounce all that he has cannot be my disciple' is a double conclusion. It is sufficiently general to include what has immediately preceded but the most natural reference is to material goods. So family, possessions and self are linked as hindrances to following Jesus. This again confirms that we were right to treat the excuses of v. 20, where marriage and property are also associated, as significant in the application of the parable and not merely as part of its narrative colour. What is especially impressive about 14.33, however, is its uncompromising tone. It goes beyond calling for the right use of wealth in generosity to the poor and calls for its abandonment. It is closer to 16.13, where God and mammon are set in opposition and to 12.29 which forbids the quest for food and clothing. Again we find the juxtaposition of sayings about the proper use of wealth and harsher sayings against its possession at all.

4. In our fourth passage, 18.18–30, dealing with the rich man who refuses to follow Jesus, we can compare Luke with Mark and identify with comparative confidence the emphases he has introduced. The chief difference is that Luke has generalized the passage, making the rich man representative of a wider group, as details show.[26] (*a*) There is not a new scene as there is at Mark 10.17. The context at Luke 18.18 is

the same as at vv. 9 and 15. The listeners are those 'who trusted in themselves that they were righteous and despised others', (18.9) of whom the Pharisee in the parable at 18.10ff. is typical. (*b*) The rich man simply speaks to Jesus out of the crowd. He neither approaches him at the beginning nor leaves him at the end (cf. Mark 10.17, 22). He is thus a representative of the crowd who are addressed through him. (*c*) Verses 24f. are spoken in his presence and the crowd's (Mark 10.23 is addressed to the disciples) and 'those who heard' in v. 26 are also the crowd. Only at v. 28 does Jesus turn to the disciples. (*d*) This is perhaps why Luke alone of the synoptists calls the man a ruler. He probably thinks of him as a member of the Jewish sanhedrin (23.13, 35; 24.20; Acts 3.17, etc.) or a synagogue ruler (8.41) and in either case a Pharisee (cf. 14.1), typical of those depicted in v. 9. (*e*) Luke omits Mark's statement that Jesus loved him (Mark 10.21), possibly because he is depicting a type of person rather than an individual, and thinks of Jesus as critical of what he represents. What Jesus says to him has wider application; it is not a 'counsel of perfection' for a favoured individual (cf. Matt. 19.21).

The ruler's question (v. 18) is expressed in the same terms as the lawyer's question at 10.25. In both passages the reply refers to the law, this time to some of the ten commandments.[27] But observance of the commandments is not enough. One thing is lacking, although it resolves itself into three related steps: possessions must be sold (Luke characteristically adds 'all'),[28] the proceeds must be distributed to the poor, and the man himself must follow Jesus. This he is unwilling to do because he is 'very rich' (v. 23).

Verses 24–30 abbreviate and streamline Mark. Verses 24–27 deal publicly with wealth. It is well-nigh impossible for the rich to enter the kingdom of God. Verses 28–30 are addressed to disciples, with significant changes from Mark 10.29f. Peter says they have left their homes (*ta idia*)[29] to follow Jesus; the list in v. 29 of what they might have left is modified: wives are added, while lands are omitted, so that the emphasis is on relationships broken rather than possessions given up;[30] the cause is 'for the kingdom of God' rather than for Jesus and the gospel, that is, it is a requirement for all disciples if they are to enter the kingdom, not just a demand related to persecution or mission, which might affect only some; the accompanying promise in v. 30 is abbreviated as 'manifold more', leaving it much less specific than Mark's catalogue of benefits, although with emphasis on the disproportion between loss and gain. Verses 28–30 are thus a comment on 'come follow me' in v. 22 and the break in family ties it implies, just as vv. 24–27 were a comment on 'sell all you have and distribute to the poor' and the difficulty that presents for the rich.

18.18–30 thus offers an alternative reply to the question asked by the lawyer at 10.25. Some of the themes we have met elsewhere are repeated and some new aspects introduced. There is the same stress on the dangers of wealth and the importance of giving to the poor. Elsewhere this is related to the idea of heavenly treasure (12.21, 33f.), the kingdom of God (12.31f.), life (12.15) or what is eternal (16.18). All these concepts are involved here (vv. 18, 22, 24f., 29f.) with the addition of salvation (v. 26). But wealth does not stand on its own: also involved is following Jesus. An aspect of what that means is shown in the reference to breaking family ties in vv. 28–30 and more is hinted at in the reference to Jesus' passion in the next paragraph, vv. 31–34. Possessions, family and taking up the cross are thus linked, as we saw them to be in 14.25–33. All this brings home the importance of the right use of wealth for Luke but warns us against isolating it as though discipleship could be expressed exclusively in such terms, although other passages might give that impression.

These four sections of Luke have brought out the main lines of his attitude to wealth. Transient worldly wealth must be used well, to win heavenly treasure, for all will experience a reversal of fortunes. Right use involves cost, for it means generosity to the poor, the empty-handed who cannot repay. Such use reflects the generosity of God. Alongside this there stands a more radical view, an either-or. One must choose between God and mammon, daily necessities and the kingdom. In any case wealth is not the only threat. Other ties, of family and self, are involved, and the challenge cannot be met without trust in God. A further point to be noted is that Pharisees are mentioned in the context of all these passages. This is clear in 14.12ff. (cf. 14.1), 16.19ff. (cf. 16.14) and is implied at 16.1ff. (cf. 15.2) and 18.18ff. (cf. 18.9f.). They also feature in 11.37ff., 12.1. The significance of this will be explored in a later chapter.

In the light of this we can now look more briefly at some other passages. In themselves they add little that is new. Their chief importance lies in the way they illustrate Luke's preoccupation with this subject. Often quite small touches illustrate it. Only by surveying them all shall we realize how pervasive his concern is. The importance will be reinforced when we look in chapter 8 at the exemplary figures in his narrative.

1. 11.39–41 is extremely difficult to translate and interpret.[31] The RSV reads: 'Now you Pharisees cleanse the outside of the cup and of the dish, but inside you are full of extortion and wickedness. You fools! Did not he who made the outside make the inside also? But give for alms those things which are within; and behold, everything is clean for you.' The saying is parallelled in Matt. 23.25f., and probably comes from Q, though not necessarily in the original order or wording. It fits uneasily with the introduction in vv. 37f. which Luke may have composed to introduce the whole passage down to v. 54, and which deals with Jesus' failure ritually to wash himself.[32] Jesus' reply is best taken as involving a double contrast, between external and internal cleanness and between vessels and people. Cleaning only the outside of the utensils for a meal is futile not only because God is equally concerned with the inside, but because the users themselves are inwardly unclean. Their attitude to vessels is a kind of parable of their attitude to themselves, and Luke has conflated parable and application: in both spheres they are concerned only with externals. Their concern for ritual cleanliness is vitiated by extortion (better translated, 'rapacity') and wickedness. The answer is (departing from RSV) to 'give alms with respect to what is within you',[33] that is, to deal with the inner selfishness by substituting generosity. The reference to almsgiving in v. 41 (contrast Matt. 23.26) takes interpreters by surprise, and some have gone so far as to suggest that Luke's version is simply a mistake in translation; but if so it coincides astonishingly well with Luke's interests and we can readily understand it, just as his Greek-speaking readers would have had to do. The use of material wealth is an indispensable spiritual test; purity before

God can only be attained by the practice of generosity. In not realizing this the Pharisees (again we note the reference to them), like the rich man of 12.20, are 'fools' (v. 40), a striking contrast to the prudent steward of 16.8. But what of the end of v. 41? Does almsgiving render everything clean, so that ritual washing becomes unnecessary? Such an interpretation might explain why Jesus himself does not wash. But the point of v. 40 is that part will not do for whole; since God has made inside and outside alike, both must be cleansed, just as v. 42 in the next paragraph does not dispense with Pharisaic practices but adds to them. Verse 41 therefore probably implies that both almsgiving and ritual cleansing are necessary for the Pharisees.[34]

2. A group of passages employs the idea of being lost or losing one's life. Of course being lost is the simple converse of being saved (cf. 6.9; 15.6, 9), and one must not claim too much for straightforward instances, but it is interesting to note the contexts in which the idea is sometimes used.

(a) In 19.1–10 Zacchaeus, a rich man, in an extravagant response to Jesus restores fourfold whatever he has defrauded and gives half his goods to the poor. So salvation comes to his house. It was in his unscrupulous accumulation of wealth that Zacchaeus had been lost, and his act of repentance marks his salvation (vv. 9f.) In contrast to the ruler of 18.18ff. Zacchaeus is a rich man who can be saved (18.24).[35]

(b) This invites further reflection on 9.23–25 (cf. Mark 8.34ff.), in which Jesus lays down conditions for discipleship. Luke makes various changes. In taking over the language of denying oneself, saving and losing one's life, and gaining the whole world, he speaks in v. 25 of 'losing or forfeiting oneself', combining terms from different contexts in Mark 8.35f. If the double expression is more than rhetorical it presumably refers on the one hand to the action of God who strips away all our gains as he did for the rich fool ('forfeits', literally, 'is fined', *zemiotheis*[36]), and, on the other hand, to what happens to us before this in the process of gaining the whole world; in such wealth one is already lost. While we must not narrow Luke's meaning unduly in vv. 23–25, the thought of possessions may well have been uppermost in his mind.

(c) Is there a similar nuance in the parable of the prodigal son (15.11ff.)? Twice the father refers to the son who had claimed his wealth and enjoyed it without restraint in immoral pursuits (v. 13, *asotos*, 'in loose living' RSV) as lost and now found, dead and now alive (vv. 24, 32). While we should not insist on pressing details of the parable which may only be intended for dramatic colouring, it is possible that by them the language already used in a general way at the end of the previous parables (vv. 6, 9) is given new depth. It was worldly wealth that was the prodigal's undoing.[37]

3. Several passages in Luke deal with the time before the coming of the Son of Man or the kingdom of God, and warn disciples against unpreparedness. In each case wealth is involved.

(*a*) 17.22–37 has parallels in Mark 13.15f. and Matt. 10.39, 24.1ff. with features peculiar to Luke. The main point is the contrast between disciples who must be ready for the day of the Son of Man and act decisively when it comes, and people generally who will be caught unawares. In contrast to Matthew's brief reference (24.38) to 'eating and drinking, marrying and giving in marriage', Luke sets before us two vignettes of daily life with its domestic and commercial activities: 'they ate, they drank, they married, they were given in marriage . . . they ate, they drank, they bought, they sold, they planted, they built', assuming a future which was to be cut short (vv. 27f.). Like Noah and Lot, disciples must break free from these things, leaving everything behind; there must be no going home for baggage. 'Whoever seeks to gain [perhaps better, 'save', NEB] his life will lose it, but whoever loses his life will preserve it' (v. 33).[38] Here it is not excessive wealth, nor even the sins upon which the Old Testament stories of Noah and Lot lay so much stress (Gen. 6.5–8, 11f.; 19.12ff.), but the daily routine which constitutes the danger, the lure of which Lot's wife could not resist (v. 32). Verse 33 thus involves a play upon the word 'life'. In a crisis we have to decide whether it is constituted by our possessions or by our standing before God. (cf. 12.15). There is, however, a difficulty, for although in vv. 31f. he speaks of flight 'in that day', that is, when the crisis comes, in vv. 34f. Luke emphasizes the suddenness and unexpectedness of the crisis, when there will be no time left for flight (in Matthew the sayings are in different contexts). Luke must have thought of the flight metaphorically as separating oneself from worldly pursuits,[39] but the point seems to be, not disengagement here and now (the activities are innocent enough, and both Noah and Lot engaged in them) so much as freedom from inner attachment so that relinquishment is easy when the time of crisis comes. This is where Lot's wife failed. She could not make a decisive break. It is a question of where the heart is (cf. 12.34).

(*b*) 21.34–36, a passage peculiar to Luke, goes further. Like 17.27f. it warns against the day to day 'cares of this life' (v. 34), the routine preoccupations of all the inhabitants of the world, but it adds a warning against 'dissipation and drunkenness'. All alike can dull the disciples' minds and destroy their readiness for the decisive moment when God's kingdom unexpectedy comes (v. 31).

(*c*) We should probably also see an echo of these ideas in the parable at 12.41–46. In v. 45 the behaviour of the irresponsible servant is characterized as maltreating fellow servants, 'eating, drinking and getting drunk'. While this may simply be dramatic colouring, we note that the parable, with the one in vv. 35–40 which it follows and amplifies, concerns readiness for the coming of the master, and follows immediately on the teaching about possessions in vv. 13–34 which we have already examined.

(*d*) We should certainly see an echo of these ideas in Luke's version of the interpretation of the sower in 8.11–15. By modifications to Mark 4.14–20 he characterizes the listeners to the word as, at the one extreme, those who fail to respond at all (v. 12), at the other those who persevere to the end (v. 15), and between them two further groups, those who give up in times of particular stress (*peirasmou*, v. 13),[40] and those who 'are choked by the cares and riches and pleasures of life' (v. 14), a fuller description than in Mark 4.19.

In this group of passages then we find a combination of the emphases we noted earlier. There is the same warning against excessive wealth and the self-indulgence that may go with it, but there is also a caution against everyday commercial pursuits that borders on the stark call to renounce basic needs in preference to the kingdom which we found in 12.29 and 14.33. Here, however, the radicalness seems to be softened; attachment rather than possession is the danger.

4. Lastly, some other passages should be noted. (*a*) Part of Luke's account of the preaching of John the Baptist is derived from 'Q' (3.7–9 = Matt. 3.7–10), but it is followed in 3.10–14 by a passage peculiar to Luke which spells out, by question and answer, what is meant by 'fruits that befit repentance' (v. 8) in preparation for the coming judgment of God, now urgently near. It cannot be coincidence that all John's replies refer to the sharing of possessions and avoiding extortion.[41]

(*b*) We may note the impact of Luke's account of the cleansing of the temple (19.45f.). He has drastically shortened Mark 11.15–17, omitting the overturning of the tables and the reference to the house of prayer being 'for all the nations'. There are probably several reasons: he may have wanted to soften the militancy of the figure of Jesus, and for him the temple is never a place of prayer for the Gentiles.[42] The effect of these changes, however, and perhaps part of their intention, is to throw into sharp relief the opposition between prayer and commerce.

(*c*) In 21.1–4 Luke reproduces the Marcan story (12.41–44) of the widow in the temple. He streamlines the narrative, omitting the reference to 'the multitude' and thus sharpening the contrast between rich and poor. Of course the narrative depends on the contrast in the size of the gifts, but by omitting Mark's 'large sums' (*polla*, 12.41, perhaps suggesting ostentation) Luke emphasizes the point that the donations of the rich are only a fraction of what they have, costing them nothing, and possibly indicative of meanness, while the widow has given away all she depended on for survival. These are not gifts to the poor, however, but contributions to the temple treasury for the worship of God, possibly gifts of gratitude in fulfilment of a vow.[43]

(*d*) In the charges to the twelve in 9.1ff. and to the larger group of disciples in 10.1ff. Luke incorporates restrictions on what the emissaries may carry with them on their journey. The passages are based on Mark and 'Q' respectively but with distinctive features.[44] 'Take nothing for your journey, no staff, nor bag, nor bread, nor money; and do not have two tunics' (9.4) is more demanding than Mark 6.8f. in excluding a staff and making no mention of footwear, both of which Mark allows, and in forbidding the possession, not just the wearing, of two tunics. In 10.4 purse, bag and sandals are forbidden. The reasons for these requirements are not stated but they can be deduced. Haste is required, as the prohibition of greetings on the road indicates (10.4) and unnecessary baggage may be discouraged for this reason. The message the travellers carry is urgent. Both passages are followed by instructions on receiving hospitality; it is possible that the more spartan demands of Luke's version may be intended to force the travellers to depend on it. The best light on these passages, however, is shed by 22.35–8 which refers back to 10.1ff. and by implication since the twelve are being addressed, to 9.1ff. also. Their going without provision for themselves is an act of faith in God, and in the event his providence does not fail them. But 22.35ff. shows that this arrangement is now a thing of the past. It suggests too a change in people's attitudes to Jesus' representatives. In the future hospitality may be refused (as already in 9.52ff.).[45]

So interpreted 9.1ff. and 10.1ff. are of limited value for our study. They are an unreliable guide to the later practice of Luke's church. Paul in Acts sets a different example (Acts 20.33–5). They illustrate in the rigour of their demands (which derives from 'Q' and is reflected in Matt.10.9f.) the call to renounce material needs for the sake of the kingdom which we found in Luke 12.29–31, but unlike that passage these instructions are addressed to people engaged in a particular task on specific occasions and should not be taken as a general guide to Christian living as Luke understands it.[46]

It is time to sum up the study so far. It is difficult to do so without blunting the edge of some of the passages, for a feature of Luke's presentation is a combination of sayings which emphasize the right use of possessions with others which stress their abandonment. Luke stresses the transitoriness of wealth and contrasts it strongly with eternal riches. The latter can only be had at the expense of the former. Only God can squeeze a rich man through the needle's eye into his kingdom. The reason is that God and wealth compete for our affection. Both demand full service and we must choose between them. At death there will be a great reversal, poverty to riches, riches to poverty. Those who renounce possessions and even the everyday concern for food and clothing thereby entrust themselves totally to the care of God. Yet simply to let go of possessions is not enough. They must be given to the poor. In this way they are made use of, and faithful handling of the world's wealth in this manner is the test of our capacity to handle the treasure of the age to come. Extensive as these concerns are in Luke, however, they do not exclude other elements in the call to discipleship. Jesus also calls for a break from family ties and a readiness to lose one's own life. In response to such renunciation there is held out to us the promise of a reward, real wealth which does not deteriorate, in heaven. We must now try to set all this in a wider context and explore some of the implications.

4

Wealth – II

In the last chapter we reviewed the passages which are evidence of Luke's strong concern with wealth. To understand them properly, however, two questions need to be explored further. One concerns his eschatology, the other the meaning of poverty.

First, let us try to clarify Luke's understanding of the moment of reversal, when the heavenly reward may become ours. One the one hand he sometimes refers to a reversal of affairs for the individual at the moment of death (12.20f.; 16.22 and probably 16.9). On the other hand, there are clear and repeated references in Luke and Acts to a future 'day' or 'hour' of universal judgment.[1] It has been widely held, since Conzelmann's work on Luke, that one effect of Luke's editing has been to discourage expectation that this 'day' is imminent and stress instead an indefinite period of waiting. More recent studies have argued for a more balanced interpretation, holding that Luke combines an emphasis on the fulfilment of hope for the kingdom in the events of the present with an expectation of a final consummation to come within the lifetime of his readers.[2] A key passage is the parable of the pounds (19.11ff.), in which a nobleman goes away to receive a kingdom and later returns. It is Luke's answer to expectations of an immediate manifestation of the kingdom, and suggests that at his ascension (cf. Acts 2.36; 3.30f.; 7.56) or possibly his crucifixion (Luke 22.69; 24.26) Jesus enters his kingly rule, thereafter exercising it invisibly until at the end of all things the kingdom 'comes'.[3] Two questions arise: what is the relation between the individual

experience of death and the future universal coming of the
kingdom? Does the one initiate a provisional intermediate
state pending the consummation of the other? Secondly, are
other passages which speak less precisely of a future partici-
pation in the blessings of the kingdom to be referred to the
universal end or to individual death?

The question of an intermediate state hinges on the interpretation of two passages, Jesus' reply to the penitent criminal,
'today you will be with me in paradise' (23.43) and his
teaching about the resurrection in 20.34–38.

23.43, as a response to 'remember me when you come in
your kingdom' in v. 42,[4] can be taken to imply a distinction
between paradise and coming 'in power' or an identification
of the two. On the first view Jesus is not able to grant the
man's request, but promises him a provisional state of
blessedness meanwhile.[5] But this hardly meets the demands
of the context. Luke is demonstrating Jesus' power to save
even on the cross, which bystanders are calling in question
(vv. 35, 37, 39).[6] The stress is on 'today'; all the man asks for
is granted in the promise of paradise, the meaning of which is
indicated in the case of Jesus himself in v. 46: acceptance into
the care of God. Anything less would not meet the case.

But does not Luke's stress on the resurrection as an
essential feature of the Christian message (e.g. Acts 2.32;
5.30ff.; 17.18; 23.6; 24.15) imply that the dead must await the
coming of the kingdom so that what the rich men in chapters
12 and 16 experienced at death was only temporary and
provisional? Here the interpretation of 20.34–38, Jesus' reply
to the Sadducees, is crucial. With Mark, Luke has Jesus
affirming the truth of the resurrection but there are important
modifications: he makes it clear that not all attain to the
resurrection, for sharing it involves sharing in the age to
come and being sons of God (vv. 35f., cf. Mark 12.25), he
omits Mark's reference to 'when they rise' and he expands v.
38 in a way which suggests that the dead are already alive in
relation to God.[7] It is difficult to resist the conclusion that
Luke intends his readers to think of the resurrection as a
privilege already enjoyed by the patriarchs and others who
have died. To interpret Luke in this way is not to attribute to
him a doctrine of immortality, for survival of death is not an
innate endowment but the gift of divine sonship for 'those

who are accounted worthy' (v. 35).[8] Resurrection is thus not
a single universal event and does not require for its consummation a location in a renewed universe coming into being
only at the dissolution of the present world order, but an
individual event in which each person at death is translated to
God's world.

It is clear therefore that the passages from which we began,
12.20f., 16.9, 22, speak of God's final determination of an
individual's lot taking place at the moment of death as 16.26
in any case implies.[9] What then are we to make of other
passages which speak of the kingdom or equivalent concepts
in future terms? Not all of them can be taken as referring to
life after individual death; certainly not 9.27, 17.34, nor
probably 13.28f., 22.29f.[10] But we cannot rule out the
possibility that Luke believes other instances to refer to an
inheritance into which one may enter at death. This may be
true of the promises attached to the beatitudes and woes
(6.20ff.), or the references to reward in 6.35, 14.14, to
inheriting eternal life in the age (or world, *aion*) to come
(10.25; 18.18, 30), or to entering or receiving or feasting in
the kingdom of God (12.32; 14.15; 18.17, 24f.; Acts 14.22).
There remains, however, an ambiguity about these passages,
which is perhaps deliberate. Because Jesus has already entered
upon his kingly rule by virtue of his exaltation, it is already
possible to enjoy its benefits.[11] For those who die before the
end there is the possibility of entering immediately upon its
joys. For the rest, entry awaits its final coming, on the day
when God has determined to judge the world and Luke is
content to allow these sayings to apply to either eventuality.
In either case what matters is our preparation beforehand, by
repentance and, as one of its fruits, the right use of wealth.

A feature of Luke's gospel is its insistence that the good
news is for the poor. This is evident at the beginning of the
sermon in the synagogue at Nazareth (4.16ff., citing Isa.
61.1ff., cf. RSV margin), in the blessings and woes which
open the sermon on the plain and in Jesus' reply to the
Baptist's question at 7.22: 'the blind receive their sight, the
lame walk, the lepers are cleansed and the deaf hear, the dead
are raised up, the poor have good news preached to them.'
Jesus' ministry to such people has already been illustrated in
the preceding chapters (cf. 5.12ff., 17ff.; 6.20ff., 7.11ff., 21)

and there are more examples later.[12] There is an anticipation
of all this in the song of Mary in 1.46ff., especially in v. 53,
'he has filled the hungry with good things, and the rich he has
sent empty away'. Already, in the expected birth of Jesus, the
great reversal has begun. Two questions suggest themselves:
how far does Luke spiritualize poverty, and how far does he
regard it as an ideal to which all Christians are called?

How far does Luke intend these passages to refer to
economic status? The fact that Mary's song so strongly recalls
the song of Hannah in I Sam 2.1ff. (esp. vv. 5, 7f.) suggests
the possibility that here at least 'poor' is being used in the
conventional Old Testament sense for the pious who depend
on God, rather than the literally impoverished.[13] On the
other hand the family of Jesus as Luke depicts them belong to
the economically poor (2.24; cf. Lev. 12.8), and a strong
argument for interpreting references to poverty generally in
an economic sense is the way in which it is linked with
physical disabilities (as in 7.22). Most disabled persons, being
unable to work, would also be poor. Linked with this is the
frequent stress on giving to the poor (as at 18.22–25). All this
suggests that 'rich' and 'poor' are not generally for Luke
merely colourful metaphors for 'proud' and 'humble'. The
beatitudes are more difficult to interpret. Matthew's version
explicitly refers to poverty of spirit (5.3), but Luke avoids
such qualifying phrases. It is clear from 6.20a that the
disciples are being addressed, but whether they have adopted
poverty (or had it forced on them because they have become
disciples) or have been called into discipleship from the ranks
of the poor as in I Cor. 1.26–29 is unclear.[14] In the former
case 6.20f. is essentially a blessing on discipleship,[15] as 6.22
certainly is, but neither alternative resolves the question
whether poverty for Luke is essentialy economic or spiritual.
It is true that Luke describes some disciples as having left all
to follow Jesus (5.11, 28; cf. 8.2f.; 18.28; Acts 3.6), but the
disciples in 6.20 include more than the twelve (6.17). Moreover, the sermon goes on in terms which suggest that the
hearers are far from destitute: they are to give and lend freely
(6.27ff.). Elsewhere too the disciples are bidden to give alms
(12.33; 16.8ff., contrast Acts 3.6). On the other hand we have
seen that the poor man Lazarus is taken to the place of blessedness after his death without discipleship being in question at all

(16.22). We should perhaps conclude that the beatitudes are not simply a description of disciples as disciples, but a blessing on those who actually experience poverty, hunger and grief, on disciples in so far as they are poor, and on the poor as potential disciples. We should also be wise to assume, however, that Luke did not intend to narrow the application too much; the power of the beatitudes has always lain in the range of experiences to which they can be seen to apply. They refer to poverty without specifying its cause, but it is poverty not discipleship which is pronounced blessed in 6.20.

Yet even if poverty has primarily an economic reference, there remains a spiritual dimension, as the use of identical language in 14.13f., 21 shows. While vv. 13f. suggest an economic reference v. 21 implies that the poor are the empty-handed who have nothing to distract them from response to God. Indeed, while the beatitudes are an example of the 'good news for the poor' of Isa. 61.1ff., they will only seem so to those who are prepared to look to God and accept Jesus' assurances in faith.

Does this mean that for Luke economic poverty is the goal of discipleship? Must all become poor if they are to be enriched? Surprisingly Luke does not advocate an ascetic ideal. It is true that he depicts Jesus as having nowhere to lay his head, and some of the twelve leave everything to follow him, supported by the generosity of others (5.11, 28; 8.2f.; 9.58) but one of the points of difference between Jesus and John the Baptist is that Jesus enters freely into normal activities of eating and drinking, so much so that he is abused for it (7.34). Luke emphasizes this elsewhere. At 5.27–32 he amends Mark 2.13–17 in such a way as to stress that Levi put on a 'great feast' (v. 29) and that the Pharisees' objection was not only to the company but to their 'eating and drinking' (v. 30). This is emphasized again in amendment of Mark in Luke 5.33–39, which unlike Mark 2.18–22 is a continuation of the same conversation. Here the objection is that Jesus' disciples substitute eating and drinking for the fasts and even the prayers in which the followers both of John and of the Pharisees engage (5.33; cf. Mark 2.18). Jesus' reply is that his presence brings such joy that festivity is inescapable. So what is seen as a danger in passages like 12.19, 45, 17.27f. has its acceptable counterpart in the life of Jesus and his disciples.

Such activities are out of reach of those who are as poor as Lazarus and would be objectionable to the throughgoing ascetic.

This conclusion is confirmed by other evidence from Luke and Acts. We note that although Zacchaeus' transformed attitude to possessions marks his salvation, he stops short of giving all he has to the poor, nor does Luke depict him as giving up his work and following Jesus. As we shall see, other exemplary characters in the gospel and Acts show the same pattern. They are well-to-do, and the emphasis is on their generosity, not on their adoption of voluntary poverty (e.g. 8.2f.; Acts 4.36f.; 10.36ff.). The Jerusalem church practises sharing of possessions so that none is in need,[16] but does not dispense with them altogether. They become dependent on others because of famine, not through choice (Acts 2.42ff.; 4.32ff.; 11.27ff.). For all the starkness of the language he uses, therefore, especially at 14.33, there is no evidence that Luke believed that Christians were called to absolute poverty in order to enter the kingdom.

Why then the uncompromising call for renunciation of possessions? Two possibilities must be rejected. It has been suggested that the different strands in Luke represent different stages in the history of the gospel tradition from the time of Jesus through to Luke's redaction, reflecting the different social conditions of each stage.[17] While this may explain the origin of the diversity, Luke's own view cannot be distilled only from the modifications he has made at the final stage. The fact that he included all the diverse traditions reveals his attitude, and the more rigorous sayings have to be treated with full seriousness. An alternative, suggested by Degenhardt,[18] is that the harder sayings are intended for church leaders, represented by the disciples in the gospel, who are expected to give up possessions altogether, while ordinary Christians, represented in the gospel by the people, are merely exhorted to generosity. But it is not clear that this distinction is rigidly observed (e.g. at 16.1–13) and there are the additional difficulties that in Acts 'disciple' refers not to leaders but to all Christians, and that renunciation of all possessions in the style of Luke 10.2ff. is not attributed to the missionaries of the early church. Indeed Luke 22.35f. seems to suggest that it is no longer to apply.

The reason for including the sterner sayings on renunciation, and widening their application as in 14.25ff., 18.18ff., must therefore lie in Luke's pastoral concern for his readers. It has often been observed that Luke appears to be more concerned for the rich than for the poor,[19] and this may very well reflect the situation of his readers, relatively prosperous and inclined to find a false security in their prosperity, vulnerable when Christian allegiance involves segregation from society (6.26) and perhaps affects business interests (cf. the suggestion of commercial pursuits in 6.34 (lending) and in 8.14; 17.28; 21.34). Luke clearly considers wealth a spiritual danger. Of course, when transferred from the setting of the itinerant ministry of Jesus to the situation of those who live in settled conditions, where, albeit without anxiety, daily necessities have to be secured,[20] the summons to sell all, give to the poor and follow Jesus would inevitably be modified in practice, but the best understanding of sayings like 14.33 is to think of them as intended to have a shock effect, in order to awaken readers to their plight. It is inner detachment from wealth which is crucial, and the best test of this is the willingness to give it away.

What then is the value of the relative poverty to which Luke summons his readers? The answer must lie partly in the empty-handedness of the poor. As we shall see in another chapter, it can be shown that for Luke entry into the kingdom of God is impossible except for the humble who trust in God; his teaching about wealth is another facet of this. Only by letting go of external support can we trust God, and those with possessions find this impossible. Possessions claim the heart (cf. 12.34; 16.14 'lovers of money'; 18.23 'became sad'). This is why the gospel can be preached to the poor and obtain a hearing while the rich generally fail to respond. By relinquishing possessions the rich free themselves for openness to God. The more stringent sayings calling for abandonment of possessions find their place here.

Is this the only value in the disposal of wealth? The question is prompted by 14.14 where the consequences of generosity are spelled out in terms of benefits for the giver rather than the recipient: 'you will be repaid at the resurrection of the just.' Is almsgiving positively a good deed to be rewarded, as in Judaism it is one of the standard acts of

piety;[21] or, more negatively, is it simply a way of getting rid
of wealth and so attaining the spiritual goal of poverty? The
former explanation is unlikely for Luke, if we are right in our
emphasis on empty-handedness, but in either view there is an
appeal to spiritual self-interest. How far does Luke consider
giving to the poor to be desirable because it brings benefit to
them?

Much will depend on how the reward is conceived. The
language of repayment and heavenly treasure can suggest an
almost mechanical system of *quid pro quo*, although we have
seen that Luke is sparing in his use of the actual word
'reward'.[22] But the variety of terms used to describe the
content of the reward and the fact that they are interchangeable (cf. 18.18ff.) should warn us against being over-literal.
The essence is communion with God, as in 6.35, 20.36. The
nature of the kingdom to which we are admitted depends on
what God is, and as 14.16ff. stresses, God is generous to
those who cannot pay. His good news is for the poor, not just
because they are ready to receive it (as 14.16ff. taken by itself
might suggest) but because, like the blind, the lepers and the
lame with whom they are linked (7.22) they need the
liberation which God offers through Jesus (cf. 13.16). This is
what makes the news good.[23] We have seen that in both
14.12ff. and 6.35f. the call to be generous is rooted in God's
generosity. We have noted too that for Luke the love
command is a unity; love of God and of neighbour are
inseparable. In Luke's eyes we are to be concerned for the
poor not just for the sake of the freedom from possessions it
brings and the possibility it thereby creates of trust in God,
but because the poor are God's concern. So, while woe is
pronounced on the rich not explicitly for their treatment of
the poor but because they already have and enjoy the comfort
of wealth (6.24), the parallels in 16.25 show what is implied
(cf. also Acts 20.35). In giving we become like God and in
refusing to give we are alienated from him. Given the fact
that the language of reward was embedded in the gospel
traditions which Luke used in his work, and in the vocabulary of biblical religion as a whole, how else might Luke have
made the point that giving to the poor benefits giver and
receiver alike; and how else might he have described how a
generous God receives one who has relinquished all for the

poor except in terms of reward, treasure and lavishness
(6.38)?

What, finally, may be deduced from this discussion for our
understanding of Christian character? The Christian profile
includes generosity. It is a response to human need and a
reflection of the love of God. There is no rejection of worldly
goods as such, for the disciples are distinguished by their
capacity to enjoy them, but possession of them and participa-
tion in everyday commercial affairs must be accompanied by
an inner renunciation. The quality of generosity can only
arise out of an inner freedom from possessions and a corre-
sponding trust in the care of God. For Luke this has a definite
other-worldly dimension. Only in the kingdom beyond
death or the last day is there real wealth. As the story of
Zacchaeus illustrates, such freedom is a grateful response to
the good news Jesus brings. This gratitude, freedom and trust
are possible only for those to whom God is a reality.

5

A Sense of God

The conclusion of the previous chapter invites us to look
more broadly at the way Luke depicts the response which
people make to Jesus.

Like other evangelists Luke reports a variety of reactions to
the events he describes. In some cases these are integral to the
development of the plot, showing cause and effect in the
sequence of events (cf. Luke 11.53f.), but surprisingly perhaps
'Luke the historian' makes little use of this device. More
commonly reactions are indicated in order to bring out the
character of the event, its astonishing or awe-inspiring
quality or the threat it poses to the unrepentant. In this way
Luke helps his readers to form their own judgment upon
what they read. Underlying this is the intention that the
reader should share (or possibly take warning from) the
response described. These reactions are thus an important
indication of Luke's expectations. While it would be a
misreading of the narrative to suggest that they are included
simply as examples for readers to imitate, they may nevertheless function as such and afford some understanding of Luke's
conception of Christian character. In this chapter we shall
take note of these reactions, relate them to other aspects of
Luke's narrative and the teaching of Jesus he reports, and
consider what lies behind them. One aspect, however, we
shall defer to the next chapter: faith requires more extended
treatment.

1. A common reaction is astonishment and wonder. In the
gospel it may be provoked by the wisdom and authority in
Jesus' teaching (4.22, 32; 20.26; cf. 2.47f.), or the authority

and power of his deeds (4.36; 8.56; 9.43; 11.14). Similarly wonder is registered at the events concerning the births of Jesus and John the Baptist (1.63; 2.18, 33), and at Jesus' resurrection (24.22, 41). In Acts wonder is occasioned, for example, by the apostles' speaking with other tongues (2.7), the conversion of Paul (9.21) and the coming of the Spirit upon the Gentile Cornelius. Luke uses a variety of terms to describe this reaction,[1] but they all express the fact that people have encountered something out of the ordinary, unexpected and unaccountable.

The meaning of what is encountered, however, is not always self-evident, and occurrences which provoke wonder often also lead to questioning. A contrast should be seen between the unreflective astonishment of those who hear what the shepherds report about the birth of Jesus and Mary's reaction as she turns over its meaning in her heart (2.18f.).[2] Wonder is also combined with questioning at 4.36, 8.25. The disciples are astonished at the report of the empty tomb, but this leads only to questions, not to faith (24.22; cf. vv. 15f., 25). Both at the expulsion of the demon in 11.14–16 and at Pentecost in Acts 2.7, 12f. astonishing events lead some to express wonder while others find an explanation in the powers of darkness or simple drunkenness. In 9.43ff. Luke makes the point very forcibly; the universal wonder at all Jesus did is set in sharp contrast with the warning of his betrayal. Readers of the gospel already know that it is central to his ministry but even the disciples to whom it is imparted find it impossible to understand. Wonder by itself may miss the point.

2. This explains the emphasis which Luke often places on the connection between hearing and doing. The image of people listening to Jesus, hearing his (or God's) word, and coming to him expressly for this purpose is a common one in Luke's narrative (5.1; 10.39; 15.1; 19.48; 20.45; 21.38). Frequently this hearing is associated with healing or exorcism. A similar picture is given in Acts.[3] It is the background for the sayings about the importance of hearing rightly. The Pharisees and lawyers heard the appeal of John the Baptist but rejected (*ethetesan*) God's will by not responding to his appeal for baptism (7.30). There is a similar risk that people will reject Jesus and those whom he sends: to do so is to reject

God himself (10.16). Such rejection occurs in the synagogue at Nazareth (4.28) and by the Pharisees later at 16.14. The consequences are disastrous; they involve God's act of judgment upon the whole nation of Israel in the destruction of the holy city (19.41–44). So there is a call for discernment, an ability to interpret the evidence which is plain for all to see, such as one would exercise in everyday life, recognizing the signs of the weather and reacting accordingly (12.54–56; cf. 19.42).

Behind this lack of discernment, however, lies the refusal of the will. Essentially, like John the Baptist before him, Jesus calls for repentance.[4] We have already looked at Luke's interest in repentance in chapter 1. Only when repentance has occurred has the message been truly heard (cf. Luke 8.12); so Luke can sometimes use the verb 'to hear' in the pregnant sense of 'hearing and responding' (8.8; 9.35; 10.16; 14.35; 16.29, 31; Acts 3.22f.; 28.28).

Such warnings are important not only for the crowds to whom Jesus preaches but for the disciples as well. They too must be careful how they hear. We have noted in the case of Mary and Martha how important hearing the word is for disciples (10.38ff.), but the discernment demanded of the crowds is also needed by them if they are not to lose what they have gained (8.18). Hence the sayings which stress doing as well as hearing. Luke's sermon on the plain ends with the parable of the two houses (6.47–9). The point of the contrast is to drive home the importance of putting into practice what Jesus teaches. In addition there are the parable of the disobedient servant, 12.47f., and the sayings in 8.21 and 11.28 in which hearing and carrying out the word of God are stated to be more significant for relationship to Jesus than the physical ties of family. In 8.21, which is parallel to Mark, Luke has modified the wording specifically to introduce the phrase 'those who hear the word of God and do it'. The correlative to the negative act of turning away from wrong in repentance is the positive practice of the teaching of Jesus.[5]

3. A reaction which on occasions betokens a deeper perception of what has occurred than wonder is fear. Sometimes Luke uses fear in a negative sense. The authorities fear the crowds, just as the disciples are terrified by what they take to be the apparition of a spirit (20.19; 22.2; 24.37). The end of

this age will be marked by terrifying events (21.9, 11, 36). Fear can also be produced by what is mysterious rather than directly menacing, and like wonder can lead to questioning (1.65f.). In some contexts fear and wonder are distinguished; at 8.35, 37, 39 Luke eliminates all suggestion of wonder in the people of Gerasa; they are simply afraid of Jesus and beg him to go away (cf. Mark 5.15, 17, 20).[6]

Fear is the regular response to visitation by an angel, and as regularly the visitor gives a reassurance that there is no need to fear (1.12f., 30; 2.9f.; cf. 24.5). This is a standard element in the Old Testament pattern which such accounts follow.[7] The source of fear here is a combination of the known and unknown. It is recognized that the visitor comes from God, but the implications of the visit are not known, and in any case God is essentially mysterious, powerful and threatening. 'Do not be afraid' is reassuring because it means that the angel has come for the good of the one visited. It is in effect a declaration of God's goodwill, which extends, as the contexts of the passages show, beyond those who receive the visitation to others who will benefit by the news.

Fear can thus be contrasted with faith. As we shall see, faith recognizes God's love and trusts in it, fear exists in the absence of such trust (8.50; 12.7, 32). But in other contexts Luke can refer to fear in a positive sense: it is the profound respect for the creator and judge that determines our behaviour as human beings and our scale of values. So in the same paragraph disciples can be urged to fear and not to fear (12.4–7). The proper response to the presence of God is to be afraid (9.34),[8] and the fear people feel at the appearance of an angel as God's messenger is not essentially out of place. Not fearing God is an expression for incorrigible wickedness (18.2, 4; 23.40) and in Acts 'fearing God' is the standard term for Gentiles who have been converted to Jewish faith and morals but have not adopted circumcision (Acts 10.2, 22; 13.16, 26).[9] As in the Old Testament fearing God embraces both faith and obedience (cf. Luke 1.50; Acts 10.35).[10]

It is not surprising therefore that fear should be a reaction in Luke to the events he narrates (cf. 1.65); it signifies people's perception that God is at work. But, perhaps because fear by itself is ambiguous, it is usually combined with other responses. In both 5.26 and 8.25 Luke expands Mark, adding

fear to astonishment in the one case and wonder to fear in the
other (Mark 2.12; 4.41). Wonder excludes craven fear, while
fear tempers astonishment with a recognition of the activity
of God. The disciples' fear in 8.25, after the stilling of the
storm, apparently differs from what they had felt just before
at v. 24 at the height of the storm. Earlier it was a sign of their
lack of faith; now it implies awe at the mystery of Jesus'
authority. If we are to detect fear behind Peter's plea for Jesus
to leave him at 5.8 (cf. 8.37) this too is tempered by wonder
in the next verse (5.9). Similarly fear can be joined with praise
(7.16); in such a combination it becomes specifically the awed
but grateful recognition of the presence and activity of God.
In 5.26 in fact all three responses, astonishment, praise and
fear, are found together (cf. Mark 2.12), and Luke's form of
the end of the sentence gives the reason: 'we have seen strange
things today' (*paradoxa*, 'beyond our expectation').

4. After a consideration of fear as the proper response to the
mystery of God, it is natural to draw attention to the
emphasis in Luke on humility. Two passages make the point
in almost identical words, 'everyone who exalts himself will
be humbled and he who humbles himself will be exalted'
(14.11; 18.14).

The saying in 18.14 concludes the parable of the Pharisee
and the tax-collector, which contrasts two attitudes to God as
expressed in the prayers of the two men. There is no
suggestion that the claims the Pharisee makes are untrue, but
he fails to humble himself before God as the tax-collector
does. His opinion of himself is consequently denied. It is not
he but the other, for all his sins, who is righteous in God's
view.

The tax-collector's plea, 'God be merciful to me, a sinner!'
is echoed elsewhere. The prodigal son returns with the
words, 'I have sinned against heaven (God) and before you. I
am no longer worthy to be called your son,' (15.18f., 21; cf.
also 5.8). But humility is also displayed by the centurion in
7.6f., who declares himself unworthy despite the testimonial
given of him by the Jewish leaders in v. 4.[11] Humility is
appropriate not only for the 'sinner' but for the 'worthy' and
the 'righteous'. It is the self-abasement before God which is
appropriate for the creature before the creator. Humility is
the recognition of the truth about oneself. This is why in

16.15 the Pharisees' claim to righteousness is false: their arrogance is repulsive to God. Not to give glory to God is to arrogate to oneself a status which human beings do not possess, as the story of the death of Herod in Acts 12.21–3 illustrates (cf. Acts 10.26; 14.15).[12] Consequently to have expectations of glory, as the people of Capernaum do, is a sign of unrepentance (10.15). One has to become like a child to enter the kingdom of God (18.16f.; cf. 10.21). Repentance means 'justifying God', that is, acknowledging his verdict upon us to be right (7.29, 35); so we in turn are justified, his verdict being that we are in the right (as in 18.14a). All this reflects common Jewish ideas as represented in the Old Testament.[13] It is important, however, to take note of the particular slant which Luke gives it. In the parable of the Pharisee and the tax collector v. 9 as well as v. 14 defines the significance which Luke sees in the story. It is a warning to those who trust in themselves as righteous and despise others. There are two dimensions under consideration, attitudes to God and to other human beings, and both are illustrated in the Pharisee's prayer. The Pharisee despises the tax-collector. It is integral to his estimate of himself that he should measure himself by the shortcomings of others. The two dimensions of his attitude are thus interwoven.

How far is this also true of the parable about places at table which precedes the other occurrence of 'everyone who exalts himself . . .' at 14.11? It is sometimes taken as straightforward advice on social behaviour at feasts, or as an illustration of modesty in human relationships generally, and is regarded as evidence of Luke's 'moralizing tendency'.[14] But 14.7–10 is introduced as a parable, and we should not regard this as meaning no more than 'example-story'. Further vv. 7–10 are linked with vv. 12–14 to form a pair of paragraphs with parallel introductions. While vv. 12–14 also deal with human relationships, we have seen that the advice to the host to invite the poor to his parties is linked to and grounded in the parable of the great feast in vv. 16–24, which depicts the hospitality of God.[15] In addition, the whole section, 14.2–24, is set at a meal table in a Pharisee's house, and implies criticism of Pharisaic ways. As 16.15 later makes plain, the Pharisees are prime examples of an attitude of arrogance towards human beings which God finds offensive; 'what is exalted among men is an abomination in the sight of God' is another formulation of the principle stated at 14.11. We should therefore assume that the same double reference applies to 14.7–10 as to 18.9–13. In the latter passage the stress lies on relations with God, in the former on relations with other human beings, but in both the implication is that these two dimensions are inseparable. Our dealings with others involve (and are a parable of) our dealings with God.

14.11 and 18.14 thus echo in two respects the reversal theme which we observed in our study of Luke's attitude to wealth. They stress in the realm of attitudes what we saw to be true in the realm of possessions: existing conditions will be reversed; the proud and the rich will become humble and poor, while the humble and the poor will be exalted and enriched. They also emphasize that the test of what pride and wealth mean is to be found in our dealings with our fellow human beings.

The importance of humility is not limited, however, to the moment of repentance. There are frequent cautions on the subject addressed to disciples. In addition to the warning against self-righteous judgment of others in 6.36ff., we have 9.46–8 in which Jesus counters the disciples' dispute about rank among themselves by identifying himself with a child, and a similar passage at 22.24–7 where greatness is defined in terms of the youngest and the servant, again with reference to Jesus.[16] 17.7ff. shows what the status of a servant means: obedience and not trading on duty done. We meet the obedience emphasis elsewhere, in 12.35–48, 16.10–12, 19.12ff., and in the emphasis we have already examined on 'doing' as well as 'hearing', and in 10.20 there is a warning not to rejoice in achievements but in the grace of God. The proper attitude for a disciple is to acknowledge his servant status and not to act towards others as though he were anything else.

5. It is the response of joy and praise, however, which is most characteristic of Luke. In the gospel he uses eleven verbs with variations on the meaning 'praise' or 'rejoice' forty-two times, against fourteen in Matthew, five in Mark and twenty in John. Of these eleven, five are used by him alone.[17] The related nouns and adjectives he uses sixteen times against eight in Matthew, two in Mark and ten in John. The contrast with Mark is especially striking, for in that gospel the

dominant reaction is fear. Luke adds joy or praise where Mark has no reaction, as in 5.25, 18.43 (Mark 2.12a; 10.52) and elsewhere expands Mark's description to include it (19.37; 23.47; Mark 11.9; 15.39). In both 5.25f. and 18.43 the result is a double response, from the person healed and from observers standing by, as in the non-Marcan 13.13 coupled with 17.

Joy emphasizes the quality of what has occurred, whether the preaching of the word (8.13), healing (17.15ff.; 19.37) or the resurrection of Jesus (24.41, 52f.). It is a welcome event because what has long been awaited has now come (as in the case if Simeon, 2.25–28), a need long felt has now been met (as in the case of the healing miracles just referred to in 5.25f.; 13.13ff.; 18.43), or an unexpected and undeserved privilege has now been granted (as with Mary, 1.46ff.). Joy is expressed in thanksgiving, which involves recognition both of the source of the benefit received and its quality as a gift (cf. 17.15, 18). Through thanksgiving joy is focussed in a discernment of God as the giver; but, as the passages cited make clear, it is a recognition, not primarily of what God is but of what he has done. In the coming of Jesus the awaited new age has dawned and people enjoy its benefits (cf. 1.78; 2.20; 7.16). It is in keeping with this that the disciples should be the ones to rejoice at Jesus' entry as king into Jerusalem (19.37), for they have seen what kings and prophets had longed to see (10.23f.). It is 'eschatological joy', the rejoicing of the end-time when the kingdom has come. In anticipation of the joy to come when the poor will be enriched and the rich impoverished it is possible to rejoice now, even under persecution (6.20–23). So the good news which the angel announces to the shepherds can be characterized as 'great joy' (2.10).

A similar atmosphere of joy permeates the narrative of Acts. Here too joy is the response to healing (3.8; 8.8) and the preaching of the word (2.46f; 8.39; 10.46; 13.48; 16.39; cf. 15.31). It is occasioned by God's work in the conversion of Gentiles (11.18, 23; 15.3; 21.20), and by the experience of persecution (5.41; 13.52).

Luke conceives of this joy as corporate and having physical expression. It is essentially shared, and its typical manifestation is a party at which there may be song and dance (cf.

15.25). Jesus eats and drinks with sinners (5.30, 34; 15.2; cf. 1.58; 7.34; 15.6, 9, 23ff.; 19.37).[18] Luke alone uses the verb *skirtan*, which means to leap or dance for joy (1.41, 44; 6.23). People may be beside themselves for joy (cf. 24.41; Acts 12.14). Further, in 15.6, 9, 22f. it is to be noted that it is the finder not the found who rejoices. The point of 7.34, 'the Son of Man has come eating and drinking ... a friend of tax collectors and sinners', is that Jesus rejoices as much as the sinners at their repentance. This joy mirrors the joy of God and the angels who form his court (15.7, 10; cf. 2.13).[19] The celebrations in which Jesus shares anticipate the feasting of the messianic banquet when the kingdom comes (cf. 14.15). But without the discernment of God at work the joy cannot be shared. Those who do not respond to the Son of Man in repentance are unable to rejoice that he comes feasting and revelling with those who do (7.34f., cf. 5.30–32; 15.1f.; 19.6f., 39f.).

The note of joy is particularly prominent in the canticles which Luke includes in the infancy narratives of the gospel (1.46ff., 68ff.; 2.14, 29ff.). The extent to which these represent Luke's own composition is disputed. The canticles of chapter 2 have the strongest claim to be Luke's own, while the fact that Mary's and Zechariah's hymns could be detached from their settings without disruption and that their contents do not entirely fit their contexts may suggest that for them Luke drew upon traditional sources.[20] But if so he has adapted them, especially at 1.48, 76. On the other hand, the appropriateness of Mary's hymn generally in Luke's setting is underlined by the close parallels with the hymn of Hannah in I Sam. 2.1–10. All the canticles draw heavily upon Old Testament language and models, and reinforce the Old Testament atmosphere which Luke, by language, style and content, has deliberately created in these chapters, and this makes a judgment on their origin particularly difficult. It has been argued that they derive from the early Christian community in Jerusalem which saw itself in terms of the 'poor' (*anawim*), in the tradition of some of the Old Testament psalms and the writings of the covenanters of Qumran. Whether or not this is so, they reflect such a piety and it is congenial to Luke. Themes which are encountered elsewhere make virtually their first appearance in these hymns: the fulfilment of God's promises through a descendant of David bringing redemption to Israel and hope for the Gentiles (1.54f., 68–75; 2.29–32), God's generosity to the empty-handed (1.48f.; cf. 10.21), joy in heaven (2.13f.), the reversal of rich and poor (1.53), and of proud and humble (1.52f.). The joy of these things is articulated in praise.

A point to be noted however is how infrequently this joy is linked to the Holy Spirit. 13.52 is the only clear instance in Acts and, in the gospel, the only references are Jesus' prayer of praise at 10.21 and Zechariah's hymn at 1.67. At 1.67 the link is established through prophecy, which is the major activity of the Spirit in Luke's view. He appears to regard speaking with tongues as a form of this (Acts 19.6), and both can involve praise (cf. Acts 2.11; 10.46). This is because the Spirit gives insight (sometimes in the form of visions) which may be formulated either in prophecy or praise (cf. Acts 2.17; 7.55; 11.5–12; Luke 10.18, 21). The implications of this for Luke's understanding of joy are important. It is not a feeling injected by the activity of the Spirit but a response to the mighty acts of God, in Jesus and in the mission of the church generally, or in the individual's own particular case; the Spirit's contribution is to give insight into the significance of what has happened.

There is, however, a note of caution: there can be a false basis for thanksgiving and joy. They may be self-centred and not truly reflect the joy of God. The thanksgiving of the Pharisee in the parable was unacceptable (18.11) and the disciples themselves must be careful that the ground of their rejoicing is not the defeat of Satan through the deeds they perform but simply that their names are included in God's register of his people (10.20). The next paragraph (10.21–24) spells out what this means: the disciples are only babes, without wisdom or understanding, yet God in his generosity has revealed himself to them. God's grace not human achievement is the cause of joy. Similarly in more than one passage Luke sets in contrast the joy of the crowds and the call of Jesus for repentance. Some hear and receive the word joyfully, but do not survive the testing that follows (8.13). In 13.26f. those who have feasted with the householder are nevertheless dismissed because they are unrepentant 'workers of iniquity'. In 11.27 an unthinking eulogy is countered by emphasis on hearing and keeping the word of God, and in 14.15ff. a similar outburst leads to the warning contained in the parable of the great feast. Joy like wonder can fail to perceive the real issues.

The primary purpose of the canticles and other references to joy and praise in Luke's narrative is to clarify the significance of what is happening and set the tone of the reader's response, like the background music of a film. In Jesus the hope of Israel is realized; the prophecies are fulfilled as he speaks and the kingdom of God is present in his exorcisms (4.21; 11.20). But it is clear that Luke intended more than this. The gospel contains injunctions to give thanks (6.23; 10.17ff.; 17.15ff.), and the parable of the two brothers in 15.11ff. implies that it is a repudiation of God not to join in his rejoicing. The references to joy in Acts show that Luke did not consider occasions of rejoicing to be confined to the time of Jesus' earthly ministry. As exalted Lord he continues his work (Acts 3.16). The thanksgiving articulates our humanity and dependence upon the creator. Luke would hardly have attempted to emphasize the joyful quality of his narrative unless he had wanted his readers to share it.

6. We may conclude this survey of responses and attitudes in Luke by drawing attention to two topics which strictly come under neither heading, but are just as important in the context of the subject of this chapter.

It is natural, when describing the responses of wonder, fear or joy which participants in the story express, to pay attention to the outward words and actions by which these emotions are revealed. Obedience, hearing and doing, similarly concentrate on behaviour. Humility too is reflected in what people say about themselves, and their behaviour towards others (cf. 17.10). We have seen on the other hand how often the outward expressions can be ambiguous; wonder or joy can arise from a misunderstanding of the true state of things.

Luke lays some emphasis on a person's inward response and disposition. He makes generous use of *kardia* ('heart'), and freely employs other terms for thought, although of course all the gospels make some reference to this.[21] The heart is the seat of affection as well as thought (cf. 1.17); it is upon thought that Luke concentrates.

Thoughts can lie hidden. One aspect of hypocrisy is the

disparity between outward appearance and inward reality (20.20).[22] Luke frequently represents the real reaction to Jesus' words and deeds as occurring in the realm of hidden thoughts, although Jesus is able to see through the outward facade (cf. 5.22; 6.8 (added to Mark 3.3); 7.31, 49; 9.46f. (open conversation in Mark 9.33ff.); 11.17). Jesus' presence is a catalyst which forces people to declare their true selves in responding to what he says and does. In this respect he brings into the present moment what will occur at the last day, when the secrets of all hearts will be revealed (2.34, 35b; 12.2f.).[23]

What happens in the heart is therefore of vital importance. Although it may be kept hidden, it determines in the long run what is said and done outwardly (6.45; 10.27), and it is by the heart that God judges (16.15; cf. 1.51). Where the heart is set indicates what our true values are (12.34). It is therefore important that the word which is the good news of the kingdom of God should be retained in the heart (cf. 8.12; 2.19) and have its effect there. But the relationship is reciprocal. The heart may be too slow or dulled by indisciplined living and the concerns of daily life for the word to have its effect (cf. 21.34; 24.25). The heart itself must be honest and good and hold fast to the word (8.15).[24] There is thus a counterbalance to the emphasis on both hearing and doing that we have drawn attention to in Luke. Inwardness is also important: what a person is within will determine whether doing follows hearing, and it is with the heart that God on the day of judgment will deal.

We have evidence here to justify our search for Luke's view of Christian character. At times Luke seems to suggest that what a person is already predisposes him to respond favourably or unfavourably to the news of Jesus. Because they are lovers of money and arrogant, the Pharisees mock and repudiate Jesus (16.14). Because they are righteous and god-fearing, men and women like Zechariah and Elizabeth, Simeon and Anna, the centurion of Capernaum and Cornelius welcome the good news and believe. Such a view appears to cut across the understanding of the gospel as a call for repentance in which the sinner finds joy in forgiveness, a view also to be found in Luke. If at times he emphasizes the former, it is because he recognizes the extent to which the latter depends on it. Total character change is difficult and rare. There is a consistency and a continuity in human behaviour which arises from the integration of the personality behind the behaviour. Luke recognizes that even though our actions cumulatively affect what we become, what we do arises from what we are. If the good news of the kingdom is to have its due response, it will arise, not from periodic words and actions but from what one is in the heart; in our terminology, from the development of Christian character.

7. We have already noted that some of the attitudes we are discussing find their expression in prayer, whether it be the joy of the thanksgivings of chapter 2 or the contrasting prayers of the parable of 18.9ff. Prayer is important to Luke. He uses a wider vocabulary for the activity of prayer than other writers and makes extensive use of Jesus and others as examples.[25] We must therefore pause to consider what this may contribute to our understanding of Christian character.

Jesus is so frequently shown at prayer in Luke's gospel that it must be regarded as an essential part of the picture Luke wishes to give. It is a detail added to Mark at 3.21, 5.16, 6.12, 9.18, 28, and occurs also at 10.21, 11.1, 22.32, 41, 23.34, 46. These prayers are frequently at moments of special significance in the narrative, and it is very likely that Luke's primary intention is to show that throughout his ministry Jesus took the crucial decisions in full dependence upon God and in obedience to his will.[26] If so, then Luke may have felt that the prayer at the Mount of Olives (22.41ff.) represented the essential content of most of the others: 'not my will but thine be done'. Thus through prayer we touch again on the theme of obedience.

But 11.1 shows that Jesus' habit of prayer is also an example for the disciples, although the link is only obliquely made. The reason why the disciples ask for instruction on prayer is that John the Baptist had instructed his disciples (and we are aware from 5.33 of differences), but they make their request after Jesus himself had been praying. Further, apart from vv. 2–4, the teaching Jesus gives them is essentially an encouragement to engage in prayer, so that the emphasis of the whole passage is on doing it rather than on how it should be done. Jesus' example reinforces this.[27]

Prayer is also prominent in Acts. It is a regular feature of the life of the church (1.14; 2.42; etc.), is resorted to before important decisions (1.24; 6.6; 13.1–3) and in times of crisis (12.5; cf. 16.25). Various aspects are depicted: for forgiveness (8.22, 24), or healing (9.40), as a regular religious duty at specified hours (3.1; 10.9, 30), as an act of praise under persecution (4.23ff.) and upon departure (20.36; 21.5). In various ways Luke keeps the idea of prayer before his readers.

Apart from Luke 11.1ff. however, Luke offers little in the way of direct teaching upon prayer. Apart from the attack on long prayers (not for their length but for their motive as a form of display, 20.47 = Mark 12.40) and the contrast between the disciples of Jesus and those of the Pharisees and John the Baptist (5.33–5), there is nothing of a polemical nature in Luke's prayer material, suggesting perhaps that it was not a controversial issue for him.[28] The incidental references, however, are instructive. Prayer is an expression of love for enemies (6.28; 23.34); continuing prayer for God's deliverance is an element in the faithfulness for which the Son of Man will look when he comes (18.1, 7f.); prayer for forgiveness is an expression of humility (18.13f.); praise is an expression of the joy which arises from the discernment of God at work. As we shall see, another element in persistence is prayer not to succumb to temptation (22.40, 46).[29] These are all topics we have discussed already, or will come to in later chapters.

It is remarkable how these are reflected in the prayer the disciples are to use in 11.2–4. The Lord's Prayer has undergone modification and expansion in the manuscript tradition, no doubt because of its regular use in worship, but there is little doubt that the tradition translated in the RSV represents what Luke wrote.[30] Its wording bears traces of his own style at some points, but there is no reason to doubt that it was already for him a traditional prayer, as the parallels with Matthew show. It begins as a prayer for the coming of God's kingdom, for God so to act that the world will be ready to ascribe to him the glory due to him (v. 2).[31] It contains a petition for forgiveness, based upon the forgiveness we show to those who are indebted to us (v. 4).[32] It concludes with a request that we should be prevented from succumbing to temptation.[33]

As a whole the prayer is cast in the form of a request, and

the teaching which follows amplifies this, picking up the reference to giving bread in the central petition of v. 3.[34] Verses 5–13 are an encouragement to audacity in prayer, asking in the confidence that the gift will be given.[35] Much of this is parallelled in Matt. 7.7–11, but Luke concludes with a reference to the Holy Spirit. There can be little doubt that Luke has introduced this modification. It intrudes unexpectedly into the context and is not taken up in what follows.[36] The intention, however, is perhaps less to reduce all God's gifts to one (there is no suggestion of this elsewhere and it would implicitly deny the content of the Lord's Prayer), than to avoid a materialistic interpretation of 'good things' (as in 12.19; 16.25). We saw at 12.29–31 that in his version of Matt. 6.31–33 Luke was careful to exclude the possibility of material gain from trusting in God.[37]

This dependence upon God as giver is epitomized in the opening address of the prayer, 'Father'. J. Jeremias has urged strongly the view that this form of address goes back to Jesus himself and is without parallel in the language of Jewish prayers, carrying in the Aramaic *abba* a strong sense of intimacy.[38] That the early church was familiar with a prayer beginning in this form is suggested by Rom. 8.15, Gal. 4.6, but so far as the gospels are concerned it is only Luke who preserves a prayer for disciples in this form (contrast Matt. 6.9). He does not preserve the Aramaic here any more than elsewhere, and it is unlikely that his readers would have known the implications of the word in that language, but they would be aware that in using this address disciples would be imitating Jesus' own practice (cf. 10.21; 22.42; 23.34, 46), and that only two paragraphs before Jesus had claimed that it was his vocation to reveal the Father to his disciples (10.21–3). What such fatherhood might mean would be further amplified by 12.22–32: they are not to be anxious for the Father intends to give them the kingdom. The Lord's prayer is thus an expression of faith; it is couched in the form of petition in the conviction that we are dealing with a God who is willing to give.

Luke sees this prayer as integral to discipleship. It is a badge of identity which distinguishes the followers of Jesus from those of the Baptist, and is to be used regularly.[39] This is not only true in a formal sense. The content of the prayer gathers together characteristics which should belong to disciples and articulates them in an address to God. Above all the teaching in which the prayer is set brings out the fact that it presupposes the generosity of God, which we saw in chapter 2 to be a characteristic of the sermon on the plain, to which faith is a response and which disciples are required in turn to express in their dealings with others.

In this chapter we have considered some of the reactions to events which Luke attributes to the participants in his story, and which he clearly tries to communicate to his readers both by his narrative and by the teaching of Jesus he records. Wonder, fear, joy all spring from a discernment of the saving activity of God. About each of these considered in isolation there is an ambivalence; they may or may not betoken a genuine recognition of the truth; in combination they are an expression of the awareness that God, who is essentially mysterious and all-powerful, has disclosed himself as compassionate and trustworthy. Humility is another expression of the sense of God. It is the recognition of how things are in the universe of which God is the creator and judge. All this finds its articulation in prayer of praise and petition, and should do so. Both praise and petition affirm God to be the source of all that is good. An important test of a true response is the willingness to allow hearing to pass over into obedience, so that repentance occurs and is sustained in a different pattern of living. But outward expression alone is not enough. That too can become a hypocritical facade. What matters is the attitude of the heart. It is in the depths of one's being that the test is ultimately applied whether one has a true sense of God. This sense of God, however, is not just a general awareness of the ever-present reality of the creator in his universe; it is the specific recognition of God active in the words and deeds of Jesus, as he affects the lives of those who encounter him. This activity continues after the ascension in the life of the church which preaches and heals in his name. The 'sense of God' is the recognition of the dawning of God's kingdom, the time of salvation. It is not a natural endowment of 'religious' persons, nor can it be manufactured at will; it is awakened by God.

6

Faith

After our discussion in the last chapter it is natural to consider Luke's understanding of faith. In the writings of Paul and John and in the epistle to the Hebrews there are developed and distinctive concepts which have tended to dominate subsequent theology, but it would be a mistake to read them into other parts of the New Testament. Luke has his own perspective which makes an important contribution to the Christian profile which we are seeking.[1]

Faith is associated with conversion. In Acts it is the basic indispensable response to the gospel which marks the moment of transition for one who becomes a Christian. 'He/they believed' (*episteuse/episteusan*) means 'he/they were converted'.[2] In 2.44 'those who believed' means 'the converts'. There is also a general word for conversion (*epistrophe*, 15.3, literally 'turning'),[3] but the use of *pisteuein* shows what conversion involves. It is an act of believing, not just of renunciation or the adoption of a new life-style or identification with a new community (cf. 14.27; 26.18).[4] Sometimes the object of believing is spelled out: the Lord, more fully the Lord Jesus, Jesus Christ, the Lord Jesus Christ, or simply God,[5] but the degree to which believing has become a technical term for conversion is shown by its use without an object. Such believing is also associated with repentance and baptism. The response is to the message proclaimed by the apostles and others; so faith is often associated with hearing. What is attained by faith is described as forgiveness of sins or its equivalent, justification, as eternal life, or more comprehensively as salvation.[6]

It is in accord with this usage that in the interpretation of the parable of the sower in the gospel Luke adds to the description of the first category of listeners from whose hearts the devil takes away the seed altogether, 'that they may not believe and be saved'. Although they hear the message they never reach the stage of conversion (Luke 8.12). Similarly in Luke 20.5, 'believe' means 'repent and submit to John's baptism' (cf. 7.30). It is a development of this tendency that on occasions 'the faith' occurs in Acts almost as short-hand for Christianity itself, the message which is preached and believed (cf. 6.7; 13.8; 24.24).[7]

But faith is more than a momentary, decisive response. It is an attitude which continues to be characteristic of the Christian from then on.[8] A common designation for Christians in Acts is 'those who have come to believe' (*hoi pepisteukotes*, 15.5; 18.27; 19.18; 21.20, 25). The perfect participle employed in the Greek implies the continuing exercise of what has been begun. At least twice Luke uses the adjective *pistos* (which can also mean 'faithful') to mean 'possessing faith' (Acts 10.45; 16.1, possibly also 16.15), virtually with the meaning 'Christian', and the present participle, translated 'believers' or 'who believes(d)' (RSV) in 5.14, 10.43, 22.19, may in at least some instances imply the continuous exercise of faith.[9] It is also important that the verb *epikaleisthai* ('to call upon'), which describes in effect the expression of faith in words, is used in the present as well as the aorist; Christians are those who continue to 'call on the name of the Lord' (9.14, 21; contrast 2.21; 22.16). It is this aspect of faith as a continuing mark of Christian living that we shall especially explore further in this chapter.[10]

Faith is also connected with healing. In Acts faith can come about as a consequence of acts of healing and exorcism (8.6, 13; 9.42; cf. 13.12). There are traces of this idea in the gospel too (5.1–11; 10.23f.),[11] but more prominent there is the tradition which Luke takes over from Mark and Matthew of depicting faith as a prerequisite for healing. Not even in Mark is this an invariable prerequisite, although at 6.6 (omitted by Luke) he suggests unbelief as the reason for Jesus' inability to heal in his home area. Faith is explicitly mentioned in Mark 2.1–12 (Luke 5.17–26) the paralytic let down through the roof, 5.21–43 (Luke 8.40–56) Jairus' daughter and the woman

with the haemorrhage, 9.14–29 (Luke 9.37–43) the epileptic
boy, and 10.46–52 (Luke 18.35–43) the blind man at Jericho.
In the case of the paralytic and the epileptic boy, the faith
concerned is not that of the patient but of friends or relatives
who are responsible. Luke retains all these passages with
modifications, and in addition has the 'Q' passage about the
centurion's faith on behalf of his servant (7.1–10) and a story,
without parallel, of ten lepers (17.12–19). In Acts there are
two further examples. In 3.16 the man at the temple gate is
healed by faith, although it is not clear whose faith it is.[12]
14.8–10 refers explicitly to a lame man's faith.

Outside these passages, however, Luke gives the impression
that he lays little emphasis on faith as the key to healing,
preferring to stress the power possessed by Jesus and the
apostles, virtually as a physical force whose flow can be
sensed, and depicting healings as acts of sovereign compassion and initiative without reference to the attitude of the
beneficiary. It is not surprising that Luke has been accused of
being the most magical of the gospel writers.[13] To do so,
however, is to ignore Acts 19.11–20, which stresses that the
name of Jesus, more powerful than pagan magic, is only
operative in those who believe in him. Also important is
Luke 10.17–20, in which the victory of the disciples over the
demons is the gift of Jesus himself, not their own achievement, and is less important than their own salvation. Where
Luke does not specifically link acts of healing and exorcism
with faith, they nevertheless occur within the context of faith
in its broader sense.

In fact where Luke does link faith and healing there are
additional shades of meaning to be detected in his narrative.
In no instance is faith simply belief that healing can take place.
To begin with Acts, it is well known that *sozein* in Greek can
mean 'to heal' as well as 'to save'. In Mark 5.34, 10.52, for
example, *he pistis sou sesoken se* is often translated 'your faith
has made you well' (RSV; cf. NEB, JB). A comparable translation is possible in Acts 14.9, the man 'has faith to be made
well' (RSV; *pistin tou sothenai*). But we note that Paul had just
been preaching the gospel (14.7f.) and the phrase is so close to
'believe in the Lord Jesus and you will be saved' (16.31) that
we are entitled to wonder whether either faith or the meaning
of *sothenai* can be narrowly restricted to healing alone.

Acts 3.16 does not use the verb *sozein*. Faith in that passage is clearly related to the 'health' of the cripple who was 'made strong'. But in 4.9, referring to this incident, Peter says, 'if we are being examined today concerning a good deed done to a cripple, by what means this man has been healed', using the ambiguous *sesotai*. 4.10 is clear enough: the man has been made 'well' (*hygies*), but this occurred through the name of Jesus, which leads to verse 12, 'there is salvation in no one else ... no other name ... by which we must be saved'. The healing of the man has thus become the basis of a statement about salvation. Either Luke is playing on the ambiguity of *sozein* or there is a real connection. The fact that the 'name' is involved in both suggests the latter. Healing is an element in the wider salvation which the name of Jesus imparts. The salvation which was given to the man encompassed more than the relief of his lameness, and the faith which was involved according to 3.16, whether it was the cripple's or Peter's, was more than a confident expectation of healing; it was a reaching out to the Jesus who 'saves'.

In the light of these passages we can turn to the gospel to see whether the same possibility of a broader interpretation of faith and healing exists there. In 8.26–39 Luke reproduces Mark's story of the Gerasene demoniac. The word 'faith' does not occur, but Luke makes two significant modifications. In v. 35 he describes the condition of the man after the expulsion of the demons. Mark (5.15) had described him as 'sitting there, clothed and in his right mind'. In Luke this becomes 'sitting at the feet of Jesus, clothed and in his right mind'. We have referred to the phrase 'sitting at Jesus' feet' already, in connection with 10.39.[14] It is the attitude of the disciple, attentive to the word. Luke intends us to think of the man as a convert who naturally wants to go with Jesus when he leaves the area (v. 38, cf. Mark 5.18). We have already been told of others, the women who, after being cured of demon possession, go 'with him' and the disciples on his journeys (8.2f.). The change in Luke 8.36 reinforces this impression. Mark's 'those who had seen it told what had happened to the demoniac and to the swine' becomes 'those who had seen it told them how he who had been possessed with demons was healed'. In Greek the verb is again *esothe*, and after the previous verse it is clear that Luke intends a wider reference. The man has been saved.

There are four passages where Luke uses the Marcan phrase, 'your faith has made you well' (*he pistis sou sesoken se*). Two are peculiar to Luke, and two based on Mark. 17.11–19 describes the healing of ten lepers. In response to their request for help Jesus sends them away to show themselves to the priests, who are required by the law to certify their cleansing (cf. Lev. 14.1ff.). We are reminded of the earlier incident at 5.12–16 (Mark 1.40–45), but in the present case it is only 'as they went they were healed'. One, a Samaritan, returns to give thanks, and Jesus remarks on the failure of the others to do the same. There are overtones here of the contrast in Luke's gospel and Acts between Jewish and non-Jewish responses to the mission of Jesus and the church, but the interesting point is what follows. It is to the Samaritan that Jesus says *he pistis sou sesoken se*. It is no doubt true that the man's faith had made him well; the trust he displayed in asking for help and his unquestioning obedience to Jesus' instruction to go and offer evidence of a cure before any had taken place could only be described as faith. Yet all ten lepers had exhibited this, and the point at vv. 17ff. is the contrast between the Samaritan and the other nine. In its context the pronouncement must refer to the Samaritan's action alone. What then is his faith? It must be the attitude which was able to discern in the healing work of Jesus the act of God, and did not take this for granted but returned to give thanks to Jesus and glory to God (vv. 16, 18). More than healing is involved here, and *sesoken se* must be translated 'has saved you'. It embraces both the cleansing from leprosy and the gratitude to God which flowed from it. Faith correspondingly includes the recognition of God's goodness which prompted the gratitude, as well as the trust and obedient response which led to the cure.[15]

7.36–50 is more complex. The precise relation of the anointing of the woman in Simon the Pharisee's house to the stories of the anointing at Bethany in Mark 14.3–9 (Matt. 26.6–13) and John 12.1–8 is uncertain. It is likely that there are several different threads interwoven, partly by Luke, partly by the tradition before him, and there is some tension as a result.[16] Some interpreters are tempted to take v. 47a, with the preceding verses, as meaning that Jesus forgives the woman on the basis of the love she shows. This would explain the position of v. 48 as a pronouncement of the forgiveness now granted. But v. 47b. and the parable in vv. 41–43 show that the woman's love is the result of her having already been forgiven, perhaps in some previous meeting with Jesus. In the knowledge of this, she expresses her devotion in an extravagant way, while the Pharisee, knowing nothing of such forgiveness, is perfunctory almost to the point of neglect in the treatment of his guest. Verse 48 must therefore be taken as a confirmation by Jesus of forgiveness already affirmed, necessary because the critical attitude of the Pharisee had called it in question. The episode as a whole illustrates the contrasting attitudes to Jesus described in 7.31–35. What then are we to make of 7.50? It is the only occurrence of *he pistis sou sesoken se* outside a healing story. There is no question of the woman having been ill or demon-possessed. She is simply described as a 'sinner' (v. 37). RSV rightly translates, 'your faith has saved you' here. But to what is Jesus referring? A reference to the forgiveness already affirmed in v. 48 would result in a double affirmation of what has been the presupposition of the story from the start, and seems unduly repetitive. It is true that a new step is taken as the other guests dispute Jesus' right to pronounce such forgiveness, but an appropriate response by Jesus would have to be addressed to them as at 5.24ff. Instead Jesus speaks to the woman. The only new factor in her situation is her expression of gratitude. Like the Samaritan leper the woman has returned to give thanks. Moreover, she has persisted in doing so publicly in the face of hostile reaction. It is hard to resist the conclusion that her gratitude and her persistence are elements in her salvation and the faith that leads to it, which go beyond the forgiveness of sins already affirmed. Because of this she can go in peace. Like Simeon in a different context (2.28ff.) she has seen God's salvation and given thanks.[17]

We now turn to the first of the two passages Luke has taken from Mark. In 8.43–48 he reproduces Mark's story (5.25–34) of the woman with the haemorrhage. In Mark the woman comes forward fearfully after her healing and tells Jesus 'the whole truth'. Being in a state of ritual uncleanness she has broken the law by touching Jesus; having imparted her uncleanness to him she could well expect a rebuke. In 8.47 Luke amplifies this, spelling out the fact that she tells the whole story, the reason for touching him and her instant cure; but she does not do so for Jesus' benefit. Luke emphasizes the public nature of her confession: 'she declared in the presence of all the people'. It is no longer a private conversation between patient and healer, in which a hidden sufferer is identified, but an act of public testimony. After this Jesus declares, as in Mark, 'daughter, your faith has made you well; go in peace' (v. 48). As in Mark this could be reassurance in place of rebuke and a way of identifying faith as the means by which she had tapped his healing power. But in view of Luke's expansion of v. 47 and in the light of what he makes of *he pistis sou sesoken se* elsewhere we may wonder whether the RSV is adequate, and whether we should not once again translate *sesoken se* 'has saved you', seeing in the woman's faith not only the confidence that healing could be received but also the willingness to make public what had happened even at the risk of attracting hostility.

In 18.35–43 Luke uses Mark's story of the blind man at Jericho (10.46–52), shifting the setting to the entry into the city to make room for the story of Zacchaeus afterwards. Again Luke repeats from Mark the pronouncement about faith. Here it is part of the formula pronouncing the cure which then follows. It is more natural in this case to translate *sesoken se* 'has made you well'. But we note that Luke expands the end of the story, having the man not only following Jesus, as in Mark, but giving glory to God. There is to be no doubt that the man recognizes the source of his cure (the theme of gratitude again). Luke modifies the beginning too. In Mark the crowd begin by being antagonistic to the man and trying to silence him, but they turn to encouragement when Jesus sends for him (10.49). In Luke they are consistently hostile. It is made clear that only Jesus responds sympathetically. Thus in this instance the man's faith includes not only the recognition that Jesus is the Son of David and the belief that as such he can restore his sight, but the refusal to be dissuaded by the crowd or allow the opportunity to pass. We are given another glimpse of faith as involving persistence in the face of hostility.

This suggestion of persistence is found in other passages

linking healing and faith where the phrase *he pistis sou sesoken se* is not used. It is present at 5.20, where Luke, following Mark 2.1–12, comments on the reaction of Jesus to the men who lower the paralytic to Jesus through the roof, 'and when he saw their faith'. In Mark too their faith is a combination of confidence in Jesus and determination to reach him. Luke if anything emphasizes this, expanding the description of their frustration and resourcefulness (cf. vv. 18f. with Mark 2.3f.). It should probably also be seen in the story of Jairus and his daughter in 8.40–42, 49–56. Unlike Matthew, who curtails the story so that it is known from the start that the child is dead and her father is asking for her to be raised (9.18), Luke preserves Mark's two stages, so that Jesus' words in v. 50, 'do not fear; only believe', come as reassurance when the news of her death seems to make further action pointless. The idea of faith surmounting discouragement is thus present in the narrative, although it is not emphasized by any redactional phrase, unless, against modern editors, we were to read the present tense of the verb 'believe'. The aorist normally adopted cannot mean 'persevere in believing' but must be translated 'have faith now', or possibly 'start believing'.[18] Luke does, however, add to Mark's 'believe' *kai sothesetai*. Here the RSV 'and she shall be well' is inadequate on any showing, for what is required in the context is not healing but deliverance from death. *Sozein* can have this meaning in Luke (cf. 6.9; 9.24; 23.37, 39; Acts 27.30f.). Perhaps Luke has simply rearranged his source, picking up the father's request from Mark's 5. 23, 'that she may be made well (*sothe*) and live' (cf. Luke v. 42), and incorporating it into Jesus' reassurance.[19] But in the process he has reproduced the formula of Acts 16.31, 'believe. . . and you shall be saved'. What Jesus says to Jairus is of wider application than the resurrection of his daughter. In all its connotations salvation becomes accessible to the act of faith which, as in the case of Jairus, must overcome mounting discouragement and fear.

The point is rather different in another passage, where *he pistis sou sesoken se* is not used, Luke 7.1–10. The healing of the centurion's servant is a 'Q' passage, although there are wide differences between Matthew and Luke outside the central conversation. In both gospels the central element is the centurion's belief that Jesus can heal at a distance, and

Jesus' comment that he has not found such faith among the Jews. Luke prefaces the centurion's statement of faith by a passage in which Jewish leaders support the centurion's request. His sympathy with the Jewish faith and people and his friendly dealings with them mark him out as 'worthy' (v. 4). But the centurion's own estimate of himself is different. In Luke he does not meet Jesus; he does not 'presume' to do so (v. 7). So what in Matthew is no more than recognition of the difficulties a Jew might have in entering a Gentile house ('I am not worthy to have you come under my roof') becomes in Luke a statement of personal unworthiness. The testimony of the Jewish elders makes it clear that this is not a confession of guilt but an expression of humility. In consequence it is not just the man's faith but the humility which led to it which Jesus praises as rare. We shall see further examples where faith is associated with humility and prayer is answered.

Lastly, we examine the healing of the epileptic boy (9.37–43). We said above that Luke tends to separate the activity of healing and exorcism from specific acts of faith while keeping it within the context of faith in a broader sense. This passage provides part of the evidence for this. Luke shortens Mark's version considerably (Mark 9.14–29). Most strikingly he cuts out Mark's vv. 28f., so that there is no discussion of the methods by which the disciples (or Luke's church) might continue such work. He also omits the discussion between Jesus and the father in Mark's vv. 21–24, thereby omitting any call for faith from the father. The episode becomes a straightforward miracle story in which Jesus' exorcism of the demon provokes praise from the crowd (v. 43). Note, however, that Jesus immediately cuts across this response of wonder with a warning to the disciples about his coming passion, which they fail to understand (vv. 44f, cf. Mark vv. 30–32, a separate incident). Before the story Luke has omitted the discussion about Elijah from Mark 9.11–13. The healing of the epileptic is thus sandwiched in Luke directly between the transfiguration, with its clear reference to the passion (9.31), and the passion prediction of 9.44. This highlights the one saying of Jesus left in the narrative (v. 41), slightly expanded from Mark. It is an expostulation with the crowd for the faithlessness and perversity of the whole generation, and a warning that Jesus' time with them is limited. Both the disciples and the father are included in this. It accounts for the failure of the disciples to heal the boy. The father too is part of the crowd. He speaks from the crowd and so represents them (cf. 11. 27; 12.13; 14.15; 18.18; 19.39)[20] It is this more general faithlessness, which fails to recognize the true nature of Jesus' presence, with the opportunity it offers and his impending passion, rather than a specific inability to believe in a miracle, which Luke highlights here. Luke uses this passage, not as a paradigm for the church's healing ministry, but to bring out the underlying issues of the ministry and passion of Jesus.

We have been arguing on the basis of a number of passages that Luke's use of the verb *sozein* and the noun 'faith' are not straightforward. It is a misfortune that in English translation we are driven to make a distinction between salvation and healing, either of which (along with 'rescue') could be conveyed by *sozein*. Luke would have been able to use the word in a way which spanned both alternatives. Certainly if he had wished to exclude wider meanings more restricted verbs such as *iasthai* were available. As a translation of *sozein*, 'saved' might fail to suggest to English readers the direct connection with healing; yet we have seen reason to think that the translation most favoured by modern versions, 'cured' or 'made well' is too restrictive, and 'saved' is actually nearer the mark. Salvation includes the condition of which gratitude and willingness to bear public testimony are the hall-mark, and finds its expression in discipleship. Luke sees faith as implying in various situations, trust, obedience, the discernment which leads to gratitude, the readiness to bear open testimony to what God has done, persistence in the face of hostility or discouragement, and the humility which, again, leads to discernment of the undeserved nature of God's grace. It is the converse of fear. Faith, indeed, is not merely the means by which salvation is attained: as outlined here it is itself an element in the condition of being saved.[21]

This is not to suggest that Luke has merely allegorized the miracle stories. There are sufficient references to healings in the summary passages of the gospel and Acts to show that he recounts specific episodes as instances of such healing and not just as acted parables of discipleship. What Luke is emphasizing, however, is that healing cannot be divorced from the wider aspects of salvation, nor is there an exercise of faith whose reference can be limited exclusively to bodily restoration.[22] It is part of the wider recognition of God's saving work in Christ and cannot be divorced from repentance, discipleship and the way of the cross. It is important to bear this in mind when reflecting on his tendency to portray healing as the almost mechanical operation of a physical force.

In the nature of the case, the incidents we have considered, with the exception of the woman in 7.36ff., have been examples of first encounters with Jesus. When considered in the context of salvation in its broader sense they inevitably invite comparison with conversion. But some of the aspects of faith we have noted, particularly gratitude and persistence in public testimony, are by their nature more than momentary. We have seen too that faith is the beginning of continued discipleship. In the case of the woman, we have had to presume a previous meeting with Jesus, so that her faith is a clear example of a continuing attitude. We have noted also that faith is often exercised on behalf of others. There is nothing in such faith that limits it in principle to an initial encounter; indeed in 9.41 the disciples are rebuked along with the crowd for their unbelief. What Luke sets before us in these stories therefore cannot be confined to the moment of conversion. The colours we have seen diffracted in his use of the word 'faith' contribute to the overall picture of what it means to be a Christian.

It might be objected that the details in Luke's narrative to which we have been drawing attention are no more than cosmetic changes which will not bear the weight we have attached to them. The objection would have to be conceded if the emphases we have claimed were not to be found elsewhere. But this is not the case, as will be seen if we explore further two of the ideas which we have noted, testimony and persistence.

While Luke does not use the concept of testimony or witness as extensively as John's gospel, it is an important idea for him, particularly in Acts. He is concerned to emphasize the public character of the Christian preaching and of the events which lie behind it. 'This was not done in a corner' (Acts 26.26; cf. 2.22; 19.17).[23] So he often relates incidents involving preaching or healing in which it is clear that they are public events, known and spoken of (e.g. 2.14; 4.10, 16; 6.8; 8.5ff.; 9.42; 14.3; etc.). The same is true in the gospel of the events of Jesus' birth (2.17f.), his preaching and teaching ministry (6.17–19; 12.1; 19.47f.; 24.19; cf. 7.11–17; 14.1–6; 18.35–43), and of his death (23.48). From time to time details in the narrative bring this out. Whether on trial or preaching, the apostles and Paul stand 'in the midst' (*en meso*) (Acts 4.7; 17.22; 27.21, 35), a natural enough detail but one which conjures up a picture of the speaker with all eyes upon him, as was the case with Jesus in the synagogue (Luke 4.20, 22). Similarly, by adding phrases to Mark at 5.19, 25, Luke emphasizes that the paralytic was laid before Jesus and healed in the full sight of all. Again at 6.8 Luke strengthens the description of the man with the deformed arm standing up in full view.[24] These details endorse our interpretation of 8.47, in which the woman's admission of her healing is an act of public witness.

According to the opening of the gospel Luke is primarily concerned in his narrative to stress for Theophilus and other readers the truth of the Christian message (Luke 1.1–4), and consequently emphasizes the role of the twelve apostles as witnesses of what they have seen and heard, the ministry and death of Jesus and particularly his resurrection. For this reason it is an essential qualification of apostleship that the twelve were with Jesus from the beginning (Acts 1.21f.).[25] They establish continuity between the time of Jesus and the church's preaching. A key word in this context is 'boldness' (*parresia*), the ability to speak out in public without mincing matters and regardless of the consequences (Acts 4.13; 9.27f.; 13.46; 14.3; 19.8; 26.26; 28.31). Because of this interest Luke does not use the word witness of Christians in general in Acts. But Paul is a witness, not only to the risen Jesus (22.15; 26.16) but more generally to 'the things concerning him', his death and resurrection according to scripture (23.11; 26.22f.). So also is Stephen (22.20), although in his case too there was a vision of the exalted Jesus which perhaps led Luke to call him a witness.[26] Nor does Luke limit preaching to the twelve and Paul (8.4ff.; 11.19ff.). He notes the effect on the people in Jerusalem of the way of life of 'all the believers' (2.44–47), and attributes to them the same boldness that the apostles

display (Acts 4.31). In 19.18f. he depicts the Christians of
Ephesus publicly renouncing their magical practices and
burning their books. In the gospel, 21.13 speaks of persecution proving to be an act of witness,[27] and 12.8f. warns
against failure in this regard. While therefore the idea of
public testimony we detected at Luke 8.47 cannot be said to
be a major theme with reference to Christians in general, it
fits well into Luke's general interests, and is indeed fore-
shadowed at 8.39. The unusual element of 8.39, 47 is the
concentration upon what God has done for the individual
rather than upon the central themes of the kingdom of God or
the death and resurrection of Jesus (but cf. Acts 3.8–10).

Frequently in Acts the ideas of witness and boldness are set
against a background of hostility from bystanders in which
suffering results or is threatened (Acts 4.13, 29; 14.3; 22.18,
20; 23.11; 26.22; cf. Luke 12.8f.; 21.13). The fact that the
woman with the haemorrhage in 8.47 bears her testimony in
a setting where she is afraid fits Luke's pattern, and leads us to
a discussion of the relation between faith and persistence.

We begin with Luke's version in 8.11–15 of the interpretation of the parable of the sower. Luke has made a number of
changes from Mark in this and in the parable itself, the most
obvious being the elimination of the distinction between
three degrees of good harvest (v. 8, Mark 4.8). He shows no
interest in different categories of good Christian, and lays all
the emphasis on the contrast between success and failure and
the reasons for the latter. Luke also makes unmistakably clear
that the parable is about Christian preaching: the sower sows
the seed which is the word of God; to accept it is to 'believe
and be saved' (v. 11). In the interpretation of each kind of soil
the emphasis is on the hearers of the word. All four groups
hear, but with the first the devil prevents the response of faith
so that there is no conversion (v. 12). In the other cases there
is response, but only in the fourth the kind of response for
which the sower-preacher hoped.

The second group make a response of faith; they are
converted as their joy shows.[28] But 'in time of temptation'
they 'fall away' for lack of root (v. 13). It is not certain what
Luke means by this. Mark (4.17) had, 'they have no root in
themselves, but endure for a while; then, when tribulation or
persecution arises on account of the word, immediately they

fall away' (or, 'stumble', cf. RSV margin). What is the meaning of Luke's word, 'temptation' (*peirasmos*)? Has he merely summarized Mark and broadened his meaning, or substituted a different concept? He has not made the change to avoid language referring to the final eschatological tribulations, for neither *diogmos* (persecution) nor *thlipsis* (tribulation) necessarily carries this reference for Luke (nor indeed in Mark 4.17).[29] Nor can the view be upheld that *peirasmos* is a word restricted to Christians who apostatize while *thlipsis* is reserved for those who persevere. This is to confuse cause and effect.[30] At the same time *peirasmos* cannot be weakened to 'temptation' in the general sense of day-to-day moral testing. Luke refers to those who are believers for a while, until a particular occasion of *peirasmos* arises. The result is not just 'stumbling' (as in Mark, if *skandalizein* has this weaker sense there) but 'desertion' (*aphistantai*). So these are not the petty temptations of ordinary life. In fact there are probably two motives at work in Luke's choice of *peirasmos*: he wishes to broaden the description of the danger to include other tests beside physical suffering, and at the same time he points to the underlying nature of such tests: they are an inducement to desert the cause.

The third group (v. 14) are also converts. This is suggested not only by the logical progression of the groups and the fact that in the parable the thorns 'grow up with' the good seed (*symphyeisai*, v. 7), but by the use of *poreuomenoi* ('as they go on their way') which is probably a reference to discipleship. These are 'choked by the cares and pleasures and riches of life'. Luke has made other small changes. It is riches, not their deceptiveness ('delight', RSV Mark 4.19), and the pleasures of life, not Mark's 'desire for other things', which constitute the threat; but it would be a mistake to think that Luke has simply externalized the dangers;[31] cares are inward enough. Nevertheless his addition of 'of life' points us to 21.34 and suggests preoccupation with the attractions of the material side of life and the rewards and anxieties which immersion in business and social contacts can bring as the danger for this group. The result is that they do not bear fruit to maturity. What has begun does not fulfil its promise because the life is choked out of it.

In contrast to all these is the final group (v. 15). They not only hear the word, they hold on to it in an 'honest and good heart', and so bear fruit. What the fruit is Luke does not indicate; for an answer we should probably turn to 3.8 and 6.43f. The stress, however, lies not here but on the final words, *en hypomone*. 'Patience' (RSV) will not do here, if that means uncomplaining acceptance of hardship or of the fact that the parousia will be delayed. The contrast is with those who desert the cause or allow themselves to be throttled by the distractions of life; this last group do not accept the word and exercise faith only 'for a while'. *Hypomone* here means perseverance, and shows what continuing faith implies.[32] It involves prolonged resistance to the temptation to give up because of persecution and other difficulties, and the ability to resist the seduction of worldly cares and interests in the midst of which one has to live. The interpretation of the parable of the sower is thus an important contribution negatively and positively to our picture of Christian faith after conversion and strongly emphasizes the idea of persistence.

Luke uses *hypomone* on one other occasion, in 21.19. Chapter 21 forms his parallel to the 'apocalyptic discourse' in Mark 13 and in part at least is based upon it.[33] His major modifications are a much clearer arrangement of material so as to distinguish the fall of Jerusalem and events preceding it from events preceding the coming of the Son of Man and the kingdom of God, and the substitution of a description of the siege and destruction of Jerusalem for Mark's 'abomination of desolation standing where he ought not' (13.14). These changes reflect Luke's distinctive view of the future.[34] In the discourse vv. 12–19 deal with the threat of persecution. There are hints elsewhere that Luke has softened references to Christians suffering for their faith. In 6.22f. he refers to hatred and general ostracism where the Matthean parallel (5.11f.) includes persecution.[35] In 21.16 he modifies Mark 13.12 to suggest that only 'some' will be put to death, and adds the reassurance of v. 18, 'not a hair of your head will perish'; in v. 15 his version of the promise of help in making a defence in court includes the assurance of the invincibility of the message they are given.[36] It is clear, however, that he does anticipate some persecution, including death, and the reassurance of v. 18 should not be pressed too far. There is a parallel in 12.4–9 close enough to suggest that Luke's thought is running along similar lines. In that passage the assurance that all the head's hairs are numbered is combined with a warning to fear God rather than those who can do no more than kill the body. The example is given of the dead sparrow which God nevertheless remembers, and the passage closes with a call for confession of Christ. In the light of this, 21.18 cannot be pressed as an unambiguous promise of physical survival. Indeed if the details of the sufferings are intended in any way to reflect what actually befell the disciples in Acts, it is clear that death is not ruled out.[37]

So it is by no means certain that in amending Mark 13.13, 'he who endures to the end will be saved', to 'by your endurance you will gain your lives' in 21.19, Luke wanted to give an assurance that Christians would escape death. He will have omitted the reference to the end because, whatever its meaning for Mark in this context, for Luke it means the end of the world (cf. v. 9), and in his perspective there is much else to happen first. *Ktesesthe tas psychas hymon* could indeed mean 'you will save your lives' in the literal sense, but we should note the parallel in Luke's other 'apocalyptic passage', 17.20–37, which we considered earlier. After a warning against being unprepared 17.33 insists on preserving one's true life before God.[38] There the threat was constituted by thoughtless immersion in everyday worldly affairs and reluctance to detach oneself from them. Here the danger is the physical menace presented by people's opposition to Christianity and its representatives. It is likely that Luke had the same point in mind and in 21.19 is saying that only persevering loyalty will preserve true life.[39]

The parallel with the interpretation of the parable of the sower in 17.33 and 21.19, linked as they are by the thought of preserving life, is striking. As in the interpretation of the parable, we have a double threat, human opposition and worldly pursuits. It may even be that the substitution of the noun 'endurance' for Mark's verb in 21.19 is intended to trigger our memory of 8.15. But we do not have to look only to chapter 17 for the parallel to worldly pursuits. It is also present in Luke 21. The chapter ends (vv. 34–36) with a warning, echoing Mark 13.33–37 but very different in detail, against being caught unawares by the coming of the Son of Man, in which the dangers are loose living and 'cares of this life', a phrase which echoes 'the cares of life' in 8.14.[40] Here is further evidence of Luke's wider concern for the persistence of faith which we saw dramatically presented in the narratives we examined above.

This discussion will help us to interpret another reference to faith in the gospel, in 18.8b, 'when the Son of Man comes will he find faith (*ten pistin*) on earth?'[41] The parable of the widow is introduced to encourage persistent prayer (v. 1), but in the context it is not prayer in general with which Luke is concerned. The passage follows immediately on 17.20ff., with which it is bracketed by the reference to the coming of the Son of Man in v. 8. In both parable and application, petition is for 'vindication' or deliverance (*ekdikesis*, vv. 3, 5, 7f.), which appears to be intolerably delayed (cf. 17.22f.).[42] Assurance is given that God will vindicate his elect 'speedily'.[43] In the context the reference must be to the coming of the kingdom of God and the deliverance from oppressors which that will bring. But will those who have been so earnestly praying actually be ready? 17.26ff. has drawn a picture of people immersed in worldly affairs and unprepared for the day. What will the Son of Man find among his disciples? 'Faith' in 18.8 is thus akin to 'loyalty'. It involves what we have seen to be implied by perseverance: being neither frightened off by hardships nor drowned in the excesses or even the preoccupations and anxieties of daily life. But it is more than obstinate immovability as a human stance; it is an attitude directed towards God, and is expressed in prayer which does not give up. This is shown not only by the context in 18.1–8 but by the end of the discourse in 21.36 which offers a striking parallel, 'watch at all times, praying that you may have strength to escape all these things that will take place' (a phrase which embraces not only the worldly temptations of vv. 34f. but all the preceding troubles and persecutions of the earlier part of the chapter), 'and to stand before the Son of Man'. Such persistence in prayer blends loyalty with confident trust.[44]

We can now deal with 22.32, 'I have prayed for you that your faith may not fail'. It is a major element in the thesis of Schuyler Brown's book, *Apostasy and Perseverance in the Theology of Luke*, that the twelve disciples, with the single exception of Judas, never lose faith in Jesus throughout the gospel.[45] He draws attention to the fact that in Luke the disciples are present throughout the passion narrative (cf. 23.49 and, at 22.53, the omission of Mark 14.50). He distinguishes between faith in Jesus as the messiah, which they begin to acquire at 5.1–11, confess (with Peter as spokesman) at 9.18–21 and retain throughout the gospel (cf. 19.37f.), and faith in the necessity of his suffering, which they are unable to understand until after the resurrection (cf. 18.31–34, 24.44–49). On this view 22.32 is an assurance by Jesus (whose prayer is efficacious) of their persistence.

But this interpretation draws an artificial distinction between the 'fact' of Jesus' messiahship and its 'modality' in suffering. Even though it is true that Luke reinterprets the 'messianic secret' of Mark so that it refers only to the necessity of suffering, 24.13–32 shows that once Jesus is dead belief that he is the messiah cannot be sustained if it is not recognized how the messiah can suffer. Brown also lays too much weight on narrative elements as indicative of faith. The disciples do not run away when Jesus is arrested because their presence is necessary as witnesses to the events (cf. Acts 10.39f.; Luke 24.48), but this fact says nothing about their faith. The theory also runs into exegetical difficulties. The saying to Peter in 22.32 has to be taken as a saying for all the (eleven) apostles, although the singular form of 'you' is used, and the 'brethren' become the 'future Christian community' since 'no strengthening' of the apostles is necessary'.[46] Peter's denial is taken to be a sin of cowardice rather than the loss of faith, for it is not Jesus' messiahship that he denies, but only his personal knowledge of him. The evidences in chapter 24 of loss of faith by the disciples also have to be explained away: thus 24.11 becomes 'prudent refusal' to accept the testimony of women; Cleopas and his companion, whose unbelief cannot be gainsaid (24.21), are to be distinguished from the eleven, who are claimed not to share it; and the unbelief of 24.41 is taken to be disbelief not in the resurrection but in its corporeal nature. None of this can be sustained. Too sharp a distinction is drawn between the eleven and the disciples (it is not only the eleven who 'persevere' in witnessing the crucifixion, 23.49). 22.32 must mean that the other apostles will lose faith and that Peter, when he has repented of his own failure, is to restore their strength.[47] The meaning of 'that

your faith must not fail' must be determined by the story of
the denial and not *vice versa*; no valid distinction can be drawn
between 'denying knowing Jesus' and 'denying him' as the
messiah.[48] Peter loses faith; he begins to recover it with his
remorse at 22.62, but we should also look at 24.34 as a further
stage, for only the resurrection can restore faith in a crucified
messiah and show the scriptures fulfilled (24.44ff.). 'Faith' in
22.32 thus means 'loyalty', but, as before, with the connota-
tion of 'continuing belief in Jesus'. The story of the passion
shows how difficult such perseverance may become, and
how much it depends on God's grace and the possibility of
restoration after lapse. It fits well into the pattern of perseverance in times of persecution which was suggested by
8.13, 21.19. This is well brought out in the narrative of Jesus'
prayer on the mount of olives (22.40ff.), which is discussed
more fully in a later chapter.[49]

These passages show how important persistence as an
element of faith was for Luke. They highlight two main
sources of danger, persecution and the temptations associated
with wealth. The narrative passages we examined earlier
cannot be expected to provide ready examples of these two
precise issues since Luke is primarily using them to make
other points and the nuances of faith are only incidental. We
have seen, however, how one context for the perseverance of
faith was the need to overcome the hostility of critics or an
unsympathetic crowd. The presence of these ideas in the
teaching of Jesus increases our confidence that Luke's modifications of the stories do indeed reflect his understanding of
the many-sidedness of faith.

This almost completes our study of faith in Luke's gospel.
Of the remaining passages 1.20, 45, 22.67, 24.25 reflect the
relationship between faith and hearing which we observed in
Acts. In Chapter 1 the responses of Zechariah and Mary to
Gabriel's announcement are contrasted, the one believing, the
other disobedient.[50] The need for belief in the word of God is
also to be seen in 24.25. The disciples on the Emmaus road
(Luke no doubt has contemporary Christians in mind) should
have been ready to believe the scriptures when they heard the
witness to the empty tomb. They should not have needed
what is subsequently granted to them, a vision of the risen
Jesus.

22.67 is more directly christological. The council demand from Jesus a declaration of his messianic claims and identity. But these are not matters open to dispassionate scrutiny, still less to hostile interrogation. Those who refused to commit themselves over John the Baptist are not going to change their minds about Jesus simply on the basis of what he says. They lack the basic disposition for faith which involves the assent of the will (cf. 20.5; Acts 5.32).

8.25 occurs in the story of the stilling of the storm.[51] It is normally pointed out that the form of Jesus' question, 'Where is your faith?' is gentler than Mark 4.40 ('Why are you afraid? Have you no faith?'), but the nature of the difference is not always made clear. In Luke the disciples do not preserve their faith and demonstrate it by their call for help, and the purpose of the question is not to deepen their faith by reflection on Jesus' power. 'Where is your faith?' can only deplore the absence of faith which their cry for help has revealed. The true distinction is that in Mark faith seems to be a faculty exercised in moments of crisis, on occasions such as this, whereas in Luke it is a continuing attitude which ought to have carried the disciples through the emergency. They ought to have realized who Jesus is and have been confident of his power. Here then is an example of faith after the initial response to Jesus, which involves a continuing trust in him as the Lord who is able to save.[52] While there is no suggestion of 'loyalty' in this context, the idea of the persistence of faith when under threat is to be found. Compare also the rebuke, 'O men of little faith' at 12.28, where also there is a call for continuing trust in God to provide basic necessities for those who relinquish their wealth for him. In the light of 17.6 we should not be far wrong in regarding 'of little faith' as meaning 'without faith at all'.

In 17.5f., the apostles' request for an increase of faith and the saying about the grain of mustard seed, we may be dealing with sayings in a series already linked in the tradition before Luke rather than arranged by him.[53] As a result we have few clues for interpreting the meaning of faith. Possibly it is faith to work miracles, but this is suggested partly by the contexts of the parallels in Mark 11.22f., Matt. 17.20, which may not be relevant, and partly by the image of uprooting a tree by command. But as this is evidently parabolic language it is difficult to be certain whether it points to other forms of miracle (such as healing) or more generally to situations where faith seems to face the impossible. The one example of 'great' faith in Luke is that of the centurion in 7.9,[54] where the miracle is performed by Jesus himself, and the faith does not relate exclusively to it. If in 17.5f. it is faith for the working of miracles, it may be significant that 17.6 is followed by a passage which undercuts any sense of self-importance among the disciples, just as 10.20 deflated their exultation over demons in 10.17. Whatever the precise reference it would be a mistake to isolate this passage from others, as though a different kind of faith were being discussed. We have seen above how Luke links faith and healing with faith and salvation. In the gospel the passages dealing with faith are grouped in two sections, chapters 7–8 and 17–18. While 'faith' does not have a single fixed meaning in each instance, this grouping may indicate Luke's ability to associate the various meanings in his mind without sharp distinction. Certainly this faith cannot be described as *one's own* power of working miracles'.[55] It is implicitly faith in God, for the point being made is that success in overcoming the obstacles (whatever they are) does not depend on the quantity of one's faith. By its very nature faith gives access to God's power; either one has it or one does not; it is akin to trust. It was that implicit trust, combined with humility, which led Jesus to acclaim the faith of the centurion as 'great'.

In this chapter we have reviewed Luke's use of the words 'faith' and 'believe'. They are markedly more common than the word 'love'. They have a wide range of applications, but we have seen reason to resist the temptation to distinguish them sharply as separate functions. Even the exercise of faith in works of healing is brought into the realm of the faith which leads to salvation. We are to think of a single faculty exercised in different ways. So 'faith' and 'believe' cover both the initial response to the Christian message, which, not surprisingly, is especially prominent in Acts, and the continuing attitude of the convert. It involves not only acceptance of the word, and trust in the power of God (or Jesus) to save, but humility, gratitude, and the willingness to bear open testimony to what God has done. Particularly evident has been Luke's understanding of faith as involving perseverance:

the tenacity of trust and loyalty in spite of the seductions of day to day life and the hostility of other people. In this emphasis we can see reflected the needs of the church which Luke was addressing. As we have observed, these sidelights of faith underline the fact that for Luke, faith is not just a preliminary condition for receiving salvation. As a continuing characteristic of the Christian it is a facet of the salvation received.

7

Discipleship

There have been references from time to time in the previous chapters to discipleship, and it is important at this stage to lay some emphasis upon it if we are to keep Luke's teaching in perspective, for it is all set in the context of commitment to Jesus and his way. 6.46, 'why do you call me, "Lord, Lord", and do not do what I tell you?' reveals the assumption which lies behind all the teaching; it is held together by the confession of Jesus' lordship and obedience to him.

When Luke is compared with Mark it becomes apparent that he has broken down the sharp distinction which the earlier gospel drew between the circle of the disciples and the crowds who come and go from time to time.[1] Mark presents a fairly consistent pattern of public teaching in parables and private explanations, with other teaching, to the disciples (cf. e.g. Mark 7.17ff.; 8.14–21; 9.28ff.). Where Luke retains this distinction it is in modified form. In some places he has teaching which is directed to disciples in a way which suggests that others are excluded from the application (e.g. 10.23f.), and teaching on repentance is regularly directed to the crowds (11.29ff.; 12.54–13.9; cf. 13.23–30), but he has nothing to match the policy statement of Mark 4.34. He preserves from Mark 4.10ff. the distinction between those who hear only in parables and those to whom the secrets of the kingdom are revealed, but softens it by substituting for Mark's 'those who were about him with the twelve . . . those outside' words which mark the distinction less sharply, 'his disciples . . . the others', suggesting boundaries which can be more easily crossed (8.9f.). Parables are offered to disciples as well as to the crowds (e.g. at 12.35ff.; 17.7ff.), and there are passages where crowds and disciples alternate as audiences with only partial change of subject matter, as in chapter 12. Peter's question at 12.41 is thus a reasonable one, 'are you telling this parable for us or for all?' In 20.45ff. the crowds are depicted as eavesdroppers on teaching given to disciples (contrast Mark 12.37f., where the crowds are the audience and the disciples are only brought in at v. 43). A similar picture is given of the audience of the sermon on the plain (6.17ff.; 7.1). At 14.25ff. teaching on discipleship is given to the crowds (cf. 9.23ff.).

At the same time Luke expands the circle of disciples so that they are less readily identified exclusively with the twelve apostles.[2] He distinguishes the two groups at 6.13 (cf. Mark 3.14), and 8.9 (cf. Mark 4.10), and alters Mark's reference to the twelve to disciples at 9.43 and 46 (Mark 9.35). For Luke the disciples are a large group, a 'great crowd' (19.17; 6.17; cf. Mark 3.7). This distinction anticipates the picture in Acts of a large company of disciples (the regular word for believers in Acts, cf. 9.1, 10, 19, 25f., 38, etc.) presided over at the beginning by the apostles (cf. 6.1ff.), who in the overall design of Luke-Acts have an important part to play in the continuity between Israel, Jesus and the church.

It may be that Luke wants to suggest by these changes the openness of the church to all who come; there is no sharp boundary between disciples and 'outsiders'.[3] But it is also the case that Luke sees the teaching of Jesus, whether on wealth or on other topics such as those in the sermon on the plain, not as a sectarian ethic significant only for the followers of a Jesus-cult, nor as significant only in special conditions of itinerancy and mission parallel to those which obtained during the journeys of Jesus, but as having universal application to all and sundry. What is said to the crowds is relevant to them as uncommitted bystanders, even though the logical outcome is that they should commit themselves to discipleship. Conversely what is said to disciples is true for them as human beings regardless of the discipleship. Only on certain topics, as when there is a discussion of the privileged insight which God has granted them or their relations with each other as a fellowship, or their responsibilities for mission, is there a restriction of audience to disciples. The implication of this for Luke's understanding of Christian character is important and will be taken up again later.

In his narrative Luke employs two models for discipleship which may be crudely characterized as the sedentary and the itinerant. The sedentary model is exemplified as we have seen by Mary at 10.39 and the cured demoniac of Gerasa at 8.35.[4] It accords with the emphasis in other passages upon hearing and doing (6.47ff.; 8.9ff., 21; 11.28), and the references to the word of God (5.1 and in modification of Mark, 8.11, 21).[5] The word 'disciple' means a 'learner', and although Luke does not exploit this fact, nor does he use the verb 'to learn' except in a secular sense (Acts 23.27), nevertheless 1.4 shows that he understands instruction to be an important aspect of discipleship[6] and he regularly represents Jesus as teaching (4.15, 32, etc.). We should note also the influence of the wisdom tradition on Luke, especially at 11.49, 21.15.[7] It is clear that, although he does not develop the idea in the direction of a parallel to rabbinic discipleship in the way that Matthew does (cf. Matt. 13.52), Luke does wish to emphasize the importance of being schooled in the teaching of Jesus if obedience, upon which he lays equal stress, is to follow.

The itinerant model we need to follow up in more detail. Luke consistently depicts Jesus (and even John the Baptist, 3.3) on the move. Small editorial changes well illustrate Acts 10.38, 'he went about doing good and healing'. In 4.43 he amends Mark's reference to the nearby towns (1.38) to the more comprehensive 'the other cities'.[8] In the narrative that follows we are given an impression of a series of episodes in different places: 5.12 ('one of the cities'), 5.17 ('one of those days', but not at Capernaum, Mark 2.1), 5.27 (not as in Mark 2.13 by the lake). One may reasonably suppose that the lakeside and Capernaum (cf. also 9.46 with Mark 9.33) are omitted because Luke wanted to avoid the impression that Jesus' ministry was concentrated on a small number of places to which he periodically returned.[9] From 9.51 this impression of circulation in Galilee gives place to a decision to travel to Jerusalem, and the rest of the gospel to 19.28 is dominated by this journey (cf. 9.53; 13.22; 17.11; 19.11), which is undertaken in response to the will of God (9.31; 13.33; 18.31ff.).

On both phases of this journey the disciples accompany

Jesus (7.11; 9.18; 10.38; 18.31). This fact will be of significance at a later stage, Acts 1.21f., 13.31. The twelve apostles are a formal body of witnesses to the resurrection, but their numbers are initially drawn and later replenished from a wider body of observers who can attest what has been said and done from the 'beginning' at the baptism of John (cf. Luke 1.2 with Acts 1.22). Luke also draws attention to this early in the gospel (8.1–3) and again at the end (19.37, 23.49). But the disciples are more than spectators as 22.28 shows; they share in the testing he undergoes.[10] This is emphasized by the way in which the account of three prospective disciples who cannot face the demands is placed at the very start of the Jerusalem journey at 9.57ff., and by the way in which teaching about following Jesus is given both before the journey begins and during its course (9.23ff.; 14.25ff.).

In Luke the crowds also follow. Although he sometimes speaks of a crowd gathering *ad hoc*, it is part of his systematic breakdown of Mark's distinction between crowds and disciples that Luke often envisages them as following Jesus from place to place. This is clear at 7.9, 11, 14.25, and probably elsewhere. At 9.11 since Luke omits any reference to crossing the lake, the action of the crowds is not, as in Mark 6.32f., an independent movement to catch up with Jesus, but a 'following'. At 18.36 the crowd, with Jesus, is 'passing through' Jericho (cf. Mark 10.46). When Jesus withdraws from the crowd, to ascend the mountain for prayer or to go to foreign parts, they are waiting for him to return (8.40; 9.37, contrast Mark 5.21, 9.14). Even at 23.27 we are given the impression of a sympathetic crowd accompanying him to his crucifixion.[11]

In these passages Luke depicts Jesus, disciples and crowds engaged in a journey in the literal sense. He leads the way (19.28) and they 'follow' (7.9; 9.11; 22.39). They are 'with' him (7.11; 8.1). But the narrative of the journey to Jerusalem has an unreal quality. Although punctuated by references to travelling and to Jerusalem as the destination, the impression remains of a circulatory tour not unlike the earlier phase, with ample time for meals in the homes of Pharisees and a stop for teaching in every town and village (13.22). Samaria is entered at 9.52 and there is an obscure reference to it at 17.11,[12] but Pharisees are unlikely to have lived there, and at 13.31 we are still in Herod's jurisdiction; as Peraea is never mentioned by

Luke, this has to be Galilee. The truth is that the journey is a framework within which Luke has fitted narratives and teaching which belong to it not in a geographical but a theological sense.[13] The literal journey is a parable of the metaphorical journey which discipleship involves, and its destination, regularly stressed, points to the end to which it leads: it is the way of the cross.

There is no fixed terminology for this following. Luke uses ordinary phrases but from time to time invests them with symbolic meaning. *Poreuesthai* can refer to life's journey (or more specifically the journey of discipleship) at 8.14 (contrast Mark 4.19), or to God's appointed way for Jesus at 13.33, but can be used of the Pharisees going off to Herod in the same context at 13.32. 'The road' (*hodos*) may bear an allusion to Jesus' way which disciples must share at 9.57, and possibly to the journey of learning with Jesus at 24.32, 35, because the context suggests it in each case, but not at 10.4; and at 18.35 Luke omits 'on the way' from Mark 10.52 where we might have expected him to keep it.[14] Not every occurrence of 'follow' expresses discipleship (22.10). Each expression has to be weighed in its context, bearing in mind, as 8.14 proves, that the idea of a journey does have for Luke a metaphorical significance. At 5.24, 8.48 for example, one can only say that a metaphorical meaning is possible.[15] Greater weight has to be attached to references to being 'with' Jesus, as in 8.38, 22.14, 28, 33, 56, 59, 23.43 (cf. 11.23 and Acts 4.13) and 'coming after' (9.23; 14.27; cf. 23.26).

With the journey theme Luke gives dramatic expression to the meaning of discipleship. The Old Testament metaphor of 'walking in the ways of God' (cf. Luke 1.6) is given sharper definition. Jesus teaches the way of God (20.21) and follows it himself. To be a disciple is to go with him along this way, to adopt the style of life which it involves and to accept the cost to which it may lead. It is a journey of learning and sharing. But it is clearly a metaphor which is applicable to those whose actual existence is settled in one location. It is also a way of living open in principle not only to those who are numbered among the disciples but to the 'crowds', although there is no mitigation of Jesus' demands for the latter group. Luke's amendment of Mark 9.38, 'he did not follow us', to 'he does not follow with us' at 9.49 opens up the possibility that Luke saw that following Jesus might be possible for those who were not 'with' the disciples. The discussion concerns the relation of such exorcists to the disciples; their relation to Jesus seems not to be in doubt.

Discipleship depends in some cases upon the invitation of Jesus, who calls particular people to follow him (5.27; 9.59; 18.22). But the position of the disciple, unlike that of apostle, is not restricted to a few selected by name. Others may volunteer, and the only principle of selection involved is the question whether they will accept the demands which discipleship involves (9.57f., 61f.). Luke omits at 18.22 any suggestion (cf. Mark 10.21) that personal attraction lay behind Jesus' invitation so that the episode takes on a more general application. At 9.23ff., 14.26ff. an open invitation is given to all who will accept the conditions. It is a matter of 'coming to' Jesus, and the initiative lies with those who do so (6.17f., 47). Even children are welcomed (18.15f.). 18.16, 24 indicate, however, what is involved in this: to come to Jesus is closely linked to entry to God's kingdom.

The conditions of discipleship are set out in three principal passages, supplemented by references elsewhere. They are 9.23–7, 57–62, 14.25–35. We have considered them already in other contexts. Between them they indicate what is involved, and it can be summarized as follows.

(a) One must break with family ties. The most rigorous statement of this is 14.26, 'if any one comes to me and does not hate his own father and mother and wife and children and brothers and sisters, yes and even his own life, cannot be my disciple'. Not only does this cut across all natural affection, it involves infringement of the fifth commandment (Ex. 20.12).[16] The language is intended to be shocking, but one should beware of reading into it more, or indeed less, than is intended. There is no suggestion here of the emotion of loathing, whether of relatives or of oneself. On the other hand, 'hate' cannot be weakened to a mere comparative, 'love less', which might imply still loving a little. As in Deut. 5.9f., 7.9f., Mal. 1.2f., love and hate refer to the choice between incompatible alternatives and to the giving of allegiance to one person or another with the actions which appropriately follow.[17] Loyalty rather than affection is at issue. The same is true of 9.59f. This is in a slightly less rigorous form than

Matt. 8.21f., where one who is already a disciple begs leave to bury his father, and Jesus demands instead that he should follow him at once into the boat and across the lake. In Luke Jesus first invites the man to follow him, and when he makes the request about his father repeats the invitation in another form which, as we shall see in a moment, is not incompatible in principle with such an action. 'Leave the dead to bury their own dead' becomes a more metaphorical statement of the severance of relationships. It would nevertheless bring home quite sharply in the patriarchal society of both Jewish and Hellenistic worlds the rigorous demands of discipleship. The point is made again at vv. 61f.

What Luke has in mind in these sayings is suggested by 12.52f., 21.16f. The coming of Jesus brings division between those who accept and those who reject him. This division will run through the middle of families and in some cases the feelings aroused will be so intense that they will lead to betrayal. Unless the would-be disciple is prepared to accept this possibility and from the outset commit himself to a single undivided loyalty, there is no hope of perseverance to the end. The same point is made elsewhere. The parable of the great feast hinted at the damaging effect of family ties (14.20) and 18.28–30 refers to leaving homes and families for the sake of the kingdom of God. Jesus himself demonstrates this break. His own family no longer have a claim upon him as they once had as family, but only like others as hearers and doers of the word of God (8.21, cf. 11.28 and 2.51).

(b) A similar rigorous choice between incompatible alternatives is demanded in the case of possessions (18.22). We have already examined this at length and need not add to our discussion here, except to point out how comprehensively family and possessions embrace the everyday lives of human beings everywhere. The point is in fact made by Luke in the phrase 'leaving everything', which he adopts from other contexts in Mark and employs at 5.11, 28 (added to Mark), 18.28, and in the comprehensive 14.33, 'whoever of you does not renounce all that he has cannot be my disciple'.

(c) The possibility of persecution implied in family division is made more explicit in the references to taking up the cross. 14.27, to which 23.26 looks back, clearly has this reference, 'whoever does not bear his own cross and come after me cannot be my disciple'.

9.23 is less clear. There is evidence elsewhere that Luke did not expect death as the inevitable price for Christian allegiance (cf. 21.16, 'some of you', with Mark 13.12). Hatred and ostracism are envisaged at 6.22, 27f. and the sharper word 'persecute' is avoided (cf. Matt. 5.10–12, 44). Furthermore at 9.23 Luke adds 'daily' to taking up the cross. Death can be experienced only once, and this addition inevitably weakens the force of the allusion to the cross.[18] To this must be added the fact that at 17.33 'saving one's life' means rescuing one's possessions, and this must encourage the suspicion that the same meaning may lurk beneath 9.24f. which spell out the meaning of v. 23. If that were so, 'taking up the cross daily' might be no more than a vivid metaphor for denying oneself generally. That Luke is interested in the day-to-day implications of discipleship is clear from his version of the Lord's Prayer, where 'daily' also appears in the petition for bread (11.3). Provision is requested for a succession of days stretching into the future. Nevertheless, it must be doubted whether the concept of suffering inflicted by others can be eliminated altogether from Luke's daily cross in 9.23 not only because of what we have seen to be the meaning of 14.27 but because of the reference to being ashamed of Jesus and his teaching before others in the immediate context at 9.26.

This conclusion is reinforced by the saying in 9.58 about the Son of Man having nowhere to lay his head, an experience which the disciple must expect to share. As in the previous verse the volunteer has offered to follow Jesus wherever he goes, Jesus' reply cannot merely refer to the self-imposed lack of a settled home but must imply that the traveller is denied hospitality, a strong gesture of repudiation (cf. 9.4f., 10.3–11). Further, if 21.16 can be cited for a softening of the idea of persecution, 21.12 (cf. Mark 13.9) indicates some general brutality ('lay hands on you') and adds the word 'persecute', omitted earlier.

(*d*) All this is involved in the demand that one should deny, even 'hate', oneself (9.23; 14.26). We have already considered the significance of 'hate'. It expresses the attitude which rejects one set of claims in favour of another. It does not imply a morbid state of self-loathing. We should perhaps also note the effect of Luke's omissions. At 9.50 he stops using Mark as a basis for his narrative and does not return to it until 18.15. A small portion of Mark is omitted in consequence. 10.1–12 deals with the question of divorce (cf. Luke 16.18). 9.42–50 deals with occasions of stumbling and related matters. Some of this is reflected in separate sayings at Luke 17.1f., 14.34, which may derive from 'Q' or elsewhere, although 17.2 in particular reflects Mark 10.42. But there is no Lucan parallel to the sayings of Mark 10.43–8 demanding the cutting off of hand or foot or the plucking out of an eye in order to enter the life of the kingdom. It may be that Luke drew back from sayings which at their literal level implied self-mutilation.

(e) The would-be disciple is thus urged to count the cost before committing himself. The point is made by means of the parables of the tower and the battle in 14.28–32. In 9.26 the analogy of the plough is used. The contrast between the aorist *epibalon* and the present *blepon* aptly expresses the contrast between having once taken hold of the plough and thereafter continually looking behind. A similar point is made at 17.31f. with its reference to Lot's wife. There must be no second thoughts.

(f) A striking feature of many of the sayings we have been reviewing is the way in which Luke has detached them from the missionary context which they are given in Mark, and made them requirements of discipleship as such. At 9.24 he omits 'the gospel', leaving only Jesus as the cause for which one should be willing to lose one's life (Mark 8.35), and at 18.29 homes and families are to be left, not for the gospel (Mark 10.29) but in order to enter the kingdom of God. The demands are thus more radical in that they affect every disciple, and not only those engaged in preaching. Nevertheless discipleship does involve mission. This is brought out especially at 9.60. Here the call to follow Jesus in v. 59 is amplified in terms of going away and proclaiming the kingdom of God. A somewhat similar shift occurs in 8.39, where the man's desire to be with Jesus (that is, to follow him as other cured demoniacs do, 8.1–3), is met by the command to return home and 'declare how much God has done'. In this way the discipleship already shown by the man in listening to Jesus (v. 35) is fulfilled. In the light of 9.60, the following saying in 9.62 should probably also be interpreted as a reference to mission: 'fit for' the kingdom of God means literally 'useful for' (*euthetos*) and the thought may well be that the disciple who has not rejected what lies behind him cannot be used in the work of proclaiming the kingdom. The probable echo of the call of the prophet-disciple Elisha at I Kings 19.19–21 would reinforce this interpretation.[19] 10.1– 16, the mission of the seventy, is also relevant here. We have to assume that they are drawn from the ranks of the disciples who have been mentioned earlier (cf. also 10.23). Their number probably symbolized the nations to whom the church will be sent after the resurrection, but the point for our discussion is that missionary activity is not confined by Luke in the gospel, any more than in the Acts, to the twelve apostles (cf. Acts 8.4; 11.19–21).[20]

This aspect of discipleship is especially brought out by the call of Peter. In Luke generally Peter occupies a more prominent position than in Mark. His status as the leading apostle in the post-resurrection church as described in Acts is reflected in the way in which he acts as the spokesman of the twelve in the gospel (8.45 (cf. Mark 5.31); 9.33; 12.41; 18.28; Acts 1.15; 2.14, 37; 5.29). Just as the twelve apostles are more clearly distinguished from disciples in general so Peter becomes more clearly their leader and mouthpiece, and at 22.32 receives a special commission for the future life of the church. In this of course Luke is only extending a tendency already apparent in Mark, and there are parallel developments in Matthew and John, but it means that we cannot automatically regard Peter simply as a representative disciple. Nevertheless, 5.1–11 is about Peter's call to be a disciple. He is not selected for his role as an apostle until 6.13f.

5.1–11 describes Jesus' first act of choosing disciples. Although the other disciples are still involved, Luke concentrates on Peter. The passage supplants Mark's narrative of the call of two pairs of brothers (1.16–20) and is located at a later stage, when there has been opportunity for Peter to witness Jesus at work (4.38). The use of Peter's boat at 5.3 also implies a previous relationship. What Peter exemplifies is not, as in Mark, instant obedience to the imperious summons of a stranger, but a response to the ministry of Jesus. The paragraph appears to be a conflation of elements from Mark's description of Jesus' public preaching from a boat, and a tradition also underlying John 21.1–11, the miraculous catch of fish.[21] The combination of these two sources is vital to the passage, for by this means Luke frames the story of the catch of fish, on the one side by Jesus' preaching to eager and receptive crowds and on the other by the promise to Peter that he will henceforth be catching men and the description of the disciples leaving all to follow Jesus. The miracle thus becomes a symbol of the mission upon which Peter is to be engaged, and whose effectiveness will depend entirely upon Jesus' word, which is the word of God he proclaims in his own ministry (cf. v. 1). The symbolic significance is underlined by the reference to James and John as Peter's 'partners' (v. 10), as they are seen to be elsewhere in the gospel and Acts (8.51; 9.28ff.; cf. 22.8; Acts 3.1ff.; 4.13ff.; 8.14ff.). The dependence of Peter's mission upon Jesus and its connection with discipleship is also underlined by 'henceforth' (v. 10); his mission begins when he becomes a follower of Jesus, and so shares his missionary journey.[22] This dependence continues even at 9.1–6, where the twelve are sent out on a journey on their own, for it is at Jesus' bidding and they report back to him (9.10).

That the missionary element in Peter's call is related to discipleship rather than his future role as apostle is confirmed by other elements in the passage: Peter's explicit obedience to Jesus' word in spite of the objections he voices (v. 5); his faith expressed in the discernment of who Jesus is, prompted by the miracle he has witnessed and shown both in the address, 'Lord', and in the act of kneeling and imploring Jesus to depart (v. 8); the confession of sin which accompanies this and the act of leaving everything to follow Jesus.[23] In some of this, the combination of awe and amazement (*thambos*) at the miracle, and the leaving all to follow, James and John are explicitly associated. It is true that the promise to 'catch men' is addressed to Peter alone, but it should be assumed that it is intended for the others also. Verse 9 suggests that Peter's reaction in v. 8 was theirs as well, and unless the reassurance Jesus gives Peter also applies to them, their action in following him at v. 11 is unexplained.

While therefore the fact that Jesus deals directly with Peter alone reflects his future pre-eminence, here as elsewhere Peter is the spokesman and representative of others; his call is the call to every believer to recognize Jesus as Lord, to confess his sins, and to leave all and follow, sharing Jesus' mission and obeying his word. His call thus illustrates in a dramatic way what we had already observed at 9.60: discipleship involves mission. At first sight this might seem to conflict with the observation that Luke has detached the conditions of discipleship from the missionary task in order to make them applicable to every believer. On the contrary, what he has achieved is to make mission one of the activities of discipleship, and therefore a task for all. The cost of discipleship does not apply only to those who are engaged in mission as an additional activity. This emphasis on mission confirms what we saw earlier in our discussion of faith. Discipleship involves declaring, sometimes in hostile circumstances, what God has done. This is because, as the stories of Peter, the Gerasene demoniac and the blind man at Jericho alike bring out, the disciple is not only an adherent but a recipient. He is one who 'comes to' Jesus because Jesus comes to him, bringing salvation (cf. 19.9f.). This notion of indebtedness underlies many of the sayings of Jesus (cf. e.g. 10.20–23).

Our study of 5.1–11 has thus reintroduced a number of themes which are new to this chapter but are discussed elsewhere. All the teaching addressed to disciples in Luke is relevant to discipleship; a full summary would involve repetition of the whole book. In particular we noted in the previous chapter the place of prayer in discipleship. Those who follow Jesus are identified and distinguished from others by the prayer they are given to use (11.1ff.). This chapter has had a more limited aim. It has sought to bring out the relationship between the disciple and Jesus as the context in which the teaching on other topics is presented. We have seen that discipleship involves going the way of Jesus, following 'after' or 'with' him, sharing both the cost and the missionary task involved. This introduces a further question. When discussing prayer we saw that Jesus is regarded by Luke as an example for his followers. Inevitably we are driven to ask how far Luke sees Christian living as an imitation of Christ.

8

Imitation?

It is clear that Luke did not write his gospel or the Acts simply to provide his readers with examples to imitate. One need look no further than the prologue (1.1–4), for all its ambiguities, or the elaborate dating of 3.1f. for evidence of Luke's intention to give an account of the past. One must accept Conzelmann's thesis that Luke sees a distinction between the time of Jesus and the time of the church.[1] The gospel is not, as portions of the Fourth Gospel arguably are, simply an extended parable of relations between the risen Christ and the evangelist's world. But Conzelmann's theory should not be rigidly applied to exclude the possibility that the gospel has a contemporary application. We have already seen evidence to suggest that this is so. We have observed, for example, how small details in the portrayal of the woman with the haemorrhage or the Gerasene demoniac point beyond the strict setting of the incident to aspects of Christian discipleship. Details in the teaching of the sermon on the plain either betray a failure by Luke to appreciate the social and religious setting of Jesus' teaching (at least in so far as Matthew suggests a more credible setting), or indicate that he has in mind the needs of his readers.

That Luke is capable of offering an account of the past with the intention that it should furnish an example is shown by Paul's farewell speech at Miletus at Acts 20.17ff. Here Paul is made to refer explicitly to his past conduct, as he hands over his ministry at Ephesus to those whom the Holy Spirit has appointed overseers. His injunctions are interspersed with references to his own behaviour which they are to call to mind (esp. vv. 31ff.). This passage may in fact be extremely important for an understanding of Luke's purpose in his two volumes. Acts 20.25–8 suggests that he wanted to summon that part of the post-apostolic church with which he was acquainted back to the standards of its foundation era; with such a purpose the past as a whole becomes exemplary. But this aim by itself cannot account for all the details, some of which are designed to address other specific problems.[2] Provided therefore that we give due weight to other intentions, we are entitled to ask to what extent Luke depicts any of the characters in his gospel as examples.

Many of the individuals in Luke's story are introduced without any characterization at all. They are simply parts of the setting for an action or pronouncement of Jesus. This is the case with the man with the deformed hand (6.6), the widow at Nain (7.11), the man with dropsy (14.2) and the high priest's servant (22.50). Even in the case of the demoniac of 4.33 the dialogue is in reality with the demon. In other cases it is tempting to see significance in the small details. The paralytic when healed goes home 'glorifying God' (5.25; cf. Mark 2.12), a Lucan addition which recurs in the story of the crippled woman (13.13). The ending of the cleansing of the leper is modified so that he is not guilty of disobedience by talking about what happened (5.15f., cf. Mark 1.45). Peter's mother-in-law when healed of a fever, which Luke represents as a form of demon possession,[3] 'served them' (4.39, as in Mark), which may hint at the service which other women, also released from demons, later perform (8.2f.). The description of Judas into whom, by contrast, Satan entered and who betrayed Jesus for money (22.3–5) probably also reflects Luke's emphasis.[4] Earlier we considered other cases where we can be more confident: the woman who anoints Jesus (7.36ff.), the Gerasene demoniac (8.26ff.), the woman with the haemorrhage (8.43ff.), Mary (10.41), the Samaritan leper (17.16ff.), and the blind man at Jericho (18.35ff.). How far the significant features of these passages are deliberately introduced it is difficult to say; Luke may only be betraying the fact that he unconsciously visualizes these scenes in terms of his own day. The same may be true of the brief descriptions of Levi and Simon of Cyrene. Both are based on Mark. The Levi episode (5.27f.) primarily introduces the scenes that follow, but Luke adds 'leaving everything', as at 5.11. So Levi illustrates the cost of discipleship (14.25–35). Luke also modifies Mark's next sentence, so as to show Levi expressing his response to the call by being the host of a great reception for Jesus, fellow tax-collectors and others (5.29; cf. Mark 2.15); as a disciple Levi immediately shares in the missionary activity of Jesus which it is the primary purpose of 5.29–32 to justify. Similarly the description of Simon of Cyrene becomes a vignette of discipleship: they 'laid on him the cross, to carry it behind Jesus' (23.26; cf. Mark 15.21); the emphasis no longer falls on carrying Jesus's cross for him, but on following in his steps.[5]

Among these incidental portraits note should be taken of those in the gospel and Acts who are examples of the generous use of wealth. The women of 8.2f. have already been mentioned. In the case of Zacchaeus, his changed attitude to wealth is the chief indication of his repentance and saved condition. This portrayal of the generous rich is continued in Acts: Barnabas (Acts 4.36f.) in immediate contrast to Ananias and Sapphira (5.1–11), Dorcas (9.36–43) whose generosity as a disciple the mourning widows attest (v. 39), and, with less emphasis, Lydia (16.14f.).

With the penitent criminal the lines are more fully drawn (23.39–43). Here too the primary emphasis lies elsewhere, on Jesus' pronouncement demonstrating his role of saviour, which is being called into question by those who witness his crucifixion (cf. vv. 35, 37, 39). For Luke the redeemer must suffer, and the crucifixion affirms rather than denies him as saviour (cf. 24.21, 26). The criminal is also one of a succession of witnesses to the innocence of Jesus (23.4, 14f., 22, 41). Even so he is carefully depicted to illustrate qualities we have encountered elsewhere, humility before God (v. 40), acknowledgment of guilt (v. 41), and faith (v. 42).[6]

Joseph of Arimathea, however, serves other purposes (23.50–53).[7] It is true that he is described in terms we meet elsewhere: he is good and righteous and looking for the kingdom of God. But he fulfils a unique role in the story of the crucifixion, which Christians are not called to emulate, and his virtues are described, not for this purpose, but to characterize him as one of the faithful in Israel (cf. 2.25). To underline the point Luke adds that Arimathea was a 'Jewish town' (23.50). So he demonstrates that even at the crucifixion Israel was divided in its response to Jesus. Even though Joseph was a member of the council that condemned him, he did not concur, and demonstrated his dissent by providing Jesus with a grave. It is not said that he was or became a disciple; if Luke intended to point to any characteristic of discipleship in his conduct, it would presumably be his courage in identifying himself before authority as a supporter of the crucified Jesus, but there is no hint in the narrative that Luke did intend this.

A more obvious paradigm of discipleship is provided by the portrayal of Peter. As we saw in the previous chapter, Peter occupies a more prominent position in Luke than in Mark, and we have to make allowances for this when interpreting Luke's narrative. Nevertheless there are two episodes in which we are entitled to think that to his sketch of a unique figure Luke has added the colours of a typical Christian. These are the narrative of his call, 5.1–11, which we examined in the last chapter, and the denial of Jesus, 22.33f., 54–62.

In 5.1–11 we saw that in addition to the strong missionary emphasis, which is parallelled in references to discipleship elsewhere, Luke's narrative highlights other aspects of discipleship: faith, obedience, confession of sin, and leaving all to share with Jesus in his journey. Behind Peter are his partners James and John for whom he acts as spokesman and whom in a way he represents.

In 22.33f., 54–62, however, Peter stands alone. Unlike Mark 14.27–31, Luke does not set the prophecy of Peter's denial in the context of a warning that all will desert Jesus, nor do the disciples run away when he is arrested in Luke, as they do in Mark 14.50, although we cannot deduce from this that they preserve their faith.[8] Peter's protest of loyalty (22.33) is more specific than in Mark; he is ready to go to prison and death, and to do so 'with Jesus'. In Acts Peter will indeed go to prison and face the danger of death (Acts 12.1ff.); but in the gospel he does not do so 'with Jesus'. Instead he follows 'at a distance' (22.54), the act of a disciple indeed, but one whose ties with Jesus are already weakening. In the high priest's house he is identified as having been 'with' Jesus (vv. 56, 59), as one of Jesus' company (v. 58), but he

denies this, and so repudiates his discipleship. What is striking about Luke's presentation is that the denial takes place in
Jesus' presence. Mark presents two parallel scenes in 14.53–
72; Peter stays in the outer court below, while the trial and
subsequent mockery of Jesus take place indoors (cf. vv. 54,
66). Peter is perhaps unaware of what is happening to Jesus.
He is reminded of his promise only by the crowing of the
cock. In Luke the trial of Jesus does not take place until
daybreak (22.66); Peter's denial occurs in the period of
waiting during the night and Jesus hears it. It is his look
rather than the crowing of the cock which brings Peter to
remorse. The denial as a betrayal of loyalty to Jesus himself is
well brought out by 'the Lord turned and looked at Peter' (v.
61), and the contrast between disciple and Lord is under-
scored by Luke's placing the mockery and beating of Jesus
immediately afterwards, before his trial (vv. 63ff.).[9] The
implications for Luke's readers are obvious: the story of
Peter's denial warns of the dangers inherent in discipleship.
To follow Jesus may indeed lead to prison and death (cf.
12.4–12); promises are easy to make but the cost must be
counted in advance (cf. 14.28ff.); essentially discipleship is
going with Jesus in his suffering. The reader knows, however, from the subsequent story, that the good news of
repentance and forgiveness which Jesus proclaims can have its
application even in cases of failure such as this. Unlike Judas,
who becomes a complete renegade, possessed by Satan,
perverting the kiss which is a sign of loyalty into a signal of
betrayal for money (22.47f.) and dying unrepentant having
forfeited his place among the twelve (Acts 1.16ff.),[10] Peter
repented, and so was restored to his place among the twelve.
In his repentance, shown by bitter tears, his faith did not fail,
and Jesus' prayer (22.32) was answered.

We turn from Peter as an example of discipleship to Mary,
Jesus' mother, starting with Luke 1–2. In recent years some
excellent studies of these chapters have been published in
English, and there is no need to repeat here the detailed
analysis which has been made of them.[11] Particularly striking
has been the agreement achieved between Catholic and
Protestant scholars on a subject where dogmatic differences
are still very strong. It is clear that, whatever the sources
upon which Luke may have drawn, the degree of symmetry

between the various episodes and the way in which the different annunciation scenes conform to Old Testament patterns indicate that Luke has impressed his own design upon the whole section.[12] It is also clear that the primary purpose is to set the scene for the rest of the gospel: to identify Jesus, and John as his forerunner, and to affirm as strongly as possible that with their birth the long awaited new age has dawned both for Israel and the Gentiles. Hence the strong emphasis upon the activity of the Holy Spirit, the sign of the nearness of the new age (cf. Acts 2.17–21); not only John (1.15, 76, 80) but Elizabeth (1.41),[13] Zechariah (1.67), Simeon (2.25–7), and Anna (2.36), are all prophetic figures. We have seen the contribution that the canticles make to this picture. Moreover, it is part of Luke's intention to stress the continuity between the Israel of the Old Testament and the Christian community of his day; it is therefore integral to his purpose to emphasize that the Christian movement has its origins in faithful Israelites, who display traditional virtues, fulfil the requirements of the law, are loyal to the temple and look for the fulfilment of God's promise to Israel.[14] There is a parallel between these chapters and the picture in the early chapters of Acts of the earliest Christian community in Jerusalem, worshipping in the temple and rejoicing in the Spirit, which again emphasizes the continuity between the old and the new.

We therefore have to ask ourselves whether Luke intends his readers to draw any conclusions for their own pattern of life from the holy men and women he describes in Luke 1–2. For his Gentile readers there is no temple and they have been released from most of the requirements of the law of Moses by decree of the Jerusalem church itself (Acts 15.6ff.). The faithful Israelite cannot be a Christian ideal in these respects.[15] In other respects, however, these men and women display qualities which Luke commends elsewhere. They pray and fast (1.13; 2.37; cf. 5.35; 11.2ff.; Acts 13.1–3), give expression to joy in thanksgiving and praise (1.46ff., 64, 67ff.; 2.20, 28ff.,38; cf. 17.18) and bear witness to what they have seen and heard (2.17, 20, 38; cf. 8.39, 47); they are righteous in God's sight (1.6; 2.25; cf. 18.14). Moreover, there are parallels between Luke's descriptions of them and of Cornelius in Acts.

Five times in Acts 10 allusion is made to the character of Cornelius as Luke describes what is for him the decisive conversion of a Gentile, to which appeal will be made in chapter 15 as evidence of God's intention for the mission of the church. In 10.2 he is described as devout, fearing God with all his household (a phrase which not only describes his technical status in relation to the synagogue as an uncircumcised worshipper but also in this context points to the inner reality which justifies the status). He is liberal in giving alms to the people (meaning, probably, the Jews (cf. v. 22), a sign of his identification with Israel), and continually at prayer. 10.4 affirms that God has taken note of his prayers and almsgiving. 10.22 repeats the description, upright (*dikaios*, 'righteous') and Godfearing, well spoken of by the whole Jewish nation (for his almsgiving). 10.31 repeats 10.4. Finally 10.34f. records Peter's conclusion, 'God shows no partiality but in every nation any one who fears him and does what is right is acceptable to him.' The content of this testimony is the same as in Luke 1–2, where every item in the list except almsgiving can be parallelled in almost identical terms (cf. 1.6, 13, 50; 2.25, 37). The repeated emphasis is to be explained by Acts 10.34f. Luke wishes to stress that salvation comes to Jew and Gentile on the same terms. Cornelius is thus as much a good Jew as Simeon, except for circumcision and the observance of the law implied by it, although his conversion still involves repentance, as it does for Jewish converts however devout (cf. Acts 2.5, 38 with 11.18).[16] But it should be noted that Peter's conclusion extends beyond Cornelius; this character is not required only of the first human link in the chain between Jewish and Gentile church but of all.

This conclusion is confirmed by the brief description of the centurion in Luke 7.1ff. It is often suggested that Luke has introduced the deputation of Jewish leaders, absent from Matthew, to prevent premature contact between Jesus and a Gentile. This can be exaggerated, since the climax of the episode remains Jesus' acclamation of his faith as a Gentile and the healing of his servant, and there is no question of Jesus going into Gentile territory. We have suggested that the force of the commendation by the Jews is to highlight the man's humility in vv. 6ff.[17] The terms of their

commendation, however, echo elements in the characterization of Cornelius: he is generous, well spoken of by the Jews
and sympathetic to their religion.

Thus the pious men and women of Luke 1–2 are not
irrelevant for Christian character. Apart from Zechariah in
one particular which we shall examine in a moment, and their
dedication to law and temple worship which is no longer
applicable to Gentile Christians, they exemplify Christian
virtues. As characters, however, they are hardly distinguishable from one another. They make their impact upon the
reader collectively, in the overall impression Luke creates out
of them, and in the cumulative force of the canticles with
their strong sense of joy at the dawning of the new age. If that
is a fair assessment, then it is important for our study that
Luke has set these characters at the beginning of his gospel.[18]
Although they are located there for another purpose they
nevertheless set the keynote for the Christian character which
Luke will set out in the pages that follow.

The one exception to the last paragraph is Mary. She
features more frequently in these chapters, she is mentioned
again by name in Acts 1.14, and more detail is given about
her. It must be recognized that the significance Luke attaches
to her derives primarily from Jesus, for it is God's act in
giving his Son to the world, in which Mary is instrumental,
that he intends to describe. The births of both John and Jesus
are miraculous. John is born of an infertile woman in the
fashion of other Old Testament figures whose very existence
is a sign for Israel of God's salvation, Isaac, Samson and
Samuel. Every conception in the Old Testament is viewed as
an act of God, and the ending of infertility a sign of special
blessing, but, as with Isaac, it is miraculous when the mother
is past the normal age. Given the pre-eminence of Jesus over
John, Luke would have needed to introduce a more miraculous sign of God's special initiative in the birth of Jesus, even
if he had not had the traditon of Mary's virginity to call upon
for the purpose.[19] In most of the scenes in which Mary
appears therefore, the chief interest lies elsewhere. The dialogue
between her and Elizabeth at 1.39–45 is primarily about the
greatness of Jesus over John and the unborn John's recognition of him. Nevertheless, the repeated references to Mary as
the story proceeds, and the fact that Luke uses her rather than

Joseph to register 'audience reaction' to events, show that
Luke has an interest in her apart from her child. The opening
dialogue with the angel shows what this is.[20]

Mary is the recipient of grace (1.28); that is, as v. 30 shows,
God has shown her special favour. It is a misunderstanding,
both of the Old Testament background and of the rest of
Luke 1–2, to think that this implies that Mary has been
selected for her inherent special qualities,[21] or simply to enjoy
privileges. The privilege is only in being selected for service,
and as vv. 48f. make clear, God's favour to Mary is undeserved
and unaccountable except in terms of his sovereign choice.
This has immediate reference to her unique role in the story
of salvation, but the overtones are wider, for God's grace is
also evident in the conversion of people to Christian faith
(Acts 11.23; 13.43; 14.3; 15.11; 18.27; 20.24, 32), and his
sovereign choice is reflected in Jesus' summons to discipleship
(Luke 5.1ff., 27; 9.59), which every servant will acknowledge
is undeserved (17.7–10). In response Mary accepts God's will
without demur (1.38), implying both that she believes without question that what is humanly impossible can be accomplished by God (cf. v. 45), and that she submits herself in
obedience. Her faith is of the kind required of disciples
(17.5f.; 18.27; cf. 9.48), and there are direct parallels between
Mary's 'let it be to me according to your word', Peter's
obedience at 5.5, 'at your word I will let down the nets', and
the prayer of Jesus at the Mount of Olives, 'not my will but
thine be done' (22.42). What makes her response especially
characteristic of the Christian, however, is the fact that in
effect Gabriel proclaims to her the good news about Jesus, the
Son of God who will occupy the messianic throne of David
and whose kingdom will have no end (vv. 32f., 35; cf. Acts
2.22–36). Thus 'for Luke she is the first Christian disciple',[22]
and her joy expressed in her hymn of praise anticipates the
rejoicing and praise of the church in Acts.[23]

It might perhaps be thought that 'believes without question'
is an overgenerous description of her response to the angel in
v. 34, 'how can this be?' A question of this kind however is
an established part of the pattern which Luke is following of
Old Testament scenes in which a birth is announced or
someone is called to the service of God (cf. Gen. 17.17; 18.12;
Ex. 3.11; Judg. 6.15). The cue is thereby given for the

heavenly messenger to explain how the message will be fulfilled. It is a device Luke uses in other contexts (cf. 24.19). No doubt is being expressed by Mary, only a statement of what is impossible, so that the angel can show how with God there are no impossibilities (v. 37).

In this she differs from Zechariah. The encounter with the angel follows the same pattern in both cases, but Zechariah's form of the question in v. 18 does imply doubt, as his subsequent dumbness and the reason for it in v. 20 show. He asks for a sign as a condition of belief, and while signs are given to Mary (v. 36) as reassurance that God can do the impossible, and to the shepherds (2.12) as a means of identifying the birth in question, Luke sees such signs as effective only where there is a disposition to believe; they are offered but may not be demanded (cf. 11.29).[24]

Further references to Mary in chapters 1 and 2 build up this picture of her as a disciple. Her obedience is incidentally touched on in her naming of Jesus according to the angel's instruction (2.21; 1.31). At 2.19 she is described as keeping and pondering in her heart all the shepherds had said, and again at 2.51 as keeping all the preceding events in her heart. This is best understood as meaning that Mary, in contrast to the transient wonder of others who heard the news in 2.18, retained the memory of what she heard and sought its meaning.[25] The stress is on understanding. That such under-standing is not easy is suggested by 2.35 and 2.48–51.

In 2.34f. Simeon prophesies what is to become of the baby Jesus. He will be a sign from God, who will be spoken against and will bring about the fall or rise of many in Israel. The inner thoughts of many hearts will be revealed.[26] The prophecy thus points to Jesus's function as judge, both in his ministry and at the end (cf. esp. 11.29–32; 12.2f.; 20.17f.), and to the reversal of high and low which his coming brings about (cf. 1.51–3).[27] This gives the context for interpreting the sword which is to pass through Mary's soul. As Mary does not feature in Luke's account of the passion it is unlikely that he is thinking of her suffering at the rejection of her son. As the 'also' indicates, she will be as much subjected to testing by Jesus the judge as the rest of Israel. In the sword metaphor there is probably a reflection of Ezek. 14.17, which speaks of God's judgment and in Greek uses the same

vocabulary. Mary will find it hard to be a believer as her son
grows up; for her as for the rest of Israel faith will have to
come to terms with the Jesus who makes rigorous demands
and is himself rejected by Israel. Not all can believe under
such conditions.[28]
  The following episode illustrates this (2.48–51). Luke gives
us a glimpse of the boy Jesus already displaying the mastery
of the law which will mark his teaching and confound his
critics during his ministry. His understanding (v. 47) is
contrasted with the failure of his parents to understand (v.
50). The translation of *en tois tou patros mou* in v. 49 is
notoriously difficult: 'about my father's business', 'in my
father's house', or even 'among my father's people'.[29] Two
assertions at least are being made: first, that God's will
required Jesus to be where his parents found him, in the
temple discussing with the teachers, and secondly, that this
has priority over the claims of family relationships. For Jesus,
Luke is saying, as for those whom he calls to follow him,
God's will involves a break with family ties (cf. 9.60; 14.26).
It is possible, however, to venture a further step: Jesus' visit
to Jerusalem takes place at the passover. It is his first, and
God's will requires him to be in the temple for three days.
Later Luke will describe another journey for the passover,
Jesus' last, again in accord with God's will, and again
culminating in the temple before his arrest and crucifixion. If
we are right that Luke depicts Mary as a disciple it is striking
that in the gospel what the disciples consistently fail to
understand is the necessity for the messiah to suffer, which
underlies his last journey (cf. 9.31 with 9.51; 9.44f.; 18.31–4;
24.25f.). On this occasion Mary does not understand, and
Luke is indicating for the reader who knows what is to come
that she is baffled not only by the break with the family which
God's will imposes but by the deeper necessity for suffering
which underlies that break.[30] Even so, Luke does not conclude on this negative note but with Mary 'keeping all these
things in her heart' (v. 51); in the light of v. 19, she is
pondering their meaning, seeking the understanding she does
not yet have. Acts 1.14 will show her, after the resurrection,
with the other disciples who now know the secret of the
crucifixion, sharing in prayer and awaiting the Spirit.
  There are no further references to Mary by name in the

gospel, but two short dialogues refer to her by implication, and before we leave this discussion we ought to consider them briefly. Both have as their central thrust the affirmation that relationship to Jesus is constituted not by physical ties of birth but by hearing and doing the will of God. They are thus related to the passage in 2.42–51 which we have just considered. 8.19–21 is based on Mark but much edited by Luke. He omits Mark 3.20f. which describes Jesus' family pronouncing him to be mad, transposes Mark 3.31–5 to a position after the parable of the sower, shifts the reference to the crowd to the beginning, so that it becomes clear that this is the reason why his mother and brothers 'stand outside' (in Mark the impression is an unwillingness to come closer: they send a message summoning him), and he softens the impact of Mark 3.33–5. There is no longer an outright repudiation of his family by Jesus. Nevertheless the family circle is widened and its basis changed: 'these, who hear the word of God and do it, are my mother and brothers' (cf. RSV). The implication is clear: Jesus' natural relatives will only qualify for a continuing relationship on the same basis as those others who now share it. Characteristically Luke broadens Mark's doing the will of God to hearing and doing.[31]

A similar comment is to be made on 11.27f. Although in form this is a blessing of Jesus' mother the reason for the blessing is the greatness of the son. As in 8.21 Jesus shifts the basis from physical relationship to hearing and keeping the word of God, and thereby throws the blessing open to all who do so. 11.28 thus prepares for vv. 29ff. which challenge the people to 'listen to' the one who is greater than Solomon or Jonah. No doubt one could say that the implication of these two passages is that the true grounds for declaring Mary blessed is that she is a disciple, but, as the omission of the name shows, Luke is not interested in the figure of Mary, whose function as an example is confined to chapters 1 and 2.[32]

From Mary we turn to Jesus. We have just seen that as a boy Jesus has to conform to the requirements he will later lay down for his disciples. That is true of his teaching on discipleship generally. To be a disciple means to go the way of Jesus with him. How far does Luke exploit this in his narrative by depicting Jesus as an example to be followed?

Our initial impression may well be, not very far. The temptations in 4.1–13, for example, are too intimately concerned with Jesus' identity as the Son of God to be treated as a model for disciples facing temptation. The baptism is too cursorily treated to be a model for the baptism of converts, with the emphasis falling primarily on the voice from heaven, although the reference to Jesus praying may be part of the general portrayal in Luke of Jesus as a pattern for prayer (3.21f.; cf. 11.1 below). Indeed it would seem that Luke has deliberately passed by some opportunities. For whatever reason, at 9.37–43 he chooses not to employ the material in Mark 9.14–21 which explores the conditions under which disciples may successfully emulate Jesus' powers of exorcism. In other passages he omits references to Jesus' human emotions. Only at 7.13 does he speak of Jesus having compassion. He omits Mark's use of the word at 5.13,[33] and in the looser parallels at 9.11, 42 (Mark 6.34; 9.22). He also omits Mark's reference to Jesus' loving the rich man at 18.22 (Mark 10.21). Instead Luke creates his effects by other narrative details, inserting 'only child' at 8.42, 9.38 (as at 7.12) to underline the need of the parent. The reason for this is probably very simple. Luke stresses that Jesus is the messiah who inherits David's throne, the prophet like Moses, greater than Elijah or Solomon, the Son of Man who will come in glory, the Son of God whose relation to the Father is unique, the Saviour and Lord (cf. e.g. 1.32f., 35; 2.11; 9.26, 35; 10.22; 11.30–32; Acts 3.21). This form of presentation is likely to stress the distance between Jesus and others rather than his example, which implies some common ground. On the other hand it is often observed that Luke only lightly alludes to the death of Jesus as an expiation for sin.[34] In this respect therefore he does not need to insist on the distance between Jesus and others, and we shall see it is especially in the narrative of the passion that exemplary traits emerge.

One passage which is often held to suggest Jesus as an example is 6.40, 'A disciple is not above his teacher, but every one when he is fully taught will be like his teacher.' Comparison with Matthew suggests that its position may be due to Luke (cf. Matt. 15.14; 10.24f.), but the sequence of thought is not very clear. The reference to the blind in v. 39 seems to prepare for the subsequent verses, 41f. The second half of v. 40, (*katertismenos de pas estai hos ho didaskalos autou*) is usually translated as in the RSV quoted above, but the Greek is perhaps more naturally taken to mean 'everyone will be fully taught like his teacher'.[35] There is little difference, except that the more usual translation leaves doubt whether the pupil will finish the course ('when (or if) he is fully taught'). How far is there a reference to Jesus as the teacher here? It is clearly intended in Matt. 10.24f., and some commentators see at least a secondary reference in the second half of Luke's verse.[36] But a reference to Jesus here is surely intrusive. It is even less likely with the translation I am proposing, for there is no suggestion in Luke that all disciples of Jesus will complete the course (cf. e.g. 8.11–15). The point is the need for the followers of Jesus to be right themselves before attempting to put others right, and the function of v. 40 is to explain the parable of v. 39. Verse 40 is itself parabolic, stating a general principle in terms of teachers and pupils. Thus interpreted v. 40 forms a link, not a break between vv. 39 and 41f., to which vv. 43–45 form a continuation. There is no hint here of an imitation of Christ.

11.1ff. is a clearer case. As we saw in our review of Luke's teaching on prayer, the disciples ask for instruction at a time when Jesus himself has been praying, and although they refer to the way John the Baptist had taught his disciples the example of Jesus is clearly intended to be the starting point, and the prayer he gives them to say begins with the opening which is typical of his own prayers. In the light of this it is likely that other references to Jesus at prayer in the gospel are also intended to build up a picture of Jesus as an exemplary man of prayer.

22.27 is quite explicit. A contrast is drawn between the behaviour of worldly rulers and that expected of disciples, and Jesus' own conduct is given as the example. In what sense he is 'one who serves' is not made clear. In the context of the last supper and in the light of 12.37 we might suspect that Luke is thinking of Jesus' ministry to believers in the eucharist; we may note also that only a few lines later Jesus speaks of his prayer for the disciples (v. 32). But the point of v. 27 is not to explore these possibilities or their implications for the disciples' behaviour but to state the contrast between Jesus and the world's rulers. Jesus is like a servant at a banquet, and so the disciples should be too.[37] The emphasis is on status rather than function.

To a limited extent, then, Luke does set forth the figure of Jesus in his ministry as an example for his readers. When we come to the passion narrative the situation is very different. Of course for Luke the death of Jesus is the death of the messiah or king of Israel and the saviour, although for his accusers such claims are false, because they are wrongly interpreted (22.67–71; 23.2f., 14, 35, 37f. and especially 39–43). However, not all aspects of Luke's narrative, which differs considerably from Mark in many places, are devoted to expounding this.[38] In particular we need to take account of five features.

(*a*) Luke's account of the prayer of Jesus at the Mount of Olives, 22.39–46 (not Gethsemane as in Mark), involves all the disciples, not just Peter, James and John. They 'follow him' (v. 39) and are told at beginning and end to 'pray not to enter temptation' (vv. 40, 46). They are not bidden to watch (or stay awake, Mark 14.34), and when Jesus finds them asleep a reason is given, and his rebuke is very mild compared with Mark (vv. 45f.). Jesus does not share his feelings with the disciples (Mark 14.34), and his prayer is described only once. The words are given in slightly shorter form. In many manuscripts vv. 43f. describe him at prayer, supported by an angel, with his sweat falling like drops of blood.

(*b*) Luke repeatedly includes affirmations of Jesus' innocence of the charges against him: Pilate (23.4, 14, 22), Herod (23.15), one of the convicts (23.41) and (in many modern translations of 23.47) the centurion, all attest this. By this Luke does not of course refer to the charge of being the messiah but to the seditious interpretation of messianic claims put upon it by the authorities (23.2, 5, 14). He has 'done nothing wrong' (23.41).

(*c*) Jesus is portrayed showing magnanimity to his enemies. It is true that Luke includes stern, almost aggressive sayings at 22.67f., 23.28–31, but he also shows Jesus rebuking the violence of his disciples, healing the injured ear of the high priest's servant (22.51) and (in many manuscripts) praying for his persecutors (23.34).[39]

(*d*) Luke does not contain the cry of dereliction (Mark 15.34). Instead Jesus' last words are given in 23.46 as an echo of Ps. 31.6, which became for later Judaism, and may possible have been for Luke, the prayer of the pious Israelite before sleeping.[40] The effect is to impart a greater atmosphere of serenity to Jesus' last hours. Luke narrates the crucifixion with less violence anyway; although Jesus is repeatedly mocked, Luke does not dwell on the beatings and omits the crown of thorns (cf. 22.63–5 with Mark 14.65; 23.11 with Mark 15.16–20; 23.25 with Mark 15.15). Jesus thus dies with greater composure than in Mark, confident of entering paradise, able to carry on a conversation with the two criminals, and entrusting himself at the last to God.

(e) Luke has a strikingly different version of the centurion's words at Jesus' death (23.47). Mark 15.39 has often been interpreted in a reduced sense to mean no more than 'this man was a divine hero–figure' of the type common to pagan thought; more recent interpreters have recognized that for Mark the words son of God must bear the full weight of his own christological understanding.[41] What are we to make of Luke's version, which literally means 'in reality this man was righteous (*dikaios*)'?

The best account that can be given of these features is to recognize that while emphasizing his role as messiah and saviour Luke has also depicted the death of Jesus as the death of a martyr.[42] Martyrdom was a theme which received considerable development in later Judaism, both before the time of Jesus and afterwards when it was also developed in Christian literature. In both cases the experience of suffering for religious belief led to reflection on its meaning, which in turn inspired the attitude with which believers faced their suffering. Christian thought was much influenced by earlier Jewish writing, particularly by Daniel and the books of Maccabees.[43] In assessing Luke against this background it is important not to place too much weight on ideas in later literature which may not have developed as early as the first century. Moreover, some features of the tradition are obviously inappropriate to Luke. It is impossible to find parallels in Luke to the martyrs' heroic endurance of extreme physical pain, their aggressive attitude in cursing their persecutors and taunting them to get on with their work; or to the view that the suffering has disciplinary or educative value for the sufferer or expiatory efficacy for others. All these ideas are to be found, for example, in II Maccabees 6.12–7.42 and in IV Maccabees.[44] On the other hand there are parallels which cannot be dismissed out of hand. Martyrdom is often seen as a contest with the powers of evil (cf. 22.3, 31, 44, 53), angels may appear to support the martyr or fight on his behalf (cf. 22.43), prayer may be emphasized as important for victory (cf. 22.40ff.), the moment of death may be marked by supernatural signs (cf. 23.44f.), and the whole event becomes a public spectacle (*theoria*, cf. 23.48), marked by mockery (cf. 22.63–5; 23.11, 35–9). The dying words of the martyr are often given at great length, and his obedience to God's will is stressed; his suffering may be described as a cup to be received from God (cf. 22.42).[45] These features are especially prominent in Luke, as the references show, although some also occur in the other gospels. Luke devotes a generous amount of space to Jesus' last words and acts (esp. 22.51; 23.27–31, 34, 42f.).

Particularly interesting are the parallels of thought to be found between Luke and Wisdom 1–5, especially 1.16–3.9. These paragraphs depict the persecution of the righteous man (*dikaios*) by the ungodly. By his manner of life he is a rebuke to his oppressors, who have made a pact with death and opted for a life of pleasure. In their resentment they try to prove false his claim to have God for his father and protector by making him suffer torture and insult and eventually bringing him to a shameful and premature death. They do not realize that beyond death the righteous are in the hands of God and out of reach of further torment. In these circumstances the ultimate test of the righteous man is the way he meets his suffering. Will he endure it with gentleness, and maintain his integrity as a righteous man, or give way and become like his persecutors? Will he still trust in God? It is important to note that in this version of the martyr-theme, the bone of contention between the sufferer and his persecutors is presented in very general terms, as a matter of moral character and trust in God. In II and IV Maccabees the issue is much more precise, the eating of pork, although of course this is only the test of religious loyalty as a whole.

There is evidence that some of the ideas in Wisdom 1–5 influenced Luke, who may indeed have known the book, although it is not necessary for our purpose to argue that he borrowed directly from it.[46] However, he does present the death of Jesus in similar terms, as the faithful endurance by the righteous son of God of the sufferings imposed on him by opponents who refuse to accept that he is God's son, and resent and mock at the challenge which his teaching and conduct present to them. In this connection we should note especially that Luke has Jesus praying to his Father (23.34, 46), and the second prayer, as we have seen, echoes Ps. 31.6, which is a prayer of the righteous (*dikaios*, 31.18). He also describes Jesus' confidence that he will immediately enter paradise (23.43, cf. Wisd, 3.2f.; 4.16ff.). Just as the oppressors of Wisdom 2.18 want to see whether God will deliver the righteous, so Jesus' mockers defy him to save himself if he is indeed God's chosen messiah (23.35).

This gives an excellent background for the words of the centurion at 23.47. It is often held nowadays that the officer declares Jesus innocent, on the grounds that it is in line with the series of similar affirmations by others which we noted above. It is probable that *dikaios* can mean this, but the real question is whether the translation fits the Lucan context.[47] There is no other instance of Luke's use of the word with this meaning in the gospel or the Acts. It cannot bear this sense a few verses later at 23.50, nor can the adverb just before at 23.41. Moreover it is not obvious what grounds Jesus' innocence would give for praising (literally, 'glorifying') God. Normally the execution of an innocent man would be deplored (cf. v. 48). As Luke usually uses the verb (*edoxazen*) in the sense of the deliberate offering of praise, it is unlikely in this sentence to mean merely that the centurion's words reflected glory on God without his intending it.[48] If, however, *dikaios* means 'righteous', and we bear in mind the background we have seen in Wisdom 1–5, then what Luke has the centurion affirm is that Jesus preserved his integrity to the last.[49] Even under the pain of the cross and the abuse of bystanders he remained a genuinely (*ontos*) righteous man, unlike his opponents who earlier in the gospel put themselves forward as such (cf. 16.15; 18.9; 20.20). Here would be grounds for praise, and we have a good reason why Luke should have substituted this for Mark 15.39. On any other view Luke's version is an anticlimax. Thus Luke may be suggesting, as does Mark, that the centurion is the first to be converted by Jesus' death.

If we ask what Luke might have considered to justify the centurion's exclamation, as he has narrated the events, the answer will have to include Jesus' attitude towards his opponents, which we noted above as one of the distinctive aspects of Luke's passion narrative.[50] He has prayed for his persecutors at 23.34, and even on the cross continued to respond as saviour to those who repent. We are reminded of the sermon on the plain, which as we saw was dominated by the call for love. That theme was inseparable from the topic of persecution and response to enemies (6.22f., 27–9, 31, 35f.). It ended on a note which we saw repeated elsewhere, that Jesus' teaching must be both heard and obeyed. This is what Jesus exemplifies in his passion. He maintains to the last the way of love and of forgiving enemies to which he has called his disciples. His integrity as a righteous man, as defined by his own teaching, is preserved.

There is thus good evidence for thinking that Luke presents the suffering of Jesus as the victorious suffering of a martyr. That the reason for this portrayal is to set Jesus forth as an example to Christians is confirmed by his treatment of Stephen and Paul in Acts. Both suffer for their faith in Christ, one being put to death, the other expecting it.[51] Stephen prays for his persecutors, sees the Son of Man in glory, and entrusts himself to Jesus as he dies (Acts 7.55–60; cf. Luke 22.69; 23.34, 46). Paul, like Jesus, goes up to Jerusalem in obedience to God, is tried by the Jewish court, the Roman governor and a puppet king, is charged with similar offences and is declared to be innocent.[52]

The stress on Jesus' innocence is best explained within this context. That Jesus was not guilty is of course common to all the gospels, but Luke's stress on innocence has often been explained as intended to commend Christianity to Gentile readers or to offer a defence before Roman authorities. On this view Luke is saying that Christians are not potentially subversive. It is doubtful, however, whether Roman officials would be much influenced by the verdict of a self-confessed criminal (23.41) or be won over by the charge that Pilate had allowed Roman justice to miscarry;[53] sympathetic readers of the entire gospel would not need reassurance anyway. The real purpose of the testimonies is to emphasize that Jesus' sufferings were maliciously caused: the Jewish leaders who

charged Jesus with sedition called instead for the release of
Barabbas, imprisoned for revolution and murder (a point
repeated, 23.19, 25); having failed to arrest Jesus in the
temple, they come out against him with weapons as though
he were a bandit (22.52). Pilate gave in to them in spite of
declaring his innocence (23.24f.). It is a common feature of
martyr-literature to make this point (e.g. Dan. 6.4f., III
Macc. 3.1–10; cf. I Peter 2.19f.) and is obviously encouragement for readers who in their turn have to face the malice of
others.

We can now go back to Jesus' prayer before the passion
(22.39–46). It is impossible here to go into a detailed discussion of all the difficulties of this passage. A good case can be
made out for the authenticity of vv. 43f.[54] If they are genuine,
they constitute a strong endorsement of the case that Jesus'
death is a martyrdom, because many of the parallels with
other literature noted above are concentrated here. Whether
they are genuine or not, the prayer of Jesus is explicitly linked
to the prayer of the disciples who have followed him to this
place (22.39). The details Luke gives are thus intended (like
the prayers of Jesus elsewhere) to provide a pattern.

Part of the difficulty of the passage is to decide, even with
the help of parallels from elsewhere, what Luke understood
to be happening. The details have been variously interpreted,
and it is impossible to form any conclusion without postulat-
ing some background ideas which may seem strange to
twentieth-century readers, although they can be shown to fit
into the perspective of biblical writers. It is probable that
Luke understood Jesus to be wrestling with Satan for the
outcome of the impending passion. In 22.31f. Jesus has
already referred to a previous contest with Satan on behalf of
the disciples conducted through the medium of prayer. Both
have presented petitions to God, and Jesus' request has been
granted that Peter's faith will not fail.[55] In 22.41ff. we see
Jesus praying against Satan on his own behalf. It is a struggle,
and God sends an angel to support him, so that he can pray
more strenuously (v. 44, RSV 'earnestly'). His prayer is that
God should accomplish his will;[56] he would like to escape the
cup of suffering involved, but the will of God is that the
messiah should suffer and so enter his glory (24.26). Jesus'
prayer then is that he should be faithful to his vocation, and

we are to think of Satan as seeking to frustrate it, as he always has (cf. 4.1–13; 23.3). So Jesus is praying that he will not succumb in the test he is about to face.[57] This prayer involves 'agony', a state of severe distress.

The importance of this passage for Luke is obvious. It is the decisive moment when God is asked to determine the outcome of what follows; the appearance of the angel indicates the answer God will give. Satan will be overcome as he has been before. But the disciples are also bidden to share in the prayer on their own behalf. They too will have to face a test. When Jesus returns to them they are asleep. It is questionable whether Luke really intends to say they fell asleep for 'sorrow' (v. 45); they do not understand that Jesus must suffer, and cannot anticipate what is to come. *Lype* can mean 'stress' in a more general sense, and Luke may be suggesting that they were utterly exhausted by the effort to pray as Jesus did.[58] However that may be, although they stay with Jesus during his passion, their faith fails, as 22.31f. suggests, and this may be seen not only in Peter's denial but in their aggressive action with the sword (vv. 49f.), which Jesus immediately countermands. Luke may be underlining this when he invests Simon of Cyrene with the garb of a disciple: only he was found to take up the cross and follow Jesus.[59] This failure Luke will have traced to their inability to continue in prayer to the end. Both Jesus' own prayer, and the disciples' share of it, will thus have functioned for Luke as examples to his readers for their own behaviour when they are called upon to suffer as believers. We have seen in an earlier chapter how important perseverance is for Luke in his understanding of faith. The death of Jesus is an example of what such perseverance means. In 22.39–46 he sets out the means by which it can be maintained. It is strenuous prayer, which God himself will sustain, which will enable the Christian to face the trial without failure, and to maintain in suffering the righteousness, especially the love even for enemies, which Jesus both taught and exemplified (cf. 18.1–8).

In this chapter we have reviewed many of the characters in Luke's narrative and tried to assess how far Luke intends to present them to his readers as examples. There will of course be a vital difference between Jesus and the rest. All the other figures approximate to the ideal of a disciple, and are offered in some sense for imitation. But discipleship depends on Jesus in the sense that he not only exemplifies the way the disciple must go but is the origin of the call to repent and follow, and the source of the forgiveness and release which constitute salvation. More than imitation is involved in the follower's relation to him.

We shall return to some of the issues raised by this chapter in our conclusions at the end of the book. In the meantime we have to ask whether there is any more systematic attempt to offer negative as well as positive examples in Luke than the references we have noted to Zechariah, Judas and Simon Peter. Before we do so, however, it is perhaps pertinent to draw attention to the obvious. We have analysed the function of Luke's narrative, showing how he depicts the various characters in his plot. But analysis cannot be a substitute for the narrative itself. In the nature of the case, examples only function as examples when the power of Luke's narrative is allowed to exercise its effect directly upon the reader.

9

The Pharisaic Mind

It is recognized that the Pharisees are a problem in the interpretation of Luke's gospel and Acts. In the gospel they are prominent as the opponents of Jesus, but in both gospel and Acts there are references which appear to put them in a more favourable light than anywhere else in the New Testament.

A clear example of their hostility to Jesus is to be found at Luke 11.53f. While neither the text nor the translation of these verses is certain the general drift is not in doubt: scribes and Pharisees set a watch on him in order to trap him into giving evidence they can use against him.[1] The sentence is peculiar to Luke, and comes as the climax to 11.38–52 in which Jesus makes a series of severe criticisms against both Pharisees and lawyers. Another example is to be found at 16.14f., where a contemptuous response by the Pharisees to Jesus' teaching about wealth leads to a vigorous attack in reply. This also is peculiar to Luke. In addition Luke has elaborated the role of the Pharisees in the group of conflict-stories taken over from Mark in 5.17–6.11 (Mark 2.1–3.6). In Mark, as commentators point out, we are provided with a series of controversial encounters which depict a rising tide of opposition to Jesus, culminating in a plot by Pharisees and Herodians to destroy him. The parties to this are variously described: scribes (2.6), scribes of the Pharisees (2.16), un-identified questioners (2.18), Pharisees (2.24), and unidentified opponents, presumably Pharisees again, who watch him (3.2). These opponents are mostly introduced incidentally as the narrative proceeds. Luke, in taking over this material,

makes the opposition more consistent and identifies the
participants from the outset. At 5.17, before any of the
incidents occur, he has 'Pharisees and teachers of the law
sitting by, who had come from every village of Galilee and
Judaea and from Jerusalem', his first mention of either group.
They form an impressive and threatening body of observers
assembled at the outset, numerically quite large, and he refers
to them in each incident, always mentioning the Pharisees by
name. No other parties are now involved; the Herodians
disappear as a group from Luke's gospel altogether, and by
continuation of the narrative the anonymous questioners of
Mark 2.18 become at Luke 5.33 the Pharisees and scribes of v.
30. Pharisees are thus made even more prominent early in the
gospel as an organized opposition. In fact their presence
indicates unusual interest and scrutiny; their reaction is not
the surprise result of casual encounter as in Mark. It is true
that Luke 6.11 ends with a milder reaction than Mark 3.6,
'they were filled with fury and discussed with one another
what they might do with Jesus', but a formal plot at this stage
of Luke's much longer story would come too early. He
comes closer to it later on at 11.53f. In addition to these there
are other passages in which the Pharisees are critical of Jesus
or he of them at 7.30, 36ff., 12.1, 14.1ff., 15.2, 18.11ff.,
19.39.

On the other hand Luke sometimes appears to put the
Pharisees in a favourable light. They invite Jesus to meals at
7.36, 11.37, 14.1, a feature peculiar to Luke. At 13.31 they
warn Jesus that Herod is about to kill him and advise him to
escape. Both in the passion narrative and in the Jerusalem
ministry which precedes it (19.45–21.38) they disappear
altogether, as though Luke did not wish to associate them
with responsibility for Jesus' death.

In Acts the picture appears uniformly favourable. Gamaliel,
a Pharisee, speaks against harrassing the Christians (5.34ff.),
and at 23.9 the Pharisees in the Council declare Paul innocent;
Luke emphasizes that there is a common bond between
Christians and Pharisees in their belief in the resurrection
(23.6; 26.5f.). The real opposition in Acts comes from the
Sadducees who deny this belief (4.1; 5.17; 26.7ff.).[2]

Luke, moreover, distinguishes the Pharisees clearly from
the scribes, while in other gospels, especially Matthew, there

is a tendency to blur the distinction. It is generally agreed that the scribes were the official interpreters of the law of Moses in the time of Jesus, and that many of them held Pharisaic views, but not all Pharisees were scribes nor all scribes Pharisees.[3] Luke reflects this distinction in 5.30, 11,45, Acts 5.34 and 23.9, and thus shows a true historical perspective.[4]

At the same time Luke shows himself, or at least his readers, to be at some distance from the Pharisees as a contemporary Jewish group with particular distinct concerns. He has to explain the difference between Pharisees and Sadducees (20.27 = Mark 12.18; Acts 23.8). The controversies Jesus has with them do not touch the degree of specific detail that we find in Matthew, or even in Mark. There is no discussion of Qorban (Mark 7.6–13), and the treatment of divorce is represented only by 16.18 (cf. Mark 10.2–12). In the sermon on the plain we saw that 6.29 reflects a less specifically Jewish context. Similarly 11.42 accuses Pharisees of tithing produce which, so far as we know, was not actually tithable.[5] It is probably a reflection of this relative ignorance of detail among his readers which leads Luke to use 'lawyer' (*nomikos*) instead of scribe at 7.30, 10.25, 11.45f., 52, 14.3 (otherwise in the gospels only at Matt. 22.35) and 'law-teacher' (*nomodidaskalos*) at 5.17, Acts 5.34 (not in the other gospels). They are the same as the scribes, as 5.17 and 21, 11.45 and 53 show, but Luke presumably felt he needed to introduce them with a less technical term.[6]

The most surprising feature of Luke's delineation of the Pharisees, however, is his emphasis on their love of wealth. It is hard to find parallels in ancient literature to the strong, categorical accusation of 16.14.[7] Mark 12.40 (= Luke 20.47) accuses the scribes of 'devouring widows' houses', but this does not identify them with the Pharisees.[8] Matthew 23.6f. incorporates much of Mark 12.39f. but not that clause.[9] It might perhaps be argued that greed lay behind provisions to exempt sons from fulfilling obligations to parents, but if so this is not brought out in Mark 7.11 or Matt. 15.5, where the point is rather that written commandments are overridden by oral tradition. Even Matthew, who develops a critical view of the Pharisees in many ways more severe even than Luke, lacks this stress on their love of money. The nearest parallel is Matt. 23.25, which accuses Pharisees of rapacity in terms which Luke 11.39 parallels and makes sharper. In Matthew the point is probably that the food in the dishes has been acquired by plunder and uncontrolled self-indulgence.[10] This of course reflects the character of the users, but even here Luke makes a more general accusation which is not confined to food and drink. In fact none of the New Testament references goes so far as the categorical denunciation of the Pharisees as a class in Luke 16.14.

The difficulty is not eased if we look outside the New Testament. There are problems in identifying who exactly the Pharisees were, because the terminology is not uniform in all the sources, so that it cannot simply be assumed that the Pharisees of the gospels are identical with those to whom Josephus refers or with the *perushim* of the rabbinic sources. It may be that different specific groups in the same general movement are mentioned in different contexts.[11] Even so it is difficult to find parallels to Luke's accusation. Josephus, on the contrary, speaks of their simplicity of lifestyle.[12] Individual cases may be instanced, but these do not amount to a general categorization; nor must criticism in rabbinical literature of the effect of Pharisaic rulings be confused with the denunciation of motive which occurs in Luke 16.14. On the other hand Luke's language cannot simply be explained as a literary convention. Although it was natural enough among Hellenistic writers to accuse philosophical opponents of cupidity, especially if they taught for money the virtues of poverty, it is not easy to show Luke following this trend in 16.14.[13]

The suggestion made in this chapter is that in Luke's gospel the Pharisees are not only the leaders of the opposition to Jesus in Galilee in the events which led ultimately to his crucifixion (which it is part of Luke's purpose to describe), but also represent a contemporary threat to his readers. Behind the Pharisees Luke expects his readers to recognize opponents of the Christian church, presumably Jewish, who are in a position to instigate persecution, whether of a relatively mild or harsher kind, thus constituting an external threat.[14] He also intends the Pharisees in his gospel to represent an internal threat because they exemplify a style of religion and life by which he believes Christians are in danger of being influenced. The faults which the Pharisees exemplify are not necessarily all attributable to an identifiable Jewish group, whether in the time of Jesus or of Luke; rather Luke has fashioned the Pharisees, who already had a negative image in Christian tradition, so that they embody those faults to which he believes his Christian readers are prone. The Pharisees express in concrete terms the nature of an influence which Christians have to resist if they are to be true disciples. This influence can appropriately be described as the 'Pharisaic mind'. The Pharisees thus represent the antithesis to the positive examples of Christian character which we looked at in the last chapter. Once this fact has been grasped we can go further, to recognize that some order (if not sequence) can be seen in the arrangement of the contents of Luke's gospel. Apparently disparate topics, especially in the central section, are held together by the fact that they represent aspects of the Pharisaic mind and in their combination constitute an inner threat to the maintenance of Christian character.

Before we can illustrate this in more detail however, we must deal with the apparently sympathetic portrayal of the Pharisees in Acts and parts of the gospel.

The striking thing about the Pharisees in Acts is not their apparently pro-Christian stance, but that they are mentioned at all. The opposition to the church is formed mainly, as in the gospel passion narrative, by the chief priests, scribes, elders and rulers, or in other contexts by Hellenists or unidentified Jews of the Dispersion. In two contexts, which may indeed be intended by Luke to mirror each other, the Sadducees are mentioned, and in both they are contrasted with the Pharisees, but it is misleading to represent them as the enemies of the gospel with the Pharisees as its friends.[15] The first occasion is in chapters 4 and 5, when the authorities, in a series of trial scenes, attempt to suppress the activity of Peter and the other apostles; the second occurs in the attempt of the authorities to dispose of Paul in chapter 23, which is again part of a series of trial scenes. In both cases Luke contrasts the attitude of Pharisees to Sadducees, and thus shows the Sanhedrin to be divided. In 5.34 Gamaliel, against the chief priest and Sadducees (5.17; cf. 4.1), advises restraint; in 23.6–9 the Pharisees, after quarelling with the Sadducees over whether the resurrection belongs to the hope of Israel, declare Paul to be innocent. But neither of these represents a verdict in favour of Christian faith. At most Gamaliel suggests that the Christian movement may play itself out, and that the Council should let events decide, lest they should turn out to be resisting God (5.39). The apostles are still beaten and forbidden to preach, although they are then set free.[16] 23.9 is even more revealing. Paul declares that the issue between him and the authorities is the resurrection (v. 6). The background to this is his account of his conversion, already narrated in 22.7ff., which for him is a demonstration that Jesus has been raised from the dead. Luke goes on to explain that Pharisees differ from Sadducees on three points, the resurrection and the existence of angels and spirits (23.7). It is striking after this that all the allegedly sympathetic Pharisees allow in v. 9 is that Paul may have met a spirit or an angel; it is on these grounds only that they concede his claim in v. 1, 'to have lived before God in all good conscience up to this day', which the Sadducean high priest from his different theological standpoint repudiates. They do not concede the crucial claim that God has raised Jesus from the dead.[17] From Luke's point of view therefore they are very far from supporting Paul's Christian claims. The risen Jesus was not a spirit (Luke 24.39).

It is true that Luke emphasises that Paul was a Pharisee, and explicitly links him to Gamaliel (22.3; 23.6; 26.5).[18] In two of the three passages, however, he goes on to stress that Paul persecuted the church (22.4f.; 26.9–11). Evidently the Pharisaism exemplified by Gamaliel did not encourage sympathy for Christian faith.

In the light of this we must give a different account of the position Luke adopts over the Pharisees in Acts. Luke insists that Christianity is the true heir of the Israel of the Old Testament. The resurrection of the messiah is affirmed by Moses and the prophets. Resurrection in general is part of this hope (cf. Luke 20.37; 24.26, 46). The Pharisees affirm this general hope, and are thus better representatives of the Israel of the Old Testament than the Sadducees who deny it. In this therefore, as in other ways, the Pharisees represent for Luke the strictest, most accurate form of the faith of Israel.[19] But even they reject the gospel, for they do not accept the specific case of the resurrection of Jesus. Because they are the strictest sect, they therefore focus in clear detail the entitlement of

Israel to inherit the promise and its refusal to do so. Of the Sadducees unbelief is only to be expected; denying the resurrection, they are not even faithful Jews. This interpretation of the Pharisees in Acts is entirely in keeping with the position they adopt in the gospel, where because of their devotion to the law they refuse to accept Jesus' dealings with sinners. It is also in accord with the curious reference in Acts 15.5 to believers from the Pharisaic party. Luke shows in this reference that their devotion to the law still sets them, believers though they now are, in opposition to the declared will of God (15.4) and the verdict of the Jerusalem council goes against them (cf. esp. 15.10, 19–21, 28). No Pharisaic Christian at the council speaks in support of Peter and James.

When we turn to the gospel, the absence of the Pharisees from the passion narrative and the Jerusalem ministry is important, but should not be misunderstood. It is a feature of the passion narrative in all the gospels. Only at Matt. 27.62 and John 18.3 do the Pharisees appear in this context. They are absent also from the passion predictions (Mark 8.31; 10.33f. and parallels). Luke differs in eliminating references not only in the passion narrative but in the Jerusalem ministry which precedes it. Unlike Matthew, who adds Pharisees at several points (21.45; 22.34f., 41; 23.2ff.), Luke 19.45–21.38 follows Mark in making the chief priests, scribes and elders, and on the occasion where the subject demands it, the Sadducees, the antagonists. In the one place where Mark mentions Pharisees Luke omits any specific reference (20.20, Mark 12.13). It is a historically credible picture. In Jerusalem the power of the Pharisees would have been more limited than in Galilee because in the city they were more in competition with other groups. In any case the Pharisees were a party not an official organ of Jewish national life, and when it came to official action it would be the accredited teachers and the members of the Sanhedrin who would have the power to act.[20] It would be natural for an account of events to emphasize their role, and Luke appears to follow tradition in this respect. The fact that he is even more consistent in his narrative than the other gospels suggests that he understood what the tradition implied. He follows a similar policy in Acts except where he wants to contrast Pharisees and Sadducees with each other.

It may be that in one instance or another Luke inherited a tradition that Jesus accepted an invitation to a meal from a Pharisee. Historically this is not intrinsically impossible. But it should be noted that the three occasions he describes have an artificial quality to them. The historical background to 7.36ff. and its relation to other gospel traditions is complicated, but the sudden reference to the name Simon in 7.40 (cf. Mark 14.3) at least encourages the suspicion that the identification of the host as a Pharisee is a Lucan modification.[21] At 11.37 there is a difficulty in that the saying of vv. 39–41 about cleansing cups does not correspond to the Pharisee's objection to Jesus' not washing himself. 14.1 also appears to introduce a series of meal-sayings, preceded by the healing of the man with dropsy, vv. 2–6, which seems out of place here as no reason is given for the man's presence. The parallel incident at 13.10ff. gives a more credible setting in a synagogue. All these passages may therefore be Luke's editorial work, but they have to be seen in a Lucan context. Unlike Mark, who frequently uses a house as a refuge from the crowds, usually without indicating whose house it is, Luke speaks of particular houses in which Jesus is a guest.[22] The reason for this is the contrast between Jesus and John the Baptist. The latter adopted an ascetic lifestyle but Jesus comes eating and drinking (7.34; cf. 5.33). This includes eating and drinking with sinners (15.2; 19.7) as well as with Pharisees. Meals with Pharisees are not therefore a sign of a sympathetic attitude on their part but evidence of Jesus' mission to all. On each occasion Jesus is critical of his Pharisaic hosts, which further contradicts the theory of good relations between them.

In any case one must give full weight to the indications of attitudes Luke gives. At 6.11, 11.53f., 14.1, 16.14 he indicates clearly that encounters between Jesus and the Pharisees take place in a hostile atmosphere. This is particularly important for the interpretation of 13.31, the advice to flee from Herod, and 17.20, the question when the kingdom will come.

Part of our argument for the evaluation of these two passages will be set out in the next chapter, and the reader will have to reserve final judgment until then, but it is important to stress that nothing in the preceding references to Pharisees in Luke leads us to expect that on these two occasions they approach Jesus out of simple goodwill. In both cases the reply Jesus makes is critical.[23] In 13.32 they are given a message to take to Herod. It is not said in v. 31 that they have come from him. If we are to think that they have, then they must be in league with him; if, as is more likely, they are not, Jesus' reply is nevertheless as critical of them as of Herod.[24] They fail to see that for Jesus death is not to be escaped, but is integral to his vocation as a prophet; he must suffer as all Israel's prophets have suffered.[25] Herod's territory is not the place for this, nor is it yet the time. Jesus must go on his journey, which will eventually lead to Jerusalem. First he must complete his ministry, which as we shall see more clearly in chapter 10, offers the opportunity to repent. By trying to move him on the Pharisees are trying to cut short their own chance of repentance. They fail to see all this because they do not recognize Jesus as a prophet sent from God. Similarly at 17.20 the Pharisees betray, by their question about when the kingdom will come, their fundamental failure to see the significance of Jesus. This is particularly ironic after an incident in which Jesus has led a Samaritan to saving faith. It is true that the Pharisees had an interest in eschatological questions,[26] but this is no innocent request for Jesus' opinion. There are indeed questions of the timing of future events to be discussed, but these are for disciples who recognize that they are in fact questions about the coming of the Son of Man. They have seen what prophets and kings desired to see (10.23f.). So Jesus turns to them at 17.22ff. The Pharisees ask about the coming of a kingdom whose presence already in their midst they have failed to recognize.[27] All that can be said to them is that there is no need to keep watching for the coming of the kingdom because it is already with them in the work Jesus is doing.

These passages thus show the Pharisees in a far from sympathetic light. Luke's attitude to them is to be judged not by guessing at the motives behind their actions where he indicates none, but by marking the tenor of Jesus' replies. We therefore have to conclude that the Pharisees are not presented favourably in any passage in Luke or Acts, and that the passages sometimes adduced for this have a different bearing. The way is thus open for us to explore what Luke means by what we have termed the 'Pharisaic mind'.[28] We can list a number of characteristics in Luke's portrayal.

1. The Pharisees resist the call to repent. They refused to be baptized by John, who called for repentance, and so they rejected the will of God (7.30). Their response to Jesus is no better (cf. 7.32ff.). John's baptism was for repentance (3.3), but they are equally unrepentant in response to the law of Moses and the Old Testament prophets. In its context the parable of the rich man and Lazarus is addressed to Pharisees who are characterized as loving wealth (16.14), and stresses the unwillingness of those whom the rich man represents to heed the scriptures, and the consequent unlikelihood of their repenting even if someone rises from the dead (16.29–31). The oblique reference to the resurrection of Jesus incidentally confirms our view of the Pharisees in Acts (cf. especially the discussion of Acts 23.9 above). This unrepentant attitude underlies all their antagonism to Jesus, as we shall see.

2. Far from repenting, the Pharisees 'justify themselves' (16.15), that is, they consider and proclaim themselves to be righteous. This attitude is memorably portrayed in the parable of the Pharisee and the tax collector (18.10ff.). The Pharisee's prayer is full of self-importance, cataloguing the sins he avoids and listing the disciplines he maintains. Yet as v. 14 makes clear, although he is one of those who are confident of their righteousness (v. 9), this status is not accorded to him by God.[29] His estimate of himself is based only on his own judgment and is profoundly mistaken. In relation to God he is therefore arrogant (cf. 16.15), thanking God for his superiority when he ought to be asking for mercy, as the tax collector in humility did.

3. The Pharisees expect public recognition for their superior standing (11.43), and this feeds their sense of self-satisfaction. Inevitably this affects their relationship with others whom they consider to be in need of a repentance from which they themselves are exempt. 'Justifying oneself' and 'despising others' naturally go together and the parable illustrates this (18.9). In consequence the Pharisees are incapable of approving Jesus' demonstrations of forgiveness, whether his verbal declarations (5.21; cf. 7.49) or his acceptance of sinners (5.30; 15.1f.; 7.39). In part their objection is to the implied authority with which he acts (cf. 5.21) but it also stems from

their sense of self-righteousness and contempt for those who do not meet their standards. Their concept of righteousness implies keeping one's distance from sinners (cf. 7.39).

4. It is not that the Pharisees' claims to righteousness are altogether false; rather they are partial and emphasize what is less important. They are punctilious in their observance of fasts (5.33) and of tithing (11.42) but they ignore justice and love (cf. 18.12). Several times they clash with Jesus over the sabbath. In 6.1–5 Luke streamlines Jesus' reply so that there is no longer, as in Mark 2.25, 27, a general statement about the priority of human need; instead only Mark 2.28 is emphasized: for Jesus and his followers, as for David and his, hunger takes precedence over sabbath.[30] In other passages, however, a more general point is made: doing good takes priority over inactivity which inflicts harm (6.6–11); exceptions should be made not only for the saving of life but for all healing (14.2–6). It may be that Luke sees both incidents in 6.1–11, gathering corn and healing the disabled on the sabbath, as examples of Jesus redefining what the law implies, so that with his coming a new code of practice comes into being (cf. in respect of fasting, 5.33ff.), but the Pharisees by rejecting his teaching in these matters show where their own priorities lie, as in 14.2–6. Similarly in relation to ritual purity: they are more interested in the external cleanness of the vessels used at the meal than in their own moral state (11.38–41).[31]

5. As the last reference shows, Luke particularly stresses the Pharisees' failure in relation to wealth. We have already discussed 16.14. The strict interpretation of v. 13 is that in their allegiance to wealth they cease to serve God at all; they are in effect idolaters. This is why they react so strongly in v. 14. It is in this regard that they fail to heed Moses and the prophets in 16.19ff.

6. The Pharisees thus have only an appearance of goodness. They are like unmarked graves, full of defilement but unrecognized (11.44). They are hypocrites (12.1). As vv. 2f. show the primary implication of this word is concealment; the contrast is between the fair exterior and the inner truth. While the truth may be concealed from human eyes, however, it is not hidden from God, who knows the heart (16.15).

7. It is obvious that underlying many of these details of Pharisaic shortcomings is their indifference to human need. In their contempt for sinners, in their emphasis upon fasting, tithes, sabbath observance and ritual purity, and in their disregard of the poor, they lack compassion. There is nothing about them of the spontaneity of generous love which marks the sermon on the plain or the parable of the good Samaritan. They do not see the service of God in terms of a simple command to love him and the neighbour (cf. above ch. 2 p. 21). They are thus the antithesis of the pattern which Jesus lays down for his followers. All this should help us in the interpretation of 5.32 and 15.7. The significance of the contrasts in these verses, 'not the righteous ... but', '... more than over ninety nine righteous people who do not need repentance', is to lay all the emphasis on those who are not righteous: Jesus came to call sinners and it is over a repentant sinner that heaven rejoices. The statements cannot be pressed to mean either that there is a group possessing unquestioned righteousness or that Jesus' mission does not embrace them. If there is an allusion to the Pharisees here it is intended ironically. The genuinely righteous, such as Simeon and Anna, welcome Jesus' coming (2.25–38). Similarly 7.47 affirms only that the Pharisee has not experienced forgiveness; it says nothing about his need of it, and the parable's reference to one who owed little should not be pressed to suggest that he was guiltless. On the contrary the sayings we have reviewed show clearly that the Pharisees need repentance as much as others, even if for different reasons, but they resist the call.

8. All this lies behind their refusal to respond positively to Jesus. The call to repent, as it applies to Pharisees, demands of them that they recognize the limitations of their understanding of righteousness and the arrogance of their attitude toward God and others, and that they have the humility to repent. This challenge Jesus represents both in his preaching and in his own behaviour. So they are unable to recognize him as a prophet from God, or to share in the general rejoicing at what he does. To them the welcome given to Jesus by the disciples on entering Jerusalem is offensive (19.39ff.). This is the last explicit reference to the Pharisees in the gospel and sums up their inability to see the obvious. The

same point underlies 5.33ff. and, as we argued above, 13.31 and 17.20. The Pharisees thus become the persecutors, looking for evidence on which they can suppress Jesus (6.7, 11; 11.53f.). Their antagonism is not merely personal dislike; it is based on his teaching and the claims implied in it, and in consequence it is directed against his disciples as well (5.30, 33; 12.4ff.).

We should perhaps remind ourselves at this stage that what we have been trying to do is to draw together the indications in the gospel of the ways in which Luke views the Pharisees. We are not attempting to assess the justice of the resulting picture as a description of an actual movement in the time of Jesus. In much of what he sets forth Luke is drawing on traditional material, as the other gospels show, but the emphasis on wealth at least is his own. However, we need to note that although he draws special attention to them, his criticisms are not confined to the Pharisees. Scribes (lawyers) are regularly associated with them (5.17, 30; 6.7; 7.30; 11.53; 14.1; 15.2); only at 10.25 is a lawyer mentioned on his own before the Jerusalem ministry begins. The most important example is 11.45, where a scribe objects that Jesus' criticisms of the Pharisees also affect them. What follows in vv. 46–52 must be considered appropriate only to the scribes, but the implication of v. 45 is that what precedes applies to both, and both groups proceed in v. 53 to lie in wait for Jesus. The distinction between woes against Pharisees and woes against scribes appears to be a distinction between general faults of behaviour and of religious attitude and specific abuses of the teaching office. If Luke thinks of scribes as belonging predominantly to the Pharisaic party, as 5.30 suggests, this would explain why he saw the criticisms of 11.38–44 applying to both.

This observation is of crucial importance when we come to evaluate Luke's references to scribes where the Pharisees are not mentioned. We have seen that Luke follows tradition in making the scribes one of the forces involved in the death of Jesus, and probably excludes reference to the Pharisees deliberately. The scribes are associated with other groups in 19.47, 20.1, 19, 22.2, 66, 23.10, and in the prediction of 9.22. The earlier references in the gospel associating them with the Pharisees, however, should lead us to assume that many of them were Pharisees and to expect them to display Pharisaic attitudes. Luke never mentions scribes of any other persuasion, and Jesus' attack on them at 20.46f. (= Mark 12.38f.) parallels much of what is said of the Pharisees elsewhere (cf. 11.43). So in 20.20 the spies whom the scribes and chief priests send to trap him are not actually called Pharisees, but are described in terms strongly reminiscent of them: 'who pretended to be righteous' (*dikaioi*; RSV misleadingly, 'sincere'). Outwardly they present themselves as devout men who keep the law and genuinely want guidance about God's will, but they are using this as a cover for a crafty move against Jesus (v. 23). Both the pretence (hypocrisy) and the claim to righteousness recall 12.1, 16.14, 18.11f. Similarly 20.39f. makes best sense if Pharisaic scribes are in mind; they would particularly welcome an argument which defeated the Sadducees.[32] This last example, incidentally, should not be pressed as an example of Pharisees favourable to Jesus. As v. 40 shows, v. 39 is in effect an admission of defeat, and Jesus turns to the attack, using their belief in resurrection by pressing upon them its implications for David's son and lord; Ps. 110, which he uses here, will be quoted again in Acts 2.34 to affirm the resurrection of Jesus. They have no answer for this. As in Acts 23 their belief in resurrection does not go far enough to embrace the resurrection of the messiah, Jesus. Lest there should be any further doubt, the critical words in vv. 45–7 follow immediately. These scribes are not 'friendly'.[33]

Some of Luke's other characters should probably be seen in the same light. The ruler of the synagogue in 13.14 is not named as a Pharisee, but the passage is very similar to 14.2–6, and the ruler displays a Pharisaic attitude and is associated with the 'adversaries' of v. 17, who are reminiscent of the scribes and Pharisees of 11.53f. Their 'hypocrisy' (v. 15) involves placing sabbath observance above human need, as at 6.6–11, 14.2–6; there is a disjunction between the impact of religion upon other activity and their response to the woman in need, and thus between profession and reality. In this case (but not in 8.41) the ruler of the synagogue should be seen as a Pharisaic opponent. There is much also to be said for regarding the ruler of 18.18 in a similar light, as we indicated in chapter 3, and we have also argued that the lawyer of 10.25

should be recognized as a hostile questioner intending to put Jesus to the test.[34]

In none of these three cases, however, does Luke name the men as Pharisees. It is not a sufficient explanation to assume that Luke was merely following a source, for we have seen that he is capable of introducing Pharisees when he wishes. Neither in these passages nor in the Jerusalem ministry has he done so, but here we cannot point to the historical logic of the tradition as the reason why Luke did not introduce a Pharisee more specifically. We have to conclude that he is not willing to use the Pharisees simply as a cipher for the opposition on all occasions. They exemplify a particular attitude, but the attitude is not confined to them. By depicting people who are not identified as Pharisees displaying Pharisaic attitudes Luke shows that the 'Pharisaic mind' is a more general danger. The crucial passage is 18.9. The parable of the Pharisee and the tax collector is not addressed to Pharisees but to 'some who trusted in themselves that they were righteous and despised others'. We have seen how the parable illustrates this attitude; but it is not confined to Pharisees. Whether one thinks of disciples here or more widely of others who listened to Jesus depends on whether one takes the passage in continuation with vv. 1–8 or in preparation for vv. 15ff.,[35] but it is plain that Luke thinks of the Pharisees only as readily identifiable examples of an attitude of mind that is more pervasive and against which people must be warned. This is also no doubt the reason why the Pharisees are not named at 11.15f. Their absence is at first sight surprising, as they are mentioned in the parallel to this passage at Matt. 12.24 (cf. Mark 3.22). Luke's version is more complex, however, for two different reactions are mentioned in vv. 15f. which would be more difficult to link with one group. But, as will be argued in chapter 10, the basic reason is that although the Pharisees exemplify these reactions they must not be made to bear the sole responsibility for the consequences of a more widespread failure.

That Luke sees the Pharisees as examples of a more pervasive attitude is shown also by 12.1, 'beware of the leaven of the Pharisees, which is hypocrisy'. Leaven is used in various ways in the New Testament: of evil influence in I Cor. 5.6–8, Gal. 5.9, of the kingdom of God in Luke 13.21

and Matt. 13.33, and of the Pharisees in parallels to the saying at Luke 12.1. In Mark 8.15 the leaven of the Pharisees and of Herod is left undefined; in the parallel passage in Matt. 16.6–12 the leaven of the Pharisees and Sadducees is defined as their teaching. The saying in Luke has a different setting, and may or may not have an origin independent of Mark 8.15. In Luke the leaven is defined as hypocrisy. As this follows immediately after 11.38ff. it is natural to interpret this in the light of Pharisaic shortcomings listed there (cf. also 20.20). Their outward pretensions differ from the inner reality. But in what sense are disciples to beware of it? One reading of the warning is to point to the reaction of the Pharisees in 11.53f. and the encouragement for times of persecution in 12.4ff., and to conclude that the disciples are to be on their guard against attack from hypocritical Pharisees. Their hypocrisy will be leaven only in the sense that the truth about them and the danger they present is hidden (cf. Luke 13.21).[36] But Luke tends to use the word 'beware' (*prosechete*) of guarding against making a mistake, or against an undesirable influence (17.3; 20.46; 21.34; Acts 5.35; 20.28). Verses 2f., addressed to the disciples, suggest that they too will be exposed if they try to hide anything.[37] It is thus the danger of being infected by Pharisaic hypocrisy against which the disciples must be on their guard. This conclusion is supported by the interesting fact that the version of the woes against the Pharisees in Matthew 23 to many parts of which Luke 11.38ff. offers parallels, includes the repeated accusation of being 'hypocrites'. This does not occur in Luke 11, but the appearance of 'hypocrisy' in 12.1 suggests that Luke's source may have contained it, and that he reserved its use until 12.1 in order to explain the meaning of a saying which in Matthew and Mark was clearly felt to be obscure.[38] If that is so, 'hypocrisy' points back to the faults of 11.38ff. and not to the hostility in 11.53f. It may well be that 12.4–12, which deals with disciples under attack, was introduced here because of the threat posed to Jesus by the scribes and Pharisees at 11.53f., but the emphasis throughout is on the disciples' response and the need to be true to God rather than bow to public opinion. To do the latter would itself be a form of dissimulation or hypocrisy (cf. 16.15; Acts 4.19f.). Thus 12.1 is primary evidence for the view that Luke sees a danger in what we have called the 'Pharisaic mind'. A similar point is made at 20.45–7, where again 'beware' occurs, and where there is a danger of imitation against which both disciples and the crowds generally must be on their guard.

It is not surprising therefore that some Pharisaic characteristics are dealt with in other contexts. Disciples are warned against hypocrisy at 6.42. Here it is the censorious attitude which is blind to one's own faults while drawing attention to the faults of others. In 12.56 the crowds are accused of hypocrisy because they are infallible judges of the weather but are incapable of recognizing the moment when the call for repentance comes. The underlying element in these as in all other occurrences of the word is the inconsistency in people's lives between their attitudes in one sphere and those in another, between profession and practice, or between appearance and reality. Similarly, warnings against the temptations of wealth are directed not only to Pharisees in 16.14–31 but to disciples in 16.1–13, 12.22–34, and to the crowds in 12.13–21. The key phrase, 'every one who exalts himself will be humbled, but he who humbles himself will be exalted', which is a comment on the Pharisee and the tax collector at 18.14 (cf. 16.15) occurs also at the end of the advice to the fellow guests at 14.7–11. It is not said that these are Pharisees, and Luke is apparently willing to leave it open.

There is thus an interplay of audiences in Luke's gospel. The same themes are introduced, now in conversation with disciples, now with the crowds or Pharisees. We need to explore this in greater detail, and show how the 'Pharisaic mind' is a key to the structure of the gospel. Wealth, pride, misplaced devotion to the law to the detriment of real goodness, indifference to human need, hypocrisy: these are elements in the Pharisaic mind which Luke believes can easily influence his readers. He introduces them in various contexts, employing the traditional sayings of Jesus he derived from Mark, 'Q' and elsewhere, to bring home the point. Because they are not exclusively Pharisaic sins, but a danger to all, he does not discuss them exclusively in contexts where Pharisees are the target. Nor do the Pharisees figure in his gospel only as examples of the Pharisaic mind. He has to combine an account of the 'things accomplished among us' (1.1) with a presentation of the teaching of Jesus for the Christian readers of his own day. But we shall find when we look at long stretches of the gospel that the Pharisees are in the background of discussion of these topics even when the crowds or the disciples are the more immediate participants in the dialogue, and that the reason why Luke can move without obvious reason from one topic and audience to another is because they all have their unity as components of the Pharisaic mind, which is a dangerous influence for disciples and would-be believers alike.

10

Luke's Structure

In the last chapter we argued that the Pharisees serve in Luke's narrative not only as participants in the story he has to tell about Jesus' ministry and rejection by Israel, but as examples of a constellation of attitudes into which his Christian readers are in danger of falling. We suggested that supporting evidence of this can be found in the structure of the gospel itself. What at first sight appears to be an unrelated sequence of stories and sayings can be seen to have a kind of unity when it is realized that they deal with aspects of the 'Pharisaic mind'; the presence of the Pharisees in the narrative at various places is an indicator of this and helps to alert us to the points Luke is wishing to make. In this chapter we must try to justify that claim.

The ground plan of Luke's gospel is extremely difficult to discern, as the many divergent analyses by scholars reveal.[1] Particularly in the central section, from 9.51 to the middle of chapter 18, where we are unable to compare Luke with Mark, it is difficult to decide whether Luke merely followed various sources as they presented themselves, making *ad hoc* alterations as he went along, or whether he worked to some master design now hidden from us; and in the latter case, whether the reason for the obscurity is the intractability of the traditions which Luke was reluctant to alter too radically to fit his scheme, or simply the fact that we have lost the key.

In recent years interest has been shown in theories which suggest a formal structure for the gospel dictated, not by lineal development within the subject matter itself, but by other factors. It has been suggested that items have been arranged in such a way as to mirror each other before and after a central point, following the so-called 'chiastic pattern' which can be detected in some ancient works; alternatively, or even in combination with this, it has been claimed that Luke's material has been arranged to follow and comment upon sections of the Old Testament, or even a complete lectionary cycle of Old Testament readings.[2] It is difficult to know what to make of these theories until their merits have been more thoroughly evaluated. That some parts of Luke and Acts reflect and repeat the sequence of earlier passages can hardly be denied. The infancy narratives in Luke 1–2 are an example. It may even be that in some cases the earlier passage reflects and anticipates the later. But it is a large step from this to claim that such patterning is universal and that the patterns account for the contents, and a larger step still to use the presumed pattern as a key to interpretation. In general such theories end up by doing violence to what would seem to be the plain thrust of the text, and ignoring evidence Luke gives of straightforward development in his narrative. Similar reservations apply to lectionary theories; even if first-century Jewish lectionaries could be reconstructed with the certainty that advocates of this approach claim, and we could be sure that Luke and his readers were familiar with their use, the alleged parallels with the gospel are often superficial and turn on incidentals in Luke's text. In the end the most important guide to Luke's gospel must be the text itself.

It may well be that the problem is ultimately insoluble. Certainly a thorough discussion would take us far beyond the limits of this book. What is offered in this chapter is simply a contribution to a debate which must continue. One should at least be sure that there is no possibility of explaining Luke's text in terms of sources, the needs of his readers and the intrinsic requirements of his subject matter before resorting to more formal and extraneous explanations. While therefore there are some references to alternative views in the notes to this chapter they are by no means exhaustive, nor is any attempt made to construct a plan of the gospel as a whole. We concentrate on illustrating the claim made in the last chapter, that the Pharisees are a key to the gospel's organization. This is not to exclude the possibility of other keys.

Some progress can in fact be made by looking carefully at

the text, noting how Luke has handled Mark, and attending to the clues he gives. Among these are his notes of time, place and movement, and the indications of change of audience. It is clear that these are important because of their elaboration (cf. e.g. 12.1), but it is difficult to interpret the clues because his habit of variation for stylistic reasons means that there are no fixed formulae to indicate the start of new sections. It is clear that some expressions tie two pericopae closely together with a note of time sequence or audience (e.g. 10.21; 11.37; 12.13 with 12.1). From time to time Luke introduces a pericope with an explanatory sentence which gives guidance for interpretation (e.g. 3.15; 19.11). Where we can compare him with Mark we may note the omission of phrases which separated incidents in the source (e.g. 18.18; Mark 10.17). We should note also the distribution of key words, which may offer evidence of thematic arrangement, and the habit Luke occasionally follows of linking two consecutive passages by anticipating at the beginning of the first the topic of the second. Thus at 5.30, by rephrasing the question, 'why do you eat and drink with tax collectors and sinners?' and making a similar modification to v. 33 (cf. Mark 2.16, 18) he joins into one the two topics of objectionable company and liberal lifestyle which are simply juxtaposed in Mark, and both pericopae now become criticisms of the disciples. Similarly 11.16 indicates that 11.29 is to follow and is to be treated as part of the debate introduced by 11.14. Retrospectively 12.47, with the double verb 'make ready or act according to his master's will' refers to both the preceding parables (cf. vv. 40, 43).[3]

Evidence that Luke arranged his gospel thematically can be found in the material basically inherited from Mark. A simple illustration is his treatment of the ministry in Jerusalem in 19.45–21.38. Luke follows Mark almost pericope by pericope. The similarity of wording in individual pericopae is generally very close, except in his version of the 'apocalyptic discourse' of Mark 13, where the distinctive Lucan view of the future affects the content and ordering more radically.[4] Only one of Mark's pericopae is omitted, the lawyer's question about the great commandment in Mark 12.28–35.[5] But Luke has made a major change to the setting of these chapters and so brought out a point of importance to him. At the beginning he omits Mark's double journey into Jerusalem and the cursing of the fig tree (Mark 11.11–14, 19–26). Indeed once Jesus has arrived at the city and lamented over it, interest shifts exclusively to the temple. Jesus is depicted as going straight in and virtually taking it over as the place where he teaches. This is brought out by two editorial summaries. At 19.47f. Luke develops Mark 11.18 so that it becomes a general description of Jesus' ministry in the temple, including the hostile reaction of the chief priests and scribes which now applies to his teaching in general and not as in Mark just to the expulsion of the traders and accompanying statement. All the material which follows in chapters 20 and 21 now illustrates this summary (cf. Luke's version of 20.1 with Mark 11.27). At 21.37f. he adds a second summary, not only rounding off the 'apocalyptic discourse' which Mark simply leaves without editorial ending, but also clamping together all the teaching which has been given since 19.48. Moreover Luke's version of the apocalyptic discourse is given within the temple not outside it (cf. 21.5 with Mark 13.1). Only at 21.37 are we given any hint that Jesus left the temple from the moment he entered it at 19.45. By these simple changes Luke imposes his own pattern upon substantially traditional material, making it illustrate a theme which is partly latent in the tradition (the official antagonism and popular enthusiasm aroused by Jesus' teaching) and partly in contradiction to it (the temple as the single centre of the teaching for crowds and disciples alike).

A second example of Luke's adaptation of his Marcan source to his own interests can be seen in chapters 7 and 8. Eighteen of the twenty-six occurrences of 'believe', 'faith' and 'faithful' in Luke occur in the two sections 7.1–8.56 and 16.1–19.27. Six of these are combined with references to salvation. In fact of the twenty-five instances of 'save' and 'saviour' and the two words for 'salvation', ten come in these same two sections.[6] In the first section, which we are considering now, the concentration of these terms is particularly noticeable from 7.50 onwards. Some of the occurrences derive directly from Mark, but Luke has added others in 8.12f., 36; and at 8.50, although both 'believe' and 'be saved' are to be found in the Marcan text at different points (vv. 23, 36), Luke has joined them together. In some pericopae there is no Marcan parallel. 7.9 is parallelled in Matthew 8.10 and must derive from 'Q'; 7.50 is peculiar to Luke. It is often suggested that the episode of the woman with the ointment, in which this verse occurs, is an illustration of the contrasting attitudes to Jesus described in 7.31–5 at the end of the story of John's question from prison about who Jesus is.[7] Jesus' reply to John in 7.22f. alludes to his mighty works, one of which is narrated in 7.11–17, and acknowledges the difficulty of recognizing him (7.23). Only wisdom's children acknowledge wisdom (7.35). The woman with the ointment and the Pharisee who entertains Jesus would thus illustrate recognition and refusal to recognize him. The importance of such recognition is that the fulfilment of God's purpose for Israel is at stake (7.29). It is not difficult to see how chapter 8 continues this theme showing by the parable of the sower what the response of faith means (8.4ff.) and how it brings salvation in the case of the Gerasene demoniac (8.26ff.). The question of Jesus' identity is linked with faith at 8.25 at the end of the stilling of the storm. The story of the centurion at the beginning of the section fits this pattern, for his faith, as we have seen, includes his humility in deference to the person of Jesus (7.1–10).[8] One has to conclude that Luke saw in the material he has used from Mark in this section the theme of faith and salvation, and has developed it; it may well have determined the selection of the non-Marcan material he has added. This is not to say that other themes are not present,[9] or that all the instances which refer to faith can be forced into one restricted meaning of the word, but it can be suggested that 'faith and salvation' constituted for Luke the central idea around which this material was gathered.

A crucial test of this approach is to be found in Luke 9. Scholarly discussion of 9.1–50 has often concerned itself with the problem of Luke's 'great omission'. Why should he have passed over Mark 6.45–8.26? A variety of reasons have been suggested,[10] but a prior question is what Luke has made of the material he has incorporated, for if a satisfactory account can be given of it as it stands, we may not need further reasons for the omissions.

9.1 must mark a new beginning in Luke. He has omitted Mark's account of Jesus' rejection at Nazareth at this point, and does not indicate how the sending out of the disciples is connected to what precedes (contrast Mark 6.1, 6f.). Either we are to envisage Jesus calling the twelve together on Jairus' doorstep, or Luke intends a fresh start to the narrative. A new stage in the narrative is also generally agreed to be marked at 9.51. Up to this point in the gospel Jesus is shown moving about the towns and villages of Galilee;[11] from 9.51 onwards he has a destination in Jerusalem, of which from time to time we are reminded (9.53; 13.22; 17.11; 19.11, 28).

The chapter begins with the mission of the twelve, and continues in turn with Herod's question, 'who is this?', the feeding of the five thousand at Bethsaida, Peter's confession, the first prediction of the passion, sayings on taking up the cross, the transfiguration, the healing of the epileptic boy, the second passion prediction, sayings on greatness and lastly Jesus' verdict on the exorcist who did not 'follow with us'. We can see the main lines of Luke's interest. One thread in the chapter is the question of Jesus' identity, raised in the rumours Herod hears, answered for the disciples in Peter's confession, and authoritatively affirmed on the mountain. Along with this goes an emphasis on Jesus' suffering and the conditions of discipleship. In the earlier part of the chapter this effect is achieved by omitting the story of the Baptist's death (Mark 6.17–29, alluded to in Luke 3.19f.) and the whole of Mark 6.45–8.26, and linking the feeding of the multitude with Peter's confession by means of the prayer of Jesus (Mark 6.46; Luke 9.18). In this way the views of the crowds about Jesus in 9.19 echo the thoughts of Herod in vv. 7f. Bethsaida (Mark 6.45; 8.22) now becomes the setting for the feeding miracle as there is no crossing of the lake. Luke's treatment of Mark in the second part of the chapter is equally instructive. He has shortened the narrative of the epileptic boy by omitting any discussion between Jesus and the disciples about their failure. They are included in the reproach of the people for their unbelief.[12] But this is not all. The episode is followed, as in Mark, by a passion prediction (9.43–5), but in Luke's treatment it is in explicit contrast to the enthusiastic wonder of the crowds at Jesus' deeds, and is accompanied by a more elaborate statement of the disciples' failure to understand. Closely following this (without the intervening change of scene of Mark 9.33) is Jesus' answer to their dispute about order of precedence, and John's question about the exorcist. These two paragraphs are linked in Luke not only by 'John answered' (9.49), making one continuous conversation, but by the repeated reference to 'the name', taken over from Mark (cf. vv. 48f.). Verses 49f. are linked in another way to the episode of the epileptic boy. Because in Luke the disciples' failure to heal has not been discussed or assigned a cause, it becomes the more ironic that they should wish to prevent another doing successfully what they had themselves failed to do, simply on the grounds that he was not a member of the group (v. 49, 'with us'; v. 50, 'with you', 'for you'; contrast Mark 9.38, 40). Their lack of humility highlights their failure to understand the way of the cross upon which Jesus is embarked and their inability to share his work. Luke may be driving the point home farther still in having Jesus take a child, set him beside him and speak of receiving 'this child' (v. 48) rather than 'one such child' (Mark 9.47), so contrasting the disciples' unwillingness to receive and help the epileptic boy.[13]

The disciples are thus set in a bad light here, which is surprising after their confession of faith at 9.20.[14] Throughout the chapter the disciples take a more prominent part in the proceedings than in earlier chapters. Up to this point they have the role largely of spectators. At 9.1 the twelve become missionaries, living up to the title of apostle given them at 6.13 (cf. 9.10). At 9.12 they initiate (as in Mark) the feeding of the multitude by drawing attention to the need, and the miracle leads directly to Peter's confession of faith on behalf of all, and perhaps serves as its foundation. By modification and extensive omission Luke has compacted out of the Marcan material a chapter on discipleship, its focus and conditions, illustrating both success and failure and underscoring thereby the precariousness of their faith.[15] Even at the feeding of the multitude the disciples have no expectation that Jesus can do anything. They start by trying to wash their hands of the problem, suggesting that the crowd go and find food for themselves, and when Jesus counters this with 'you give them something to eat' (v. 13, *hymeis*, emphatic), their only response is to suggest that they go shopping. It is not necessary to argue that discipleship is the only topic in chapter 9 (9.9 for instance prepares for 23.8) in order to suggest that it is the focal point for the material which Luke

has derived from Mark. It is also important to note however
that although there is undoubtedly a transition at 9.50,
discipleship continues to be the theme at least until 10.24.[16]
This is not the only point at which theme and structure
appear to be in conflict in Luke, a fact which complicates the
task of analysis.[17]

There is thus plenty of evidence that Luke was able to
impose his own interests on material which originally carried
other emphases. It encourages us to look for signs that the
Pharisees also function in parts of the gospel as a focus for the
material Luke gathers together. In our study we shall concentrate on chapters 11 to 21, but there is one section in the
earlier part of the gospel where Luke clearly makes them
serve in this way. We saw in the previous chapter that in
taking over Mark 2.1–3.6 Luke has made the Pharisees more
prominently and consistently the opposition to Jesus,
assembling and identifying them from the outset at 5.17. The
reason for the assembly of opposition at this stage of the
gospel is presumably to form a contrast with the welcome
Jesus has received in 4.31–5.16, so that both the positive and
negative responses which occur to the synagogue sermon at
Nazareth (4.16–30) are further illustrated, before the next step
forward is taken with the selection of the twelve apostles and
the exposition of Jesus' teaching in 6.12–7.1.[18] The distinctive
features of Luke's version are the exclusive identification of
Pharisees and scribes as the ones who articulate this opposition and the way in which they are written into the narrative
to make this plain. There are thus good grounds for seeing a
similar role elsewhere.

1. We begin with chapters 14–16. In chapter 14 it is easy to
detect Luke's editorial hand, grouping together pericopae on
apparently diverse topics by giving them the setting of a
meal. 14.1 describes how Jesus was invited to a leading
Pharisee's house for a meal on a sabbath and how they were
all watching him.[19] This refers back to 11.54, where we are
told that from then on the scribes and Pharisees were lying in
wait to trap him by something he said. 14.2–6 describes the
healing of the man with dropsy and a controversy with the
scribes and Pharisees about sabbath observance. The setting
seems unlikely and is probably evidence of Luke's editing.[20]
14.7–11 contains the parable about places at table, with its

lesson on humility. It is addressed to the guests, who go for the best seats. The parable fits the setting reasonably well, although it is about a feast at a wedding. It is followed by advice to the host (the Pharisee) to invite the poor to any lunch or dinner party. At 14.15 one of the other guests utters a benediction on those called to the supper of the kingdom, and Jesus replies with the parable of the great feast, which we have seen to deal with the refusal of the rich to respond to God's invitation to the kingdom and his pressing invitation to the poor. All except the first of these pericopae have some intrinsic connection with meals, but why has Luke linked them by their introductions to the *same* meal, and what have they to do with the Pharisees, who are not named after v. 3? Our discussion of the 'Pharisaic mind' in the last chapter suggests that they all have a bearing on aspects of Pharisaic behaviour, as Luke himself depicts it. Pharisees are accused of inhumane action on the sabbath in 6.1–11, arrogance towards God and desire for prominent positions in 11.43, 16.15, 18.11f., 20.46 and wealth, which leads them to reject Jesus, in 16.14 (cf. 11.39). 16.14 also illustrates, in their mockery of his call for almsgiving, their attitude to the poor (cf. 20.47). So it is not inappropriate that Jesus' teaching on these subjects in chapter 14 should be given at the table of a leading Pharisee. In vv. 2–6 Pharisees and scribes are explicitly criticized.

At 14.25 the scene changes. The meal is forgotten and Jesus addresses the 'many crowds who were journeying with him'.[21] The theme is the cost of discipleship, and the change of audience is appropriate for this. The Pharisees can hardly be considered likely recruits after 11.54, 14.1, while the crowds who are sharing Jesus' pilgrimage to Jerusalem at one level need to be warned of what it will mean to share it at another. Yet, as we have seen, the subject matter of vv. 25–35 is in fact a continuation of the earlier part of the chapter: to follow Jesus involves a denial of self and a break with both family ties and the possession of wealth, just as response to the invitation to the feast involved a break with family and business interests to which those without possessions find it easier to respond.[22] There is nothing about vv. 1–24 which applies only to Pharisees nor anything in vv. 25–35 which applies only to the crowds.

So it is not surprising that at 15.2 the Pharisees and scribes reappear. There is a verbal link between chapters 14 and 15 in that 14.35 ends with a call for the one who has ears to hear, and 15.1 opens with the tax collectors and sinners hearing while their critics show themselves to be deaf. But the connection is more substantial than the use of a catchword. The parable of the great feast concerned the refusal by invited guests and the welcome given to the poor, and alluded to the Pharisees on the one hand and the empty-handed on the other. These are the subjects of chapter 15. Chapter 15 has always been seen to have a unity of theme in the three parables of the lost although it is not always recognized that the indignant elder brother belongs to the unity. Throughout the chapter the concern is with rejoicing over the recovery of the lost and repentant, as expressed in feasting (15.23, 25, cf. vv. 6, 9), and the refusal of others to share in it (vv. 25ff.). This theme is emphasized at the very beginning, in the objection 'This man receives sinners and eats with them' (v. 2). This unity of subject is reinforced by other linguistic bonds: 'lost' (vv. 4, 6, 8, 9, 17 (RSV 'perish'), 24, 32), 'sinner' (vv. 2, 7, 10, 18, 21), 'repentance' (vv. 7, 10; cf. vv. 29f., no celebration for the elder brother but for the one who returns), 'rejoicing' (vv. 5, 7, 9, 32, cf. 23, 25). So the contrast between the joy of Jesus with those who repent and respond to him and the critical attitude of Pharisees to both is well brought out.

At first sight 16.1 marks a complete change. Jesus addresses disciples, who have not featured in the narrative since 12.41. The subject now is the right use of wealth and the need for radical action. In fact, however, the themes of both chapters 14 and 15 are combined here. Underlying the action of the steward is the thought of repentance: he has to act decisively and quickly (cf. v. 6). This repentance is expressed in the way wealth is handled. 16.1ff. therefore continues the line of thought initiated at 14.1 (cf. also 16.13 with 14.33). These are also the themes of the latter part of the chapter. The parable of the rich man and Lazarus addresses a call for repentance to the rich (cf. v. 30). Like 14.35 this chapter also closes with the need really to heed what is superficially heard (vv. 29, 31).

So it is no surprise to find the Pharisees again at v. 14. There is no indication of a change of scene at v. 1 and we should assume that, as elsewhere, Jesus is depicted as turning from a wider audience to speak to his disciples. At all events the Pharisees hear what is said in vv. 1–13 and reject it with scorn. There is nothing exclusively reserved for disciples in what is addressed to them; all that is important is that it should be clear that they are also included in what has already been said to Pharisees and crowds. The Pharisees are expressly designated as lovers of money in 16.14, and this not only explains their reaction to what has gone before but identifies them as the target of the parable which follows. This is confirmed by the tailpiece which stresses that those who have the law and the prophets but ignore them will not be brought to repentance by a resurrection (16.31).

16.14–18 are among the most difficult verses in Luke's gospel. It is hard not only to interpret vv. 16f. with confidence, but also to see the connection between these and the other verses. The most likely explanation is that some of them at least were already linked in tradition and were introduced by Luke because they were part of a chain which he was using for other purposes (cf. 17.1–4 below). Thus v. 18, which is the most difficult to account for, may originally have been connected with v. 17 as an illustration of the permanence of the law.[23] Luke may have understood vv. 16f. to be saying that since the time of John the preaching of the good news of the kingdom has meant that the poor and outcasts (previously excluded) have begun to storm their way in; but law and prophets retain their force, for they still call for the repentance essential for entry to the kingdom, a call which the rich such as the Pharisees refuse to heed.[24] A reference to the law at this point is in any case not out of place, as the Pharisees are seen, with the scribes or lawyers, as having the law as their special preserve. But we note that it is not only the wealth of the Pharisees or their attitude to the law and prophets which is castigated here but their pride; they are arrogant towards God, and present themselves to others as righteous, although such status is one they have accorded themselves. We are reminded of 14.11, and will find a similar note struck later at 18.9ff. Luke does not limit his criticism of the Pharisees to one issue at a time.

Chapters 14 to 16 thus form a unit in which a number of themes is interwoven: wealth, arrogance, the interpretation of the law against the advantage of those in need, hostility to sinners contrasted with their welcome in the kingdom of God as expressed by Jesus, and the need to hear the call to repent as the tax collectors and sinners already do. The Pharisees are not explicitly addressed by Jesus at all points, but they are the group who represent in themselves the evils which he attacks and who give these chapters their unity.

2. We now turn to 19.28–21.38. At 19.28 the goal of the journey to Jerusalem which was begun at 9.51 is reached. Jesus initiates arrangements for his entry to the city. We have already seen how Luke has edited the Marcan account of the Jerusalem ministry, framing it with summaries at 19.47f. and 21.37f. Within that section there is no reference to the Pharisees by name. He follows Mark in making chief priests, scribes and elders the principal antagonists, and we discussed reasons for this in the last chapter. The last explicit mention of the Pharisees is at 19.39 at the entry to the city.

Behind the structural unity of 19.47–21.38 which we have already discussed there is also a thematic unity. The various elements are concerned with the identity of Jesus and the consequences for Israel in general and Jerusalem in particular of rejecting him. 20.1–8 in its Lucan setting is a question about Jesus' authority for teaching. 'These things' in 20.2 refers to the previous verse, not, as it apparently does in Mark 11.27, to his expelling traders. The reluctance of chief priests, scribes and elders to commit themselves over the Baptist when challenged to do so recalls 7.29f. The parable of the vineyard (20.9–19) is addressed in Luke to the people (v. 9), not as in Mark to the leaders, although they are well aware of the implications (v. 19). It is about rejecting God's son, and the consequences for the vineyard. 20.20–6 is only nominally about tribute to Caesar. Its central thrust is the attempt of the same authorities to trap Jesus and their failure to do so, because although they put up a righteous front he is aware of their craftiness (vv. 20, 23).[25] The implication is that their acknowledgment of him as a true teacher is hypocritical. As in other episodes they are revealed as men who do not accept his authority. This christological emphasis comes to the fore again in vv. 41–4, the question about David's son. Luke has omitted from Mark the discussion of the great commandment, making this question follow immediately after the discussion with the Sadducees about the resurrection. He

ties the two passages closely together by addressing Jesus'
question to the scribes who have just commented on the
resurrection-saying, omitting Mark 12.35 which introduces a
separate scene. The lordship of the messiah is affirmed in
terms of Ps. 110.1, which will be used again at Acts 2.34 to
affirm the resurrection and exaltation of Jesus in the first
missionary sermon of the church. Coming straight after the
reply to the Sadducees with its statement that those who are
counted worthy of the resurrection are 'sons of God, being
sons of the resurrection' (v. 36), the general discussion of vv.
27–40 is given a clear christological application. The resurrection shows Jesus to be the Son of God.[26]

So the controversies close, but other teaching follows, first
warnings to the disciples (and the people) against the ways of
the scribes and the rich in two paragraphs (19.45–21.4) more
closely linked than in Mark, then the discourse on the future
(21.5–36). Two distinctive features of this in Luke are the
prophecy of the destruction of Jerusalem, clearly distinguished
from the signs of the end, and the warning to disciples in vv.
34–6 which we discussed in chapter 3. The reason for the fall
of Jerusalem should be noted. It will occur in the 'days of
vengeance' (v. 22). In the light of 20.15ff., 23.28–31 and 13.34f.
we can deduce what this means. Luke sees in the fall of
Jerusalem the judgment of God for its rejection of the messiah.
The Jerusalem ministry thus drives home a clear message in
preparation for the narrative of the death and resurrection of
Jesus. While the people welcome Jesus, the leaders refuse to
recognize him as the messiah and seek to destroy him. The
consequence will be that the Jewish nation will lose its role as
the people of God and Jerusalem will be destroyed.[27]

These themes have already been stated earlier, however, in
the narrative of the entry into Jerusalem in 19.28–46. While
the disciples hail Jesus as king, a fact so patent from the
mighty works he has done that even the rocks could acclaim
it, the Pharisees object, revealing their own failure to see. The
consequence is Jesus' lament, spelling out for Jerusalem in
explicit terms the connection between their rejection of him
and God's rejection of the city. Israel's apostasy is symbolized
in the abuse of the temple by the traders, which Jesus
rectifies, not only by expelling them but by replacing them,
using it as the auditorium for his own teaching.[28]

There is thus a link between the Jerusalem ministry and what immediately precedes it. The whole of 19.28–21.38 holds together. This reinforces the argument of the last chapter that the scribes in chapters 20ff. are to be identified as having Pharisaic sympathies. Not only are they shown to exhibit similar moral and spiritual attitudes they occupy an identical place in Luke's overall theological scheme.

The role of the crowds however is less clear. In Acts 3.17, 13.27 the people of Jerusalem are associated with their leaders in responsibility for Jesus' death. The same is suggested by the lament over Jerusalem (Luke 19.41–4; cf. 13.34f.) and by the reference to the Pharisees speaking 'from the crowd' in 19.39. The crowd do not welcome Jesus at the entry; only disciples do so. The people as well as their leaders are responsible for rejecting Jesus and for the consequences. Yet from 19.47 onward the crowd is depicted as enthusiastically attending on Jesus, and is contrasted with the leaders (note the elaborate 19.47; 20.1) even at the crucifixion (23.27, 48).[29] It is difficult to account for this, although the ambiguous nature of popular enthusiasm is often suggested in Luke (8.4ff.; 11.29; 14.25), and in addition he has to account historically for the fact that the leaders had such difficulty in carrying out their plan to get rid of Jesus.

3. The section between the two we have just considered, 17.1–19.27, is more difficult to analyse. It is not clear in the first place where a new beginning should be made. 17.1–10 resembles 16.16ff. in having the appearance of a string of only loosely connected sayings. Some interpreters are inclined to regard 17.1 as beginning a new section, while others consider a fresh start to be made at 17.11, where the renewed reference to the journey to Jerusalem seems to mark the end of the previous scene, which on this understanding would continue from chapter 16.[30] A new beginning is certainly indicated by the similar sentence at 19.28, which marks the entry to Jerusalem. Other geographical notes in the section, combined with the passion prediction at 18.31–4, show the end and climax of the journey getting progressively closer (18.35; 19.1, 11). What is less clear is whether all the stages in the journey also indicate substantial breaks in the subject matter. In 17.11 the reference to Samaria and Galilee, though difficult to reconstruct geographically, is necessary in order to explain

how a group of lepers contained a Samaritan as well as Jews, and the reference to Jerusalem might have been introduced as part of this.[31] We need therefore to ask what thematic links there are between the components of these chapters, which might help to clarify the structure.

A factor in the sequence of some at least of the material is the fact that it had already been connected in the tradition before Luke. He is mainly following Mark from 18.15, with omissions and additions. A case can also be made for a traditional connection between the sayings in 17.1–4. There are parallels to these, not in precise wording but in general subject and in sequence, in Matt. 18.6f., 15, 21f., 35. But in addition we have already seen in chapter 6 that there is a thematic unity in 17.22–18.8 in the summons to disciples to persevere until the Son of Man comes.[32] We need to explore the possibilities further.

Apart from 19.39, which we noted above, 17.20 is the only explicit reference to the Pharisees in Luke's narrative after chapter 16 (18.10f. occurs within a parable). They ask when the kingdom of God is to come, but Jesus turns from them to the disciples almost immediately. As we saw in the last chapter, their question is not an innocent request for an opinion but a sign of their failure to recognise Jesus for what he is. The important fact to notice however is that 17.20 is part of a larger pattern. Two very similar complexes can be detected, 17.11–18.8 and 18.35–19.27. The question about when the kingdom comes, asked at 17.20, is introduced again at 19.11, where Luke prefaces the parable of the pounds with the remark that because Jesus was near Jerusalem the kingdom of God was expected to come immediately. Only a paragraph before 17.20, at v. 11, there is another note about Jesus going up to the city. Both at 17.20 and at 19.11 moreover, this speculation about the coming of the kingdom is immediately preceded by stories which form the basis for the kind of reply Jesus gives in 17.21; in 17.12–19 there is the cleansing of the ten lepers, in 18.35–43 the healing of the blind man, and in 19.1–10 the story of Zacchaeus. The last is explicitly linked with 19.11, where Luke introduces the parable of the pounds by 'as they heard these things'. In each of these three stories the theme is salvation in the present (17.19; 18.42, 'your faith has saved you'; 19.9, 'today salvation has come to this house . . . the Son of Man came to seek and save the lost'). In each case too the recipient is a member of a rejected class: the Samaritan 'foreigner' (17.18), the blind man to whom the crowd are hostile and Zacchaeus, a chief tax collector, rich, a sinner, and the object of 'murmuring' (19.2, 7). In both 17.20 and 19.11 therefore speculation about a future coming of the kingdom is linked with Jesus' nearness to Jerusalem and betrays failure to recognize its presence in what he is already doing. In 19.11 there is an added irony. In 18.31–4, just before the two salvation stories, Jesus has predicted his passion, 'Behold, we are going up to Jerusalem . . .' The disciples do not understand this. It is not clear in 19.11 who 'they' are who speculate that the kingdom is about to appear, but their speculation betrays profound misunderstanding of what Jesus' arrival in Jerusalem will mean, misunderstanding which the disciples certainly share.[33]

In both 17.20ff. and 19.11ff. Jesus meets questions about the nearness of the kingdom with a double response, part applicable to critics, part to disciples. We have seen how this is developed in 17.20–18.8. For critics (vv. 20f.) there is only an invitation to see what is true now but hidden from them. For the disciples (vv. 22ff.) there is a call for faith in the sense of perseverance and trust.[34] Incidentally we note that 17.25 also includes a reference to Jesus' approaching rejection and death, reinforcing the other references. In 19.11–27 the parable of the pounds contains both a warning of judgment on those who refuse to accept the rule of the king (vv. 14, 27) and a warning of the need for the king's servants to be faithful in his absence (v. 17). Both passages imply a long interval when the king or the Son of Man will be absent (17.22; 18.7 and 19.12, 'a far country'). The point relating to critics in these two passages is the same as that made in the section on the Jerusalem ministry (19.28–21.38): failure to recognize the significance and authority of Jesus will lead to judgment; in that section the critics are identified in 19.39 as Pharisees and in chapter 20 as scribes. In 17.20 also they are Pharisees. The Pharisees overtly or implicitly are thus representative throughout of those who fail to recognize Jesus for what he is.

So far we have tried to show that 17.11–18.8 and 18.35–19.27 are not random collections of separate items but

integrated complexes following a similar pattern and driving
home similar points about the response to Jesus by both
opponents and disciples in preparation for events in Jerusalem.
By 19.28 we are ready for what is to come, a final demonstration of the same issues in Jerusalem itself. As Luke expresses
it at 19.28, 'when he had said this he went on ahead going up
to Jerusalem'. Nothing more needed to be said. But the
consequence is that although the account of the entry to
Jerusalem, which forms the first restatement of the issues,
with the final explicit reference to the Pharisees added to the
Marcan source in 19.39, is structurally part of what follows,
it also acts as a bridge with what has gone before. While there
is a division in the gospel, the themes continue, and the
Pharisees are associated with them on both sides of the
divide.

What about the material in 18.9–34 between these two
sections? At 18.15 Luke reverts to using Mark as a source,
and on that ground his 'central section' is often thought to
end at this point, but he gives no indication of any division
and we are no more entitled to postulate one simply on the
basis of sources here than elsewhere. There are four main
pericopae in this section: the parable of the Pharisee and the
tax-collector at prayer, the welcome to children, the episode
of the rich ruler, and the prediction of the passion. Earlier we
drew attention to the implications of the passion prediction in
18.31–34 for the interpretation of 19.11, but it is better to
regard 18.35 as beginning a new sub-division in view of the
form of the sentence, and take the passion prediction with
what precedes. As a reminder of the goal of the journey, it is
an ironic comment on Peter's observation that the disciples
have left everything to follow Jesus; in reality they have no
idea what such an act implies. We note that the second and
third of these four pericopae are more closely connected than
in Mark. The crowd who bring the children at 18.15 are also
present for the dialogue with the ruler at 18.18 and its
immediate sequel in vv. 24–7.[35] Only at v. 28 does Jesus turn
to the disciples. These two passages both concern what
is required to enter the kingdom. The first and second
pericopae are also connected. Luke omits Mark 10.16 which
describes Jesus blessing the children. All interest in Luke is
thus focussed on what Jesus says about them: it is necessary to

be like a child to enter the kingdom. But the parable of the two men at prayer has a similar message. It is about humbling oneself before God, and not being arrogant towards him or others (vv. 9, 14). We therefore have two subjects in the first three pericopae, which have already been associated elsewhere with the Pharisees, pride and wealth. The link is obvious in 18.9–14 (cf. especially 14.11; 16.14f.) and equally true of the rich ruler by whom Luke, as we saw, may have intended a Pharisee. Thus the Pharisaic image lurks behind these passages as much as, according to our argument, behind the rest of Luke 17.11–21.38.

The integrated character of the whole of 17.11–19.27 for which we are arguing can be seen also from linguistic data. It is to be noticed how frequently the idea of the kingdom and the king occurs: 17.20f., 18.16f., 24, 29, 19.11f., 14f., 27, and in the next section at the entry to Jerusalem, 19.38, and at 21.31. Some of these have a clearly future reference, but we have seen how for Luke speculation about when it will come is irrelevant unless first Jesus is recognized as the king in whom the kingdom is made real. The recurrence of this idea is not of itself enough to bind the passages together, but confirms the conclusion already drawn, and is to be added to the evidence provided by the occurrence of words for faith and salvation noted above.[36]

In the light of this discussion what are we to make of 17.1–10? Since all the rest can be seen to be part of a design, it is unlikely that these verses are not part of one, in spite of their somewhat random appearance. The question is, do they belong with what precedes or what follows? Some have argued for taking 17.5ff. with 17.12ff. and 18.1–8 on the grounds that all deal with aspects of faith.[37] Tempting as this is, it should probably be resisted, not simply because 17.11 by resuming the journey motif gives the impression of a break, but because in 17.19 faith, interesting though we have found it to be, is subsidiary both to salvation, which we have suggested is important as preparation for 17.20, and to the surprise of Jesus that only one, a foreigner, has displayed such faith. 17.5–10 should therefore be taken with what immediately precedes. Verses 6 and 7–10, as we suggested earlier, combine to form the answer to the apostles' request in v. 5. They are to beware of the arrogance which may follow from success.[38]

It is best therefore to take 17.1–10 primarily with chapter 16 although they perhaps also form a bridge to the next section. It is probable that in these sayings Luke heard echoes of the teaching of the previous chapters. Disciples are addressed. After the warning to the Pharisees in 16.14–31 Luke sees the need to bring the message home explicitly to disciples. The 'little ones' of 17.2 are therefore probably the poor like Lazarus. Disciples too must be on their guard against despising them. Because Jesus is the friend of sinners, the disciples too must forgive their brothers who sin and repent (note the key words of chapter 15).[39] Disciples too must beware of the arrogance and reliance on their achievements which is the undoing of the Pharisees.

We have argued for a strong bonding within each of the three sections, 14.1–17.10, 17.11–19.27, and 19.28–21.38, and also between them, and have suggested that the bonds are formed by certain key ideas all of which have their focus in the Pharisees and the scribes who are associated with them. It would be possible to argue that these sections in fact form one unit. Not only is the kingdom, so prominent from 17.20 onwards, first mentioned in 16.16, but there are very strong echoes of chapter 15 in the story of Zacchaeus, 19.1–10. All the key words recur: tax collector, sinner, lost, murmuring, seeking, joy. The joy is grounded in Zacchaeus' repentance and is expressed in a feast, and it is pointed out that v. 10 echoes Ezek. 34.16 which speaks of God as Israel's shepherd (cf. 15.3–7). But we should beware of overriding Luke's own signs of subject division. Although, as we have said, 17.11 is not as strong a break as might appear, it does indicate a change of scene and resumption of movement, as does 19.28. We should therefore think of three sections in this part of the gospel. But the story is continuous, for it is the narrative of Jesus' journey to the cross. The themes continue through all three sections, and the key to them all is provided by the Pharisees.

4. We can now turn back to 11.14–13.35. The dominant note sounded in this section is the call to repentance, and it is instructive to see how apparently disparate paragraphs are related to this, and the part played in it by the Pharisees and scribes. As was observed earlier in this chapter, 11.14ff. and 29ff. form a single discussion, even though vv. 27f. and the

beginning of v. 29 intervene. The basic sequence is probably dictated by the order of 'Q', for a similar order, with the exception of Luke 11.24–6, is followed in Matt. 12.22–45. There are also parallels in Mark 3.22–30 and 8.11–13, which have certainly influenced Matthew and just possibly Luke also. There is no parallel to Luke's vv. 27f. Luke has integrated the two discussions, concerning the expulsion of demons and the demand for a sign, by introducing them both at vv. 15f. and indicating at v. 18b that at present Jesus is replying to the first point.[40] The two responses of the crowd in vv. 15f. to the expulsion of the demon are both indications of unbelief, the one misinterpreting the power of God as demonic, the other demanding a sign when they already have a sign in Jesus himself (cf. 7.22). Verses 27f., the bystander's blessing on Jesus' mother, prepare the way for what follows. The important question is not Jesus' greatness as a wonder worker but the response of obedience to the word of God which people make: the Queen of Sheba went to learn from Solomon's God-given wisdom, and the Ninevites repented at the preaching of Jonah, but 'this generation' fails to repent when confronted by one greater than either.[41]

11.33–36, most of which is also 'Q' but found in different contexts in Matthew, can be seen to follow on. Jesus is the light visible for all to see; but a lamp is of no benefit unless the inner light of the eye makes sight possible. So Jesus is veiled in obscurity and people demand validation by a sign; they are too blind to acknowledge him. If, however, one does see clearly and recognize him, then he will bring total illumination.

This analysis of 11.14–36 clarifies the meaning of v. 29a, 'when the crowds were increasing'. It does not indicate a change of scene or a shift to a fresh topic. It simply emphasizes the response of the crowds to Jesus and contrasts it with the fundamental need for repentance which they are failing to heed.

11.37–54 presents a series of criticisms of Pharisees and scribes (lawyers). Although there are parallels in Matthew 23, they are not verbally close, nor in the same sequence, and it seems that any common source was several stages back in the tradition. Luke's version is clearly organized. Criticisms of the Pharisees are followed by others relating to the scribes, who are however also implicated in the first group (v. 45). An important turning point in the narrative is then reached at vv. 53f. The opposition to Jesus is crystallized and this fact influences the following chapters. Part of the function of vv. 37–52 is to show what led to this development, but there are also important links between these verses and what has gone before. Verses 34–6 had emphasized the importance of what a person is inwardly if he is to make a response to Jesus. Inward wholeness will lead to total illumination. Verses 38–41 also stress the need for inward purity (expressed in generosity) if everything is to be clean. Inwardly the Pharisees are full of wickedness.[42] In vv. 47f. the lawyers for all their piety show themselves as unrepentant as their ancestors; 'the wisdom of God' (v. 49) and 'this generation' (vv. 50f.) pick up the phrases of vv. 29–32. The connection between vv. 14–36 and vv. 37ff. is also emphasized by the temporal link at v. 37, 'while he was speaking'. It seems that the function of this section is to spell out in specific terms in relation to the Pharisees the more general call to repentance already proclaimed to the people, and to describe its outcome, in which the people are also implicated. This may be the reason why the Pharisees are not mentioned at vv. 15f., as they are at Matt. 12.24. The Pharisees exemplify sins of which Israel as a whole is called to repent. They are not the only culprits, and responsibility for Jerusalem's fall is not to be laid exclusively upon them but upon the whole 'generation'. This is brought out in what follows.

At first sight 12.1 with its elaborate opening looks like a new beginning. But we saw in the last chapter that 'hypocrisy' refers back to the criticisms of the Pharisees in 11.38–44, and may have been held over by Luke from his source of those verses expressly to provide a summary of them here.[43] Moreover, 12.1 is closely linked with 11.53f. by 'in the meantime'. The reference to the gathering numbers of the crowd does not necessarily mark a new beginning; we have just seen that at 11.29 such a note can function rather as a background for a warning by Jesus. Here however 12.1 also serves as introduction to what follows, to v. 13 as well as v. 2; Jesus speaks 'first' to disciples. These paragraphs deal with different topics: vv. 2f. warn disciples against hypocrisy in themselves; vv. 4–12, with the opening words marking a change of topic, [44] discuss loyalty under persecution, vv. 13–21 address the crowds on the dangers of greed, vv. 22–34 turn back to the disciples on the subject of anxiety and possessions generally. All these are aspects or consquences of the hypocrisy of the Pharisees delineated in 11.38ff.: dissimulation and self-deception in 11.44 (cf. 20.20), greed in 11.39–41 (cf. 16.14), and its outcome, a hostility to Jesus that leads to active persecution in 11.53f. As we suggested at the end of chapter 9, vv. 4–12 stress the need for disciples to be true to their confession, where denial would itself be a form of hypocrisy. Verses 1–34 therefore are held together by the ideas suggested by the threat posed by the Pharisees, externally by their hostility, internally by their influence. Not only disciples but people more widely are threatened by the latter, and Luke indicates this by the changes of audience. By gathering together both audiences at the start in v. 1 he indicates that this is so.

Running through the teaching on possessions in chapter 12 is a note of urgency. For the rich man building his barns, time was too short! This note comes to the fore in 12.35ff., where we move away from wealth to the theme of readiness, although this includes obedience and a sober lifestyle. The parables of vv. 35–40 and 42–6 are brought together in vv. 47f., which form the real answers to Peter's question at v. 41. The parables speak of readiness for the Son of Man's return, but we saw in chapter 4 that for Luke the moment of death may have an equally decisive significance. So the urgency of these parables is similar to that of the parable of the rich fool at vv. 16–21.

At 12.49–53, still keeping the note of urgency, Luke touches on the theme of persecution which we left at v. 12. Verses 49f. are most easily interpreted with reference to Jesus' own suffering in Jerusalem, and the urgency in this respect is the shortness of time before it is accomplished. [45] But this has two implications. One is that he must impress on people the need to repent while there is time; the other that people will respond to him either positively or negatively, and the divisions caused by this ('henceforth') will set members of the same family against each other. The idea of division is dealt with in vv. 51–3, the need to repent from v. 54 onwards. At v. 54 Jesus turns back to the crowd and reiterates the call to repentance last sounded at 11.29ff. The 'also' indicates the connection; the 'henceforth' of v. 52 also applies to them. The time is short; they have only one more chance (13.6–9) yet they seem incapable of seeing the warning or evading the judgment which will otherwise surely come. This too is hypocrisy (12.56).

This brings us to 13.10. From this point in chapter 13 the thread is more difficult to discern. 13.10 is not connected to what precedes by any strong temporal or geographical link, but two features of the healing of the woman suggest a connection. Although it is the ruler of the synagogue who voices criticism of what Jesus does, he is a spokesman of a larger group of 'adversaries', and we should probably think of the Pharisees and scribes of 11.53f., although they are not named. Moreover, Jesus accuses them of hypocrisy, in this case in failing to see that after eighteen years there could be no delay in healing the woman. The point, however, is not that she could have been healed earlier, but that now that Jesus has come there must be no further delay. They fail to recognize who is with them and the urgency his presence creates.

The woman is a daughter of Abraham and in her God's promises to Israel are fulfilled (cf. 1.54f., 72f.). Against the background of rejection and refusal to repent which Jesus is facing it is a small beginning, but a promise of what is to come. The two parables of mustard seed and leaven in vv. 18–21 make this point (v. 18, 'therefore'). But this growth will depend on the rejection of Jesus which the unrepentance of Israel will bring about. This is brought out in what follows.

Verse 22 marks a change of setting and audience. We are reminded of Jesus' progress to Jerusalem. But v. 23 takes up the two preceding parables. Is the number of those who are to be saved to be only small? The answer of vv. 24–30 is both yes and no. There are general parallels in Matt. 7.13f., 22f., 8.11f., 19.30, but the point is different. Where Matthew thinks of the choice between wide and narrow paths, Luke stresses the one gate which, because of its narrowness, it is an effort to enter.[46] The time is short, and action must be taken now. Where Matthew refers to Christian workers repudiated at the judgment, Luke depicts Jesus' hearers, rejected because they have not repented.[47] Luke presents vv. 28f. in reverse order to Matthew, so that two separate points are made, first that the hearers will find themselves excluded from the kingdom which Abraham and the patriarchs and prophets (and, perhaps, by implication, the daughter of Abraham of v. 16) inherit, and secondly, that others will come and take their place, a hint of the Gentile mission of the future. Now we know what the parables of mustard seed and leaven were alluding to.[48] Why then the reminder of the journey to Jerusalem in v. 22? Partly because it is a reminder of the urgency facing Jesus' hearers: he will not come this way again; partly because it prepares for vv. 31–5. Jesus is indeed going on his way and cannot be hurried. So the parable of vv. 23–30 and the dialogue of vv. 31–5 are bound together. It is 'at that very hour' that Luke introduces the suggestion that he should escape from Herod. As we have seen, this is not friendly advice from well-wishers. The Pharisees fail to recognize who he is, or the divinely ordained time scale and culmination of his mission. They try to move him on and cut short the opportunity for repentance which, as Jesus has just stressed, faces them.[49] It is not surprising that Pharisees should do this in view of what has been said of them in the preceding chapters. But the fault is not theirs alone; it is true of all the children of Jerusalem, which is why Jesus will die in that city, and the city in turn become desolate.[50]

Thus the Pharisees offer a key to the sequence of ideas in 11.14–13.35. They are not named between 12.1 and 13.31 but their spirit broods over much of what intervenes. The marks of their hypocrisy are taken up in chapter 12, and as the examples *par excellence* of those who refuse to repent they appear at the end of chapter 13. So the way is prepared for the role they assume in 14.1–17.10; not repenting themselves they refuse to share the joy of those who do.

The interpreter of Luke's gospel, particularly the material on repentance, often faces a dilemma. Why has Luke included these sayings? Sometimes the emphasis seems to be quite clearly on the past. Jesus called the people to repentance but they refused to listen. That is why God has permitted Jerusalem to be handed over to Gentiles and the temple demolished. He appears to be dealing with the difficulty that Christians claim continuity with the Old Testament but the Jewish people, whose claim to continuity seems so obvious, have not responded to the Christian mission. 19.41ff. and other passages would support this view. On the other hand it is difficult to maintain that Luke supposed such sayings had nothing to say to his contemporaries about their own lives and response to Jesus, or that he believed his readers should identify themselves with Jesus' audience only when he was speaking to disciples. As we have seen the distinctions between audiences are not reflected in the content of the discourses, and it is difficult to see why he should have needed to include so much material to illustrate the preaching of Jesus simply as a thing of the past. Repentance is a theme in the church's preaching in Acts, as we saw in chapter 1, and the material in the gospel must be treated as a contemporary call to the reader to avoid the error into which Israel fell. At various points one of the two interests, the historical and the contemporary, comes to the fore without any clear line being drawn between them. This is true of Luke's portrayal of all Jesus' audiences, the disciples and the crowds, as well as the Pharisees. The view taken in this book is that of the two, the contemporary is the dominant interest, and it has been the aim of these last two chapters to show this particularly in relation to the Pharisees.[51] Historically they were agents in the opposition to Jesus, particularly outside Jerusalem. This is why they disappear by name from the passion narrative. But predominantly for Luke they are contemporary figures, known in part no doubt from contemporary Judaism, although not at close quarters, but contemporary particularly in the sense that they represent the vices which Christians must at all costs avoid. So important is this function in Luke's mind that the Pharisees recur at various stages in his narrative in ways which can only be explained on the assumption that they were in his mind all the time. They are the key to the structure of much of the gospel. In them are associated the failings attacked by Jesus in passages which apart from this appear to have no obvious connection with each other.

11

Conclusions

This has been a limited study. On the one hand I have had to select certain details, and the previous chapters have illustrated how difficult this can be, for we have frequently found one theme leading into another. In spite of this a number of topics which are of major significance for Luke, including the person of Christ, the work of the Spirit, salvation and mission, have been virtually ignored. The gospel, like the Acts, is a kaleidescope of swiftly changing emphases, and for our own purposes we have selected certain colours, but we cannot escape being aware that they have their full significance only as part of the whole. On the other hand the study has been limited by Luke's own selectiveness. We have very little idea, for example, of the qualities he would consider essential to a good marriage, or what, apart from obedience (2.51), should be expected of children. We do not know whether the delineation of Christian character which has emerged from his work is the complete picture he would set before us if he were writing a work specifically dedicated to that theme.

We acknowledged at the outset in chapter 1 that Luke was not writing a study of Christian character but a gospel. Nothing we have discussed subsequently has led to a modification of that view. Nevertheless, the fact that we have been able to draw out so much that has a bearing on Christian character indicates how important a concern it was for him. We have not asked an irrelevant question.

It would be possible on the basis of what we have done to try to locate Luke's position in the history of ideas. There is an obvious field of comparison in the rest of the New Testament and other early Christian literature, where there are similarities and differences both of method and of content. The other gospels use a similarly oblique method of presentation, but neither John nor Mark offer the same diversity of content (John's ethic is virtually exhausted in the command to love one another), while Matthew discusses more specific issues against a background of more detailed engagement with Jewish views (as in the sermon on the mount). The epistles on the other hand (particularly the Pastorals), the Didache and some of the Apostolic Fathers have more systematic sections of teaching, though with wide differences of content. One key often used in such comparisons is to relate the style of the teaching given to the eschatological perspective, although it is not clear that ethical teaching must invariably become more specific as the expectation of an imminent end recedes.[1]

Another field for comparison lies in Jewish and pagan literature. In neither case are we presented with a single homogeneous view. In Judaism the rabbinic writings represent a later consolidation of older and more diverse attitudes. They tell us little or nothing about the views of Sadducees, Essenes (for whom the Dead Sea Scrolls are the best evidence) or Zealots, of those who belonged to none of the sects in Palestine or of the widely scattered communities of the gentile world, of whom the works of Philo and other Greek Jewish writings are the legacy but are not necessarily wholly typical. The same applies to the non-Jewish world. Certain generalizations are easy to make. Humility and service were despised as servile, though slaves often occupied positions of great responsibility. But such generalizations mask the pluralism of ancient society, and the views of the various philosophical schools whose writings have survived, influential as they were, must not be treated as a complete guide to the expectations and norms of ordinary people who are much less accessible to us.

An alternative direction in which our study might develop would be to try to read off from it an analysis of the social situation of Luke and his readers. Sociological analysis has been a developing interest in recent New Testament study and is important for our overall historical view.[2] Some very general conclusions can easily be attempted. The degree of attention given to questions of wealth and the dangers of business pursuits must suggest that Luke was writing for those who were involved in trade as part of their everyday lives, but not at a level which put them beyond the reach of everyday anxiety. They are also in a setting where public opinion matters, and where they can easily become the object of hostility, abuse and petty persecutions. For these and other reasons they are likely to have been town dwellers. Whether this makes them bourgeois is perhaps a matter of termin-ology.[3] If we try to be more specific, however, difficulties emerge. Are we to think of Jewish or pagan society or some mix of the two, and to what extent are Luke and his readers alienated from contemporary culture? To what extent should details be pressed? Do the frequent references to dinner parties really tell us anything about social class, and would the answer be different for Jewish and pagan society?

All of these lines of inquiry would require further very detailed study and would extend the compass of this work considerably. It will perhaps be more useful at the end of an already long and detailed study to ask some more general questions about the picture which has emerged.

1. The first is whether Luke can fairly be said to have moralized the gospel. It is clear from the evidence assembled in this book that Christian character was important for him. He was concerned about tendencies in the church as he knew it which he believed to be a departure from the purity of earlier days and saw in the teaching and ministry of Jesus clear warnings which he tried to bring out. The question that has to be asked is whether in the process of bringing this concern to the fore Luke has taken any further steps along the road which leads from an understanding of Christianity as essentially a response to the good news of Jesus Christ towards an understanding of it as a code of moral conduct with religious sanctions.

Such a formulation of the question of course involves some presuppositions and value judgments. It assumes that the primitive (and purer) form of the Christian message was a simple declaration of the death and resurrection of Jesus, to which faith was the response and love the practical conse-quence, which gradually gave way, as early enthusiasm died, the expectation of an early end to all things diminished and the church became institutionalized, to a detailed, rigid and uninspired moral code. Such a view of developments is simplistic and lacks hard evidence, and betrays a modern assumption that it is better to be given a simple moral principle and be allowed to work it out for oneself than to be told in detail what to do. It also assumes that developments are for better or worse simply in relation to what has gone before rather than to the requirements of a changing environment. It is hard to see how the church managed to survive the ages of martyrdom if in fact it had been reduced to nothing more than a religious institution and a moral code.

When that has been said, however, changes must be evaluated. There is some validity in the distinction between a simple moral principle and a detailed code (compare I John with James or the Didache), and it is important to try to specify where Luke stands.

Luke has certainly reinterpreted some traditional sayings. By referring to taking up the cross 'daily' (9.23) he has transformed it from a summons to martyrdom (as it appears to be in Mark) into a call to accept the kind of hardships which may be encountered from day to day, whether the petty burdens of self-denial, or the externally imposed sufferings of the hostility of others, which is what Luke seems especially to have in mind (cf. 9.26; 14.26f.). At the same time he has detached cross-bearing from the cause of 'the gospel' and made it more generally the calling of every disciple, not just the missionary (9.24; Mark 8.35). This concern for day-to-day discipleship is reflected also in the Lord's Prayer (11.3) where bread is asked for 'day by day'. It is important, however, to be clear about the change which has occurred. If the image of the cross is initially a symbol of martyrdom, any reinterpretation is likely to seem trivializing; but such a symbol can only retain its power while there is a realistic expectation of its fulfilment. In contexts where martyrdom is not widely expected reinterpretation is inevitable, and the test is whether the symbol retains a sense of challenge and rigour, or has been reduced to representing minor inconveniences. There is no evidence that Luke has trivialized it in this sense. Indeed, if his portrayal of the death of Jesus does show him as the exemplary martyr, he may still have expected the image to retain for some readers its original force. To the extent that he has detached it from the missionary enterprise in which only some may be engaged and made it applicable to all Christians he has in fact intensified it (cf. 14.27).

Another instance sometimes cited for a moralizing tendency in Luke is his use of *peirasmos* (temptation). It is suggested that in 11.4 it no longer carries the original significance of the final test of apostasy to which all believers will be put before the kingdom comes, but (in line with the prayer for bread 'day by day') refers to day-to-day incitements to moral failing. It is hard to discuss the merits of this claim because there is so little evidence either way. It is entirely possible that the meaning has been broadened to include general incitement to sin, but it is much harder to show that there has been a shift away from one meaning to another. The theory that *peirasmos* in the Lord's Prayer originally referred to the final test is in any case open to challenge, as the absence of the definite article in Greek (the only version of the prayer we have) does not support it. On the other hand Luke's general image of the word, especially at 22.40, 46 does point to something more akin to the final test.[4] While therefore Luke's language was capable of bearing a moralizing interpretation there is no hard evidence that he intended a major shift of meaning.

Another passage often quoted in this connection is 14.7ff., the parable of places at table, which, it is claimed, is a straighforward piece of moral advice about social conduct. We have already given reason to question this reading of the passage, which ignores Luke's description of it as a parable and the overtones of the concluding maxim (vv. 7, 11).[5]

The weakness of this view of Luke as a moralizer is that it separates his teaching about behaviour from its roots in the gospel proclaimed by Jesus. This is why chapter 5 on the 'sense of God' is important to the study as a whole. The teaching on conduct is interwoven with passages which speak of the good news, and the overall profile of Christian character includes joy and humility. These are essentially responses to something given, not attitudes manufactured to order. Due weight must also be given to the fact that Luke's ideal is far from being merely external, as we saw from his emphasis upon the heart and his attack upon hypocrisy.

In fact, as we saw in Chapter 2 Luke is nearer to stating the Christian obligation in terms of a single moral principle than Matthew or Mark, though he does not go so far in this direction as John. It is true, as we noted at the conclusion of that chapter, that we might have expected, from the prominence of the idea in certain passages, that the word would be more widely used in the rest of the gospel and in Acts. To some extent that impression is modified by his teaching on generosity to the poor and by the example in the gospel and Acts of those whose conduct exemplifies love. But this cannot detract from the prominence he gives to the idea of love in the key passages we have studied. For him love to God and fellow human beings is one command, and the sermon on the plain lacks the additional material in Matthew's sermon which might distract from its centrality. While therefore it is true to say that Luke is concerned with the quality of Christian character to an extent that some other New Testament writers are not, it does not follow that he has thereby significantly shifted the understanding of Christianity in a moralistic direction.

2. Secondly, we need to consider whether Luke encouraged a conformist attitude to the *status quo* in society. It is true that he assumes that, until the kingdom of God comes the Christian will live out his life within the framework of the given political and social institutions. In chapter 21 political instability is a sign of the nearness of the end or of God's judgment upon Israel, and his references to ringleaders of revolts against Roman rule do not betray any sympathy for them (Luke 23.18f.; Acts 5.36ff.). This leaves Luke open to modern criticism at two levels, one that he was instrumental in giving Christianity a decisively conformist political stance, the other that his remedies for social problems, because they were conceived in terms of individual response, were inadequate.

The charge that Luke was politically conformist is especially associated with the work of S. G. F. Brandon, who claimed that Luke in particular was responsible for turning an essentially revolutionary Jewish movement akin to the Zealots into a world religion designed to enable its adherents to live acceptably and at peace within the Roman state. But the thesis that Jesus himself was a Zealot-style revolutionary cannot be sustained, for it is built upon the premise that Roman justice never miscarried and that Jesus' crucifixion as an insurrectionary must therefore reveal more of his aims than the rest of the gospel evidence put together. It is particularly difficult to cast Luke in this conformist role when it is his gospel alone which describes Simon as a Zealot (6.15) and contains the saying of Jesus about the purchase of a sword (22.36), upon which Brandon so much depends, but which on his view Luke ought to have suppressed.[6]

A less extreme form of this view is often taken by those who see Luke's two volumes as an apology addressed to the Roman authorities on behalf of Christianity, or more specifically on behalf of Paul. In this view Luke plays down potential sources of friction between Christianity and the state, depicting Roman officials in a favourable light, and recording their verdict of acquittal on those believers brought to trial before them. Those who find it incredible that an apology addressed to the state would actually take the form of the gospel and Acts as we have them may alternatively suggest that Luke's motive may have been to allay the anxieties of potential converts (like Theophilus?) who feared that the new faith might be incompatible with their Roman citizenship. Aside from the question whether any of the New Testament writers were interested in dressing up their convictions to make them more attractive, and the fact that Theophilus, being totally unknown to us, can be made to fit almost any role we care to cast for him, we have offered arguments in Chapter 8 for thinking that these theories are a misreading of the evidence. The stress in passages which maintain the innocence of those who are accused (Jesus, Stephen, Paul) is on the malicious character of the charges brought against them. One can readily imagine the experience repeated in the lives of Luke's readers, and it is against that background that he depicts the bearing and witness of the accused. The favourable attitude of Roman officials generally in Acts has much to do with the contrast they present to the unreasonable hostility (as Luke sees it) of Jewish authorities who ought to have recognized in the message about Jesus the fulfilment of the Old Testament.

In the gospel Herod and Pilate are hardly presented in a sympathetic light.

It is not surprising that Luke should have assumed that Christians would have to live within the framework of the existing state. The possibility that a minority Christian movement could have any meaningful impact even upon local politics was so remote that it can hardly have been considered, and there is no evidence in the New Testament that it ever was considered, except possibly in the special circumstances of Rome, where the Jewish community had a history of communal disturbance, if Romans 13.1ff. is to be read as discouraging an actual tendency. On the other hand it is perhaps easier for us than for Luke's contemporaries to discount the revolutionary impact of his language about the coming of the kingdom of God and the Son of Man. It is true that for him the coming of the End is no longer imminent, as it clearly was for sections of the church at an earlier period (I Thess 4.13ff.; Rom. 13.11; I Cor. 7.29ff.) but there is no evidence that he and his readers did not take the language seriously. While we have evidence that some references to the future kingdom may be concerned with what happens at the death of an individual, not all can be related to this, and they carry strong implications for the current political order.[7] As Luke 21 illustrates, he understood the teaching of Jesus about the future to refer to two moments, the destruction of Jerusalem and Jesus' final coming. As he writes the first of these lies in the past and represents a fulfilment of the sayings of Jesus in the realities of power politics. There is no reason to think that Luke was less realistic in his expectations of the coming of the Son of Man. If it was right to argue in Chapter 4 that his language about poverty cannot be restricted to a 'spiritual' meaning, no one who takes the Magnificat seriously can fairly accuse Luke of being unwordly in his religion. Some of his original readers may have been more anxious than we imagine that their Christian allegiance might indeed bring them under suspicion from political authority. If that is true the most one can say of Luke, as of other New Testament writers, is that they took the alternative option of waiting for God to act against evil in the world, rather than the Zealot one of acting in his name.[8] That is hardly a conformist stance.

This has a bearing on the other aspect of the accusation against Luke. We have become increasingly conscious in the twentieth century that the problems of poverty and injustice on a massive scale cannot be met by private charity but only by action at international level, including changes in the economic system. Latin American theologians in particular have pressed this view of the problem. It goes without saying that there is no suggestion of a solution of this kind in Luke's material on poverty. There is no awareness of the economic, political or social causes of poverty although the climatic factor of famine is of course recognized. The Christian response is personal and individual, although individuals may band together for this purpose (Acts 11.27ff.). While the first Christians in Jerusalem hold all things in common, this is voluntary (Acts 5.4) and it is not presented as a solution to general economic problems.

Of course it is anachronistic to criticize Luke for neglecting disciplines of economic and social analysis which had not been developed. But we must not ignore the implications of the sayings on repentance and the repeated warnings of the dire historical consequences if the repentance does not occur. There can be little doubt that Luke saw the fall of Jerusalem in AD 70 as the consequence of Israel's rejection of the Messiah,[9] and that rejection was rooted, as the Pharisees illustrate, not simply in a verdict on whether he was or was not the one who was to come, but in a refusal to be open to the needs of the sick, the disabled and the poor. In this those who were responsible for leadership are particularly held responsible for what will come upon the nation as a whole. Luke's teaching is powerful testimony to the conviction that sin has social and political consequences which can only be averted by repentance. This does not offer a corporate structural solution to the problems of society but it does recognize to some extent the fact of corporate responsibility.

3. How distinctive is Luke's ideal? Earlier in this chapter we spelled out what would be involved in setting Luke within a framework of the history of ideas. It is possible to ask, however, not what a modern historian would judge to be the distinctiveness of Luke in comparison with other writers but what Luke himself considered the distinctiveness of his ideal to be as he contemplated the world about him.

How did he expect the Christian who embodied the traits of Christian character to differ from neighbours and friends? This would be an easier question to answer if we were more certain of the society in which Luke and his readers lived. One of the puzzles of Luke is that while he is clearly aware of the Hellenistic pagan world, can write in the classical style when he wishes (1.1–4) and is able to quote pagan poets (Acts 17.28), he makes relatively little allusion to the ideas and values of that world. The subject matter of the gospel naturally orientates him toward Jewish society but neither there nor in Acts where he has more reason to refer to pagan society does he come to close grips with contemporary culture.[10] We are thus in great difficulty in trying to perceive how he felt his ideal of character to be distinctive as against Jewish and Hellenistic ideals.

There are two exegetical aspects to this question which must be dealt with at this point. The first is the fact, commented on in Chapters 7 and 10, that it is impossible to draw clear lines of distinction between the content of the teaching addressed to disciples and that addressed to the crowds, except that the themes of mission and persecution are restricted to disciples. Topics such as wealth and the cost of discipleship are addressed in different passages to both disciples and crowds. The implication seems to be, on the one hand that the lifestyle to which disciples are called is not to be peculiar to them, but has relevance and application to the as yet uncommitted bystanders, and on the other, that in being summoned to a true lifestyle, the crowds are in effect being called to discipleship. The importance of this must be stressed. Luke's ideal is not a sectarian one for devotees of a private piety. It is God's will for all, and all people are summoned to it in order to respond to the will of their creator (cf. also Acts 14.15–18; 17.22–31).

Secondly, there is Luke's portrayal of those who have not yet responded to the invitation to become disciples. In Chapter 8 we took note of the way in which Luke begins his gospel, setting before his readers a number of godly men and women, including especially Mary, who, in addition to the part they play in the birth of John and Jesus and the insight they give through their words to the meaning of those events, set the moral tone for what follows. They are exemplary characters. Luke not only stresses that the historical roots of the Christian gospel lay in essentially Old Testament piety, he offers that piety as a pattern. So Mary is portrayed as an ideal Christian. Essentially the same piety is extolled in Gentiles who come to Christian faith (e.g. Acts 10.1ff.; cf. 17.11). We therefore have to ask whether for Luke there was anything distinctive about Christian character which differentiates the believer in Christ from Jews or pagan Gentiles at their best.

'At their best' is obviously an important qualification. Luke has both Jewish and Gentile instances of those who do not represent the best and we have argued that the portrayal of the Pharisees reflects this. It is also important to recognize that the Gentiles of whom he particularly approves are those who have been influenced by Judaism. It is in fact the Old Testament tradition of piety which he commends, although, as we observed in an earlier discussion, for his Gentile readers there will be no obligation to keep the law or worship in the temple. Is there anything new in Luke's ideal by which he would have expected Christian to be distinguished from Jew?

The continuity between Luke's ideal and Old Testament piety is theologically grounded in his thesis that Christianity is the fulfilment of the hope of Israel (cf. Acts 26.6f.). So it is appropriate that the lawyer should be directed back to the Old Testament for the commandment which is the answer to his question about inheriting eternal life (Luke 10.25–9) and it is not surprising that unlike Mark, Luke does not present Jesus' teaching as new.

Nevertheless, there are two aspects of Luke's portrayal of Christian character which give it, in his eyes, a novel and distinctive quality. The first is that, as we have already noted, his teaching about character cannot be divorced from the rest of his theology. This is the importance of those traits which we considered in Chapter 5 under the heading 'a sense of God'. The driving force for the new lifestyle is the humility, fear, wonder and joy which arise from the action of God upon people's lives. It is well illustrated in the story of Zacchaeus, whose generosity to the poor springs out of the generous gesture of Jesus toward him. Particularly in the early part of the gospel the fact that God has taken a new, long-awaited, and decisive initiative for Israel and the

Gentiles is emphasized repeatedly. It forms the focus of the canticles in chapters 1 and 2 and of the opening sermon in Nazareth in 4.16ff. (especially v. 21, 'today this scripture has been fulfilled in your hearing'). In Acts it is the invocation of Christ which releases forgiveness of sins and the gift of the Spirit (e.g. 8.39; 16.34). This is one aspect of the distinctiveness of the Christian character. Taken item by item, many of the traits we have noted can be urged upon those who are not committed to discipleship, and are characteristic of Old Testament piety. But taken as a whole they are distinctive because they cohere in faith in the God who has sent Jesus as Messiah, Saviour and Lord.

The second way in which Luke's ideal is perceived by him to be distinctive is concerned with the treatment of enemies. Whether or not historically speaking the command to love one's enemies was an original and novel element in the teaching of Jesus, it is clear for Luke it is a central feature and a distinguishing mark of disciples. We have already recalled how Luke's presentation of the teaching in the sermon on the plain emphasizes the centrality of love. We can, however, take the point further. It is with love for enemies that the exposition is mostly concerned. It begins with this point in 6.27 after the beatitudes and woes, and most of the examples relate to it. It is this, not love *per se*, which distinguishes disciples from 'sinners', for even 'sinners' show love to those who love them (6.32–4). In view of the prominence of this point, and the programmatic nature of the sermon as the first sustained passage of teaching for disciples in the gospel, it must have the quality of a manifesto.

Two observations confirm that judgment. When he wishes to sum up the good news proclaimed by Jesus and to be proclaimed by the church, Luke speaks of forgiveness (1.77; 4.18; 24.47; Acts 2.38; 5.31; 10.43; 13.38; 26.18). This is the theological undergirding for the ethics. It is appropriate that disciples should love their enemies, because this is what God does (6.35). Secondly, we saw that the death of Jesus is presented by Luke as a martyrdom, in which Jesus leaves an example to the disciples of faithfulness to his own teaching. Central to that picture is the forgiveness of enemies. Although the text of 23.24 is not supported by all the manuscripts, there are good reasons for thinking it to be genuine, and it coheres both with the rest of the passion and with Stephen's conduct at his death. In this particular feature Luke's treatment differs from many of the martyrologies of the ancient world, and Luke can hardly have been unaware of what he was doing. It reinforces the view that for Luke the central and distinguishing mark of Christian character is the way in which one responds to enemies with love.

4. This leads us to a final question, concerning the significance of Luke's work for today. His gospel and the Acts reflect a world long past, many details of which we cannot now recover, and many aspects of which now seem alien. In his attitude to miracle and the supernatural he displays a freshness and naivety denied to the twentieth-century Westerner. He belongs, as we now cannot, to a pre-scientific and pre-technological age. Along with technology has come, in many respects, a kind of self-confidence. Publicly at least we do not look to God to explain the inexplicable, nor do we doubt the capacity of science, given time, to solve many of our problems.

Of course it is easy to generalize on topics such as this. There are many parts of the world today hardly touched by Western secularism or communist atheism, for whom Luke's attitude to the supernatural world would occasion no difficulty. It is possible to use the products of modern technology without having to face the questions posed by the understanding of the world which has produced the technology. But as soon as one moves from being a user to becoming a producer and researcher, the questions begin to arise. It is true that there are signs in Western secularized society of a revival of interest in religion, indeed in the occult, which may well testify to the inadequacies of a culture which tries to ignore the spiritual dimension of human existence, but there is also the danger that the revival will take the form only of a private escape from the public culture, leaving a deep dichotomy between the private and individual and the public and corporate worlds in which people have to live. Such a solution is a long-term recipe for malaise, and in the tradition of the gospels would be more harshly written off as hypocrisy. It is true also that there is awareness in the other great world religions of the dangers of secularism, and particularly in some forms of Islam strenuous efforts to resist it. It remains to be seen whether the other world religions will be more successful than Christianity has been in this regard. All of this points to the distance between the twentieth century and the world of Luke.

There is increasing recognition also, as we have mentioned, that the problems of poverty cannot adequately be met by the response of generosity and the sharing of possessions which Luke urges unless their causes are also addressed. This requires action on an international scale to modify the present economic system if the problems of global poverty are to be dealt with. Sadly, growing recognition of this fact is not so far matched by adequate action by governments. As we have acknowledged Luke cannot take us very far in these matters.

Nevertheless the issues which Luke raises in his gospel remain surprisingly pertinent. In spite of the obvious differences, the situation of twentieth-century Western Christians is in many respects strangely similar to Luke's, and more so now than for a considerable time past. They are a minority in a world which contains a diversity of cultures, religions and ethnic groupings, and which is morally both conservative and permissive, and materially divided both nationally and internationally. In spite of more highly developed democratic institutions, many of the decisions which affect people's lives today are as much beyond their influence as any in the Roman Empire. We continue to see brutality in our time quite comparable with anything Luke knew. Like those for whom he wrote we tend to look back to an earlier age as a more golden period for the church. The numerical strength of many Western churches is to be found in middle-class suburban areas which bear many similarities in outlook to those of the small urban trades-people for whom Luke seems especially to have written. Should we not allow ourselves to be interrogated more thoroughly by his gospel and examine again our preoccupation with the getting and preserving of wealth, our attitude to enemies, our complacency and self-confidence, our indifference to poverty, the extent of our willingness to be humble and our capacity for gratitude?

If so, it is not just to the churches that Luke speaks. As we have seen, he draws no rigid boundary between disciples and crowds, church and world. All alike are called to repent and to follow the way of Jesus. The strength of the pattern he sets before us lies precisely in the fact that it is not a private obligation but the way for all peoples. Distant though his voice may sound, Luke speaks to society generally and not just to the church.

But if the transformation of society is to occur it is essential that Christians should be aware of their distinctiveness from it. There are numerous calls in the gospel for disciples to leave all and follow, to break with family ties and to accept the possibility of opposition and even martyrdom in order to be faithful to the way of Christ. One of the problems of the Western church is that it is living with its own prodigal son; having created a Christianized society over many centuries the church now finds itself in company which has largely repudiated its origins. It is more difficult now for the Western church to see itself over against the prevailing culture than it is for churches in Asia or Africa. The emphasis Luke places upon open witness to a potentially hostile world is one that needs to be heeded.

Interestingly the issue upon which many Christians today would argue that the church ought to take a clearer stand, that of sexual morals, is not one which features prominently in Luke. He deals with divorce only at 16.18, with incidental references to sexual sins at 15.30, 18.11,20, Acts 15.20. These are enough to give a hint of his general view, and to show it was an issue upon which Christians needed to differentiate themselves from others, but in spite of the sexual permissiveness of much of Hellenistic society it is not upon this but upon the use of wealth and the treatment of the neighbour, especially the enemy, that he concentrates, in other words upon issues of economics, community and peace.

Each of these is a complex and technical field, and there is no simple way in which we can translate Luke's teaching into action in the national or international sphere. He considers love of one's enemies to be a distinctive mark of a disciple of Jesus but makes no attempt to apply that in the realm of wars between nations. He inveighs against the arrogance which leads people to despise others but does not ask whether the prevalence of poverty and demon-possession are symptoms of deeper disturbance in the community in which people had to live in Roman-occupied Palestine. He encourages the

giving of one's possessions to the poor, in both individual
and communal terms (Acts 11.29f.) but does not analyse
causes or suggest administrative remedies by government. In
that sense Luke offers no blue-print to the modern world.

Nor is it a simple matter of changing individuals in order to
put the world right. The notion that if only all the world's
inhabitants were truly converted all its problems would
disappear is facile, both in its ignorance of the complexities
and conflicts of genuine interest and well-being which enter
the scene at the level of relationships between communities
and nations, and in its dangerously optimistic view of human
nature, even after conversion. Luke's portrayal of the disciples and of Jesus' teaching to them as well as the crowds on
repentance, does not encourage the belief that original sin
is easily eradicated. Nevertheless, underlying the technical
aspects of the world's problems is the question whether we
have the will to resolve them, and the readiness to pay the
price involved. The response of the Western world in terms
of voluntary giving to the Ethiopian famine in 1985, for
example, is remarkable, but it must be judged to be for the
most part a giving from surplus. We still await the adoption
of any remedy for that and similar needs which requires as its
price a genuine modification in Western living standards. It is
at this level of attitudes and will that Luke challenges both
church and society today. The importance of public opinion
in such matters is obvious, especially, but not exclusively, for
democratically elected governments; equally important is the
contribution of those who set the trends for public opinion,
and here Christian witness has a part to play.

Luke's central concerns are thus still pertinent today. Can
generosity to the poor be translated into genuine action for
the eradication of poverty by the sharing of the world's
limited wealth, allowing that this must mean deprivation for
those who are at present, even in relative terms, the rich?
Can humility and compassion for the neighbour be translated
into genuine frameworks for community, at local, national
and international levels? Can love for one's enemies, even
after injuries have been suffered, be translated into genuine
measures for peace? Can the love of neighbour which is
inseparable from the love of God be translated into justice?

What of that other central concern of Luke in his picture of discipleship, the 'sense of God' which is the mainspring of the rest? In many ways this is the major casualty of Western secularism. Here again Luke is pertinent, for he raises the question whether the other changes in attitude can come about or be sustained without this. It is not, however, a return to the pre-scientific outlook of Luke which is needed, but a recovery, within the new insights of the scientific age, of joy in the goodness and generosity of God to which his writing bears witness. If it is to come about, it will surely be in the pattern which Luke himself describes, as response to what is declared in the gospel and attested in the lives of those whom God has touched.

Our reflections at the conclusion of this study thus lead us back to two points which have been made before but which deserve repetition. In this book we have tried to draw attention to various strands which are woven into the tapestry of the gospel which Luke presents. It has been helpful to do so because they are sometimes neglected and their relationships to each other not recognized. But when that has been done they still need to be seen in their setting. No analysis of the component strands can substitute for the effect of the tapestry as a whole. There is no substitute for the emotive impact of Luke's gospel itself, in which the good news in its totality is related.

The particular strands upon which we have concentrated have been those which give colour and shape to Christian character. We have seen what sort of person Luke expects the Christian disciple to be. We have seen how Luke has spelled that out both by his presentation of the teaching of Jesus and by the examples of godly men and women, supremely by the example of Jesus himself. Our judgment of what a person is cannot be totally separated from what that person does, nor can good actions be considered without reference to the person whose actions they are. Nevertheless, at a time when much emphasis is laid on policies and programmes in church and society it is important to recover from Luke an awareness of the importance of what is 'in the heart'. More important in Christian discipleship than what a person does from time to time is what he or she is, because it is the foundation of what is done, and because the character of the disciple is testimony to the good news of God.

Notes

Frequently quoted works are cited by author's surname or an abbreviation and listed on pp. 211f.

1. Introduction

[1] J. Murray, *A New English Dictionary on Historical Principles*, Oxford 1893, II 280f.

[2] See, e.g. B. H. Streeter, *The Four Gospels*, London, rev. ed. 1930, 150ff.; W. G. Kümmel, *Introduction to the New Testament*, London, rev. ed. 1975, 38ff.

[3] For criticism of Streeter, see e.g. A. M. Farrer, *On Dispensing with Q*, in D. E. Nineham, *Studies*, 55ff.; W. R. Farmer, *The Synoptic Problem*, New York 1964, and for replies, e.g. G. M. Styler, 'The Priority of Mark', in C. F. D. Moule, *The Birth of the New Testament*, London 3rd ed. 1981, 285ff.; C. M. Tuckett, *The Revival of the Griesbach Hypothesis*, Cambridge 1983. Mark actually has more instances of *didaskein, didaskalos, didache* with reference to Jesus than any other gospel, but is little more than half the length of Matthew or Luke. For 'Q' see C. K. Barrett *ET*, LIV, 1943, 320ff.; for 'Proto-Luke' see Streeter, op. cit., 199ff.; V. Taylor, *Behind the Third Gospel*, Oxford 1926, and, in criticism, Kümmel, op. cit., 130ff. For a general introduction see Fitzmyer, 35ff.

[4] For general works on form and redaction criticism see M. Dibelius, *From Tradition to Gospel*, London 1934; R. Bultmann, *History of the Synoptic Tradition*, Oxford 1963; V. Taylor, *Formation of the Gospel Tradition*, London 1935; N. Perrin, *What is Redaction Criticism?* London 1970; J. Rohde, *Rediscovering the Teaching of the Evangelists*, London 1968.

[5] J. Drury, *Tradition and Design in Luke's Gospel*, London 1976; cf. M. D. Goulder, *Midrash and Lection in Matthew*, London 1974.

[6] As, e.g. C. F. Evans, 'The Central Section of St. Luke's Gospel', in Nineham *Studies*, 37ff., Drury op. cit., 75ff., 160. For lectionary theories, see below pp. 145f.

[7] For example, *dei*, 'it is necessary', is a favourite Lucan word, sometimes added to Mark (4.43), but at 9.22 it is also found in the parallel Mark 8.31.

[8] See below pp. 146f.

[9] See Kümmel, op. cit., (n. 2) 147ff.; Fitzmyer, 35ff.; B. E. Beck, *NTS* 23, 1977, 352, Wilson, *Law*, 112, cf. Maddox, *Purpose*, 7–9.

[10] Details of the occurrence of these nouns, and associated verbs and adjectives in Luke and Acts are as follows:

	Noun		Verb		Adjective	
	Luke	Acts	Luke	Acts	Luke	Acts
chara (joy)	8	4	12	7	0	0
pistis (faith, faithfulness)	11	15	9	37	6	4
eirene (peace)	13	7	0	0	0	0
agathosyne (goodness)	0	0	4*	1*	16	3
agape (love)	1	0	13	0	2	1
makrothymia (patience)	0	0	1	0	0	0	+ adverb 1
hypomone (endurance)	2	0	1	1	0	0
tapeinophrosyne (humility)	0	1	0	0	0	0
epieikeia (gentleness)	0	1	0	0	0	0
enkrateia (self-control)	0	1	0	0	0	0
pleonexia (covetousness)	1	0	0	0	0	0
porneia (fornication)	0	3	0	0	0	0
cf. *porne* (harlot)	1	0	0	0	0	0
chrestotes (kindness)	0	0	0	0	2	0
praytes (meekness)	0	0	0	0	0	0

*different verbs: *agathopoiein* (Lk), *agathoergein* (Ac).

Statistics from R. Morgenthaler, *Statistik des neutestamentlichen Wortschatzes*, Zurich and Stuttgart 1958, incorporating corrigenda.

[11] Excluding the Pastorals. The verb *enkrateuesthai* occurs twice in I Cor.
[12] *Porneia, echthra, zelos, thymos, hairesis, methe*, with various meanings.
[13] Luke 24.47; Acts 2.38; 3.19; 5.31; 8.22.
[14] Luke 5.8ff., 20ff., 29ff.; 7.36ff.; 15.1ff.; 18.9ff.; 19.1ff.; Acts 2.38; 3.19; 5.31; 10.43; 13.38; 22.16; 26.18.
[15] *Opheiletes* Luke 13.4; *opheilein* 11.4 (but cf. also 7.41; 16.5, 7; 17.10); *anomos* 22.37 (=Isa. 53.12), Acts 2.23. For the Old Testament see *TDNT* I, 267ff.
[16] The nearest to a purely sociological use of 'sinner' is Luke 24.7, where the Gentiles are intended, but it is far from certain that no more is meant; cf. 23.34. 6.32–4 (contrast Matt. 5.47) similarly does more than describe a social group.
[17] See below ch. 3 p. 31.
[18] For details see Fitzmyer, 469f., 591f., Jeremias, *Theology* I, 109ff.
[19] Although it is frequently claimed that the woman of 7.36ff. was a prostitute, Luke does not say so; evidently he did not think the nature of her sin was significant for the story; Fitzmyer, 689.
[20] Marshall 607. See further Bailey, 161ff., who unfortunately does not explore sufficiently what the cultural assumptions of Luke's readers might have been.
[21] Haenchen, 449f., 468ff.; Bruce, 299f., against *BC*, V, 204ff., but see Wilson, *Law*, 87.
[22] Cf. ch. 8 p. 110.
[23] Wilson, *Law*, 28.

[24] For the meaning of this, cf. Marshall, 516ff.

[25] But note Luke's stress on the heart, to be discussed below, ch. 5 p. 65.

2. Love

[1] For a detailed discussion, see Marshall, 243ff.; Fitzmyer, 627ff.

[2] Fitzmyer, 627; cf. Dupont, I, 299–342.

[3] *Gar* for instance must mark the continuation of a passage rather than a new beginning (against Fitzmyer, 643).

[4] (a) The emphatic 'you' (*hymin*) is only present in the woes (vv. 24, 25a, and as a variant, vv. 25b, 26), suggesting a change of addressees from the beatitudes, and while both vv. 22f. and v. 26 refer to Jewish attitudes ('their fathers'), it is hard to see a historical context for their 'speaking well' of Christians. But Dupont is too precise in identifying the 'you' in v. 26 as unbelieving Jews (III 95, less confidently 97); rather they are uncommitted listeners in the crowd, actually present on the scene. (b) The emphatic *hymin* at v. 27 marks a change back to disciples (Fitzmyer, 637). (c) At v. 39 there is a change of topic but not of audience. Verses 39–45 are governed by the idea of speech and instruction (cf. v. 45), and in this vv. 43f. differ from the parallel Matt. 7.16–18. But 'them' (*autois*), v. 39, is too general for restriction to the twelve. (d) Verse 47, 'everyone', suggests the inclusion of the crowds.

[5] In 6.34f. the point is probably not getting back the capital sum lent, nor the interest on it, but being able to count on a loan for ourselves when our turn comes to need one, i.e. the rich lending to the rich (cf. Marshall, 264).

[6] On the reverential passive see Dalman, 224–6.

[7] Fitzmyer, 635; D. R. A. Hare, *The Theme of Jewish Persecution of Christians in the Gospel according to St. Matthew*, Cambridge 1967, 53f. (social ostracism but not a formal ban); but cf. Marshall, 252ff.

[8] Fitzmyer, 640; cf. 17.9; but it is possible to see *charis* as God's approval (cf. 1.30) or as a quality of character of which God approves, cf. 2.52; Acts 2.47.

[9] Bornkamm, Barth and Held, 16, 60, 123; Hill, 110; cf. Fitzmyer, 631.

[10] They are discussed in Marshall, 440–6.

[11] See R. Bultmann, *TDNT* II, 479ff.

[12] Note that at 4.36 Luke omits any suggestion that Jesus brings a new teaching; contrast Mark 1.27. Cf. below ch. 8 p. 110.

[13] Marshall, 446 rightly rejects the suggestion of G. Sellin that 'who is my neighbour?' means 'who belongs to the people of the covenant?' The lawyer is to imitate the Samaritan, not regard him as a fellow Israelite because of his compassion for the victim.

[14] In the light of 16.15 we should probably conclude that Luke intends v. 29, 'desiring to justify himself', in an unfavourable sense also.

[15] Cf. Wilson, *Law*, 15, 24.

[16] MSS differ in vv. 41f. as to whether Martha is rebuked because she is fussing over many things when the need is for only few things (for the meal) or for only one (namely being a disciple like Mary). Some MSS have other variations. They do not affect the basic point: either way Mary has chosen what is essential and must not be diverted. See Marshall 450ff.

[17] C. Spicq, *Agape in the New Testament*, St Louis and London 1963, I 119; cf. Marshall, 498.

[18] Marshall, 496f.

[19] F. Büchsel, *TDNT* III, 942.

[20] Creed 166; Godet II, 80; cf. Thompson, 180.

[21] There are some remaining examples of *eleos* referring to God's love for Israel in Luke 1, but they do not bear directly on the present discussion.

3. Wealth – I

[1] For recent studies see Degenhardt, *Lukas*; Dupont, *Béatitudes*; Johnson, *Possessions*; R. J. Karris, 'Poor and Rich: the Lukan Sitz im Leben' in Talbert, *Perspectives*, 112–25; Mealand, *Poverty and Expectation*.

[2] The problems are surveyed in Marshall, 614ff.; cf. also Fitzmyer, 1095ff. and *Essays*, 161–84.

[3] Jeremias, *Parables*, 46f. Verses 8–13 are unlikely be Lucan in origin, as they lack a clear progression of thought. There are catchword links and v. 13 is parallel to Matt. 6.24. Against Marshall 619 and *JTS* n.s. 19, 1968, 617–9, I take vv. 8f. as separate sentences, v. 8a as the householder's reaction, v. 8b as an explanation of it at the end of the parable, and v. 9 as Jesus' application of the parable.

[4] Note the association of words, lost in English, between *oikonomos*, 'steward', and *oikous*, 'houses', vv. 1,4.

[5] J. D. M. Derrett, *NTS* 7, 1961, 198ff., and for Gentile practice, *Studies in New Testament* I 1–3. But it is difficult to sustain his translation of *epenesen*, v. 8, as 'ratified' (*NTS* 7, 210, n. 3). For a less technical version see Fitzmyer, *Essays* 174ff.

[6] For parallels in the Dead Sea Scrolls for this usage, cf. Ellis, 201, and Marshall, 621 citing H. Kosmala. In Luke, see 18.6; cf. 11.13 for a similar use of 'evil' simply to contrast human nature with God's goodness, and the use of 'sinners' in contrast to disciples at 6.32–4. 'Mammon' means wealth, but not necessarily in a bad sense, for a good sense is implied in the contrast of v. 11.

[7] This reading of 16.9 is confirmed by the interpretation of chapter 12 given above. *Ek tou mamona* is rightly translated 'by means of mammon'. The 'friends' to be acquired are not good works (as Jeremias, *Parables*, 46, n. 85) but the recipients of generosity. The 'failure' of mammon refers not to running short of cash but to the ultimate failure of all things at death. The subject of 'they may receive' (*dexontai*) may be the friends or more probably the angels of God as at 16.22 (conceivably God himself, cf. 12.20).

[8] *Allotrio* (v. 12, 'another's' RSV) is sometimes interpreted as 'belonging to God', contrasted with 'your own' (Marshall, 623), but 'your own' must be God's gift also. The word doubtless echoes the steward's handling of his master's goods in the parable, but it can also mean 'foreign' as at Ex. 2.22, Acts 7.6, with reference to Israel's exile in Egypt. The contrast may then be between the treasure of the land of exile (this world) and that of the promised land (the age to come), to which the disciples now belong, and for which they must prepare. In v. 11 'unrighteous' (see n. 6) and 'true' imply the same contrast. There is no noun with 'true' in Greek; 'mammon' is implied; RSV supplies 'riches'.

[9] *Eis ten genean heauton* ('in their generation' RSV) must mean 'in their dealings with their society' (against Derrett, *NTS* 7, 1961, 365 n.1). For this

meaning of 'generation', see Leaney, 222: society with a particular moral character rather than contemporaries in a particular period of time.

[10] An alternative view of the parable is presented by Bailey, 86ff. The debtors have rented land and must pay a proportion of the produce. Before the news of his dismissal gets out and he is still taken as acting on orders ('quickly'), the steward reduces the amounts owing. The master, a generous man, must uphold this action or appear mean. The steward trusts his mercy and gains a good reputation for himself. This view is attractive but concentrates on the original parable rather than Luke's understanding and mistakenly sets aside vv. 9–13, allowing theories about the structure of the passage too much weight.

[11] Jeremias, *Parables*, 178f., 183; Marshall, 633; Fitzmyer, 1125ff. Cf. also below ch. 9 p. 136.

[12] Marshall, 636.

[13] Basically the first born had a double portion, Deut. 21.17. For details see *Mishnah* B.B.8–9, and for the joint holding of inherited property cf. Marshall, 522.

[14] Note the plurals 'them' and 'you', hardly just the two brothers. Luke uses elsewhere the device of a speaker from the crowd, which enables him to present Jesus replying to the whole group represented by the individual. Cf. 11.27; 14.15, and especially on 18.18 below.

[15] Either version fits v. 14. NEB prepares for vv. 13–21, RSV for vv. 22–34 and so for the passage as a whole. With RSV are Turner in MH III, 146 and AG, 656; with NEB and JB, Zerwick *Analysis*, I, 230; Creed, 173. NEB would surely require *oude* for *ouk*.

[16] *Apaitousin*, 'ask back'. Either the subject is the angels or the plural is an oblique reverential reference to God (cf. n. 7 and ch. 2 n. 6); but God is the speaker here.

[17] Cf. Ps. 14.1; 53.1; 94.8; Luke 11.40. Contrast 16.8.

[18] For the verbal echoes cf. *euphrainou*, 12.19; *euphrainomenos*, 16.19; *ta agatha*, 12.18, 16.25; *anekleipton*, 12.33; *hotan eklipe*, 16.9.

[19] E.g. Marshall, 264.

[20] Cf. Marshall, 584–7; Hill, 301f.; Jeremias, *Parables*, 63–70; Fitzmyer, 1050ff.

[21] Verse 24 is intelligible as part of the parable in spite of the plural 'you', which remains difficult if it is taken as Jesus' comment (cf. the singular in v. 16). Perhaps here and 19.26 similarly Luke is sliding into application without abandoning the parable (cf. Jeremias, *Parables*, 177f.). A reference to sending portions to absent guests (Marshall, 591) is unlikely, for Neh. 8.10–12 does not refer to guests who have refused to attend; the host is simply determined not to leave vacant places for anyone who might change his mind.

[22] For their wealth cf. Jeremias, *Parables*, 177. That the guests are formally invoking the exemptions permitted in Deut. 20.5–7 to avoid partaking in the Holy War and its victory feast (J. D. M. Derrett, *Law in the New Testament*, London 1970, 126ff.) is incredible in Luke's setting. In any case the parallels are far from exact.

[23] Grundmann, 295, 299 argues that the poor, etc., of vv. 13, 21 represent unclean categories excluded from the congregation (II Sam. 5.8; IQS 2.4ff.;

cf. IQSa 2.5–7; CD 13.4–7; Marshall, 584). But the reason Luke explicitly gives is their inability to return favours.

[24] Or Jesus, if v. 24 is his comment on the parable.

[25] Of course nothing should be made of 'compel' (*anankason*) in v. 23 which merely means 'don't take no for an answer'. Cf *parabiazesthai* in 24.29; Acts 16.15.

[26] So also in part Marshall, 683ff.

[27] There is no reference to loving God, unless there is an echo of Deut. 6.4 in 'no one is good except one, God' (*heis ho theos*) v. 19.

[28] As at 5.11, 28 (cf. Mark 2.14). 'All' is a word of which Luke is particularly fond.

[29] *Ta idia*, Mark, 'everything'. Cf. Acts 21.26; AG, 370.3.b. 'Property' is also a possible translation and it has been claimed that Luke here depicts the disciples as having abandoned private property (Johnson, 162, 177), but this does not correspond with the changes Luke makes in v. 29.

[30] *Oikia* should probably be translated 'home' here rather than 'house'. Though *oikos* is Luke's more usual word for 'household', *oikia* is not always restricted to bricks and mortar, cf. 10.7; 20.47 (so too Marshall, 688). The changes Luke makes in v. 29 explain why he can say 'manifold more' in v. 30 (in some manuscripts 'sevenfold more'), in contrast to 12.31 where material needs are in view.

[31] The difficulties are discussed in Marshall 490–96, whose general conclusions are followed here. There are two main approaches: (*a*) to limit the reference throughout, as in Matthew, to vessels contaminated by the users' greed; *hymon* in v. 39 is taken with *harpages* ('the inside is full of (contaminated by) your rapacity'), and *ta enonta* in v. 41 then refers to the (metaphorical) contents of the cup ('give alms from what is in it', i.e. from what you have acquired by your rapacity); (*b*) to take *hymon* with *to esothen* ('the inside of yourselves') parallel to the 'outside of the cup', and to supply a further *hymon* with *ta enonta* ('what is within you'); there is then an overlapping reference to vessels and users: 'within you are full of rapacity and wickedness . . . give alms with respect to what is within you.' For all the difficulties, (*b*) is a more satisfactory rendering of the Greek.

[32] Against Marshall, 491, 495, once Luke's version of v. 41 is admitted to be secondary, the possibility that it was linked to vv. 37f. in 'Q' is lost. Verses 37f. deals with washing persons, vv. 39–41 with washing cups. Only Luke's editing produces a link, slight as it is. The real point of vv. 37f. in Luke is to introduce the whole section.

[33] Taking *ta enonta* as accusative of respect; RSV only fits a reference to the contents of the cup. Cf. Marshall, 495.

[34] It is no argument against this that Jesus does not practise the ritual. He is not depicted as tithing either, in spite of v. 42. These imperatives are directed to Pharisees; Christian readers are not expected to observe them.

[35] See Marshall, 696ff.

[36] Commentators tend to regard the two words as synonyms and to treat *zemiotheis* as a commercial metaphor of loss as opposed to gain in v. 25a (cf. Marshall, 375; Fitzmyer, 788). This is normal New Testament usage, though it is not a common word. But the meaning 'fine', 'penalty' is well established in Greek and should be considered here; cf. I Cor. 3.15, though

there is no suggestion in Luke of the use to which Paul puts it. Rather we should think of 12.20.

[37] See above ch. 1, p. 13.

[38] Cf. Marshall, 666.

[39] Marshall, 664.

[40] See ch. 6 pp. 83f.

[41] The point about soldiers being satisfied with wages is of course not to discourage salary increases but to prohibit supplementing them by extortion from a defenceless population.

[42] Marshall, 721.

[43] Cf. Marshall, 750–52.

[44] Marshall, 349ff., 353f., 412f., 417f.; Fitzmyer, 751ff. Matt. 10.9f. incorporates features from both Mark and Luke. Luke's word for 'money' (*argyrion*, silver) seems to imply Greek coinage rather than the Roman copper of Mark, perhaps reflecting the respective milieux of the gospels.

[45] The translation of 22.36 is difficult. See Marshall, 824f.

[46] See ch. 4, n. 16. I do not discuss here the 'communism' of Acts 2.44f., 4.32ff., as it falls outside the scope of this book, but it should be observed that what is described there is not renunciation of material wealth but voluntary sharing (cf. 4.34f.; 5.4). The idealistic language suggests that Luke admires this mutual concern and encourages its imitation (cf. 20.35), but he does not describe the practice outside Jerusalem.

4. Wealth – II

[1] Cf. 9.26; 10.12, 14; 11.2; 12.39f., 46; 17.24ff.; 18.8; 21.25–36; 22.18; Acts 1.11; 17.31.

[2] Conzelmann, esp. 95–136, and in criticism, E. E. Ellis, 'The Function of Eschatology in Luke' and W. G. Kümmel, 'Luc en accusation dans la théologie contemporaine', both in F. Neirynck, *L'Evangile de Luc*, Gembloux 1973, 141ff., 93ff.; S. G. Wilson, *NTS* 16, 1970, 330ff.; Maddox, *Purpose*, 100ff.

[3] Maddox, *Purpose*, 50, refers the parable to the rejection of Jesus by the Jews at the crucifixion, but the rejection occurs in the parable after the departure to the far country and must refer to the time of the church.

[4] Manuscripts vary between 'into' (*eis*), referring to the beginning of Jesus' rule, and 'in' (*en*; RSV), referring to Jesus' coming possessed of power, without indicating when the power was assumed. The former is probably the better reading (Metzger, *Commentary*, 181, but cf. Marshall, 872).

[5] This view is based on the Jewish understanding of paradise. Cf. Jeremias, *TDNT* V, 769–71.

[6] Cf. Dupont, *Béatitudes*, III 133–35.

[7] Cf. IV Macc. 7.18f.; 16.25, a close parallel.

[8] 20.34–8 is Lucan work and other data must be interpreted in the light of it. 'All' in v. 38 must mean 'all who are worthy' after v. 35. This is the 'resurrection of the just' to which 14.14 refers, a phrase which combines a reference to those who qualify with an allusion to the quality of life to which they are raised. In both passages Luke is interested in resurrection only as entry to bliss, but there is no conflict with Acts 24.15, which also alludes to

the lot of those who are not 'counted worthy'. Cf. Luke 12.5, 46; 16.23–26. If anything, it is Acts 24.15 which is unrepresentative of Luke (against Conzelmann, 110f.). The physical character of Jesus' resurrection body is stressed (Luke 24.36ff.) to prove he has risen, but (in spite of Acts 26.23) has no bearing on Luke's view of the general resurrection.

[9] This view is essentially Dupont's *Béatitudes*, III 109–147. 12.5 is also best taken this way, as Dupont does. In the light of it, however, his insistence that Luke does not speak of judgment at death (III 139–42) seems mistaken.

[10] 17.34, literally 'on this night', refers not to the night on which Jesus speaks but to the time just mentioned in the context, as in other examples of *houtos* (cf. 1.39; 6.12; 13.22; 19.15; 21.22 (after *tote* 'then'), 23.7).

[11] Even in the gospel Luke can depict Jesus as already the Lord (e.g. 12.41f.) and the kingdom as already present in his ministry (11.20; 17.21) – against C. F. D. Moule (as cited in ch. 7, n. 23) 159ff. In Acts though he is absent his work continues through his name (3.16). This suggests that Luke saw 11.20; 17.21 as true of the time of the church also; cf. Acts 16.17f.; 19.11f.

[12] Johnson, 139 thinks the tax-collectors are included among the poor because they are outcasts; Mealand, 57 rightly regards them as rich.

[13] Manson, *Sayings*, 47; R. E. Brown, *Birth*, 350–65.

[14] Cf. Marshall, 249.

[15] This is a view of Dupont, *Béatitudes*, III, 21–28, 96f. He takes all four beatitudes as a comprehensive description of one group, but there is no need for this.

[16] On the contrary, Acts 4.34f. depicts a church which, because of the sharing of goods, was without poverty (cf. Dupont, *Béatitudes*, III, 194).

[17] This is D. L. Mealand's thesis (ch. 3, n. 1.).

[18] Cf. ch. 3, n. 1., esp. pp. 27–36, 208ff.

[19] Cadbury, 262f.; Karris (ch. 3, n. 1.) 114, 116.

[20] The sayings about anxiety, 12.22ff., particularly derive their force originally from their reference to those who had literally abandoned everything to follow Jesus (Jeremias, *Theology* I, 236).

[21] E.g. Tobit 12.8–10; cf. Matt. 6.1–18.

[22] Above, ch. 2 p. 20.

[23] It is sometimes argued that *euangelizesthai* in Luke-Acts means no more than 'to preach', without emphasis on good news, partly because it seems to be interchangeable with *keryssein* ('preach'), *didaskein* ('teach') and other verbs, partly because good news is thought inappropriate at Luke 3.18 (and at Acts 14.15; Rev. 14.6). Luke uses the noun 'gospel' only at Acts 15.7; 20.24 (Fitzmyer I 148, 173f.). The idea of good news is strong however in the Isaiah quotation at 4.18, echoed at 7.22, and is likely to have left its mark on other instances (Marshall, *Historian*, 123f.). Moreover, the notion that a summons (and implied invitation) to repent before the coming of judgment cannot be good news deserves to be questioned. The chance of repentance is a gift of grace (cf. Luke 13.1–5).

5. A sense of God

[1] *Ekstasis, existanai, thaumazein, thambos, ekthambos, ekplessesthai.*

[2] For this interpretation of 2.19 see *MNT*, 147–52 and below ch. 8 p. 114f.

[3] Luke 5.15; 6.17f.; 7.22; 10.24; cf. 2.20; Acts 2.33; 4.20; 8.6; 10.44; 13.7, 44; 22.15.

[4] Surprisingly Luke does not reproduce Mark 1.15, perhaps because he prefers to link repentance with the coming of Jesus rather than the nearness of the kingdom; but his alternative account of the opening of Jesus' ministry brings out the issues clearly enough (4.16ff.). For repentance and conversion cf. Fitzmyer, 237ff.; Marshall, *Historian*, 193ff.

[5] In 6.43–6, however, as Luke has it, the 'fruit' required is expressed in speech.

[6] Luke stresses the fear behind their request at 8.37 and omits the wonder at the man's reports of his healing (v. 39; Mark 5.20).

[7] See *MNT*, 113.

[8] By moving the reference to fear from its position in Mark 9.6, Luke makes the cloud of the divine presence rather than the transfiguration its cause. For the difficulties of the details 9.34 see Fitzmyer, 802; Marshall, 387.

[9] Cf. H. Balz, *TDNT* IX, 207,213.

[10] G. Wanke, *TDNT* IX, 201–3.

[11] See below pp. 78f.

[12] Luke has modelled this narrative on II Macc. 9. Cf. B. E. Beck in Horbury and McNeil, 29.

[13] Cf. e.g. I Kings 8.31ff.; 21.27ff.; II Kings 22.18f.; Isa. 2.12ff.; Ezek. 28; Job 8.1–8.

[14] A. Jülicher, *Die Gleichnisreden Jesu*, Tübingen 1910, II, 246–254; R. Bultmann, *History of the Synoptic Tradition*, Oxford 1963, 104, 178f.; M. Dibelius, *From Tradition to Gospel*, London 1934, 119, 248 (Luke misunderstanding his source); R. N. Soulen, *Handbook of Biblical Criticism*, London 1977, 82, 119ff.

[15] Cf. above ch. 3 p. 35.

[16] Cf. below ch. 10 p. 151 and n. 13.

[17] Luke only: *ainein, anthomologeisthai, eulogein, skirtan, synchairein*; others: *agallian, doxazein, eucharistein, exomologeisthai, megalynein, chairein* (expressions of blessing/glorifying human beings are not included in the count).

[18] In 5.30, 34 the issue is eating and drinking; it is not just the neglect of fasting but the positive celebration to which the Pharisees object (cf. Mark 2.16, 18). The time will come when in the absence of Jesus fasting will become appropriate again (although it has only a limited place in Acts); until then not even compulsion can impose fasting (v. 34).

[19] For God and social rejoicing cf. A. F. Walls, *NT* 3, 1959, 314–6.

[20] For recent discussion of the canticles see Brown, *Birth*, 346–65, 377–91, 425–7, 456–60; Fitzmyer, 357–62, 375–9, 397, 422, where evidence for the statements made here can be found.

[21] *Dialogizesthai* and *dialogismos*, in the sense of thought rather than discussion. Cf. also *en heauto legein*. *Kardia* occurs 22 times in Luke as against 11 in Mark, 16 in Matthew, 7 in John, and 20 times in Acts.

[22] 'Pretended to be' (RSV) translates *hypokrinomenous*, the verb related to 'hypocrisy'.

[23] For 2.34ff. see below ch. 8, pp. 115f., for 12.2f. see ch. 9, pp. 141ff., ch. 10, pp. 165f.

[24] 'Honest and good' (*kale kai agathe*) probably reflects the term commonly used in Hellenistic morals of perfect behaviour, *kalokagathos*. The phrase should be taken with 'holding fast' rather than with 'hearing'.

[25] For studies of Luke's ideas of prayer see O. F. Harris *Prayer in Luke–Acts*; A. A. Trites 'The Prayer Motif in Luke–Acts' in Talbert *Perspectives*, 168–86. For vocabulary see Harris, 13ff.

[26] Harris, 197.

[27] Harris, 73ff., Jeremias, *Prayer*, 9f.; *Theology* I, 193f.

[28] Harris, 217–20.

[29] Below pp. 85, 119.

[30] Cf. Marshall, 454ff. for the longer form and other alternative readings.

[31] Cf. Ezek. 36.23; Marshall, 457; Jeremias, *Theology* I, 198. *Hagiastheto* is a 'reverential passive' (cf. ch. 2, n. 6), meaning 'cause your name to be acknowledged as holy'.

[32] *Opheilonti* may be retained from the source (cf. Matt. 6.12) in the Hebraic understanding of sin as a debt to God (cf. Marshall, 460f.), but it is tempting to see also an echo of the call for generosity to debtors in 6.31–5. Otherwise Luke could have written *hamartanonti* to match *hamartias* in the previous line.

[33] *Me eisenenkes* means 'do not allow us to give way to' rather than 'lead us not into', cf. Marshall, 461f. Without the definite article it is doubtful whether 'temptation' can mean the final eschatological test (Jeremias, *Theology* I, 202; *Prayer*, 29).

[34] *Epiousios* ('daily' RSV) probably means 'for the coming day', cf. Marshall, 458f.

[35] For *anaideia* as the petitioner's audacity, see Harris, 87. It is doubtful whether it can refer to the householder's unwillingness to be put to shame (Marshall, 465). It means the deplorable absence of proper shame rather than the desirable freedom from it. Rabbinic parallels (Jeremias, *Parables*, 158, n. 27) are irrelevant for Luke's Greek. In spite of the apparent parallel to the judge in 18.1–8 the attention is focussed here on the petitioner's action (as on the widow's).

[36] As in Matthew, the preceding verses require a reference to 'good gifts' in v. 13.

[37] Cf. ch. 3 p. 32 and 18.28–30, p. 38.

[38] Jeremias, *Prayer*, 17–21; *Theology* I, 61–8, 197.

[39] Note 'each day' (*kath' hemeran*) and the continuous present tense *didou* in v. 3 (cf. Matt. 6.11).

6. Faith

[1] For a study of faith in Luke–Acts cf. S. Brown, 36ff. In addition to the difficulties noted below, his work suffers from too rigid a distinction between faith at conversion and the continuing faith of Christians, as though one did not imply the other unless explicitly mentioned. Luke's use is more fluid. For the New Testament generally, cf. *TDNT* VI, 174ff.

[2] Acts 4.48; 8.12f.; 9.42; 11.17, 21; 13.12, 48; 14,1; 15.7; 17.12, 34; 18.8; 19.2, 4.

[3] The related verb at Acts 3.19; 9.35; 11.21; 14.15; 15.19; 26.18, 20; 28.27; (cf. also Luke 1.16; 22.32).

[4] With S. Brown, 42 against Haenchen, 437 n. 3 on 14.27.

[5] Acts 5.14; 9.42; 10.43; 11.17, 21; 14.23; 16.31, 34; 18.8; 20.21; 24.24.

[6] See Acts 4.4; 8.12; 10.43; 13.38f., 48; 14.9; 15.7, 11; 16.31; 18.8; 20.21; 26.18; and cf. 2.37f. with 2.40f. and 44. Cf. Haenchen, 412. A distinction is sometimes drawn between faith in the message and faith in Jesus, but 20.32 shows how for Luke one stands behind the other.

[7] It is not agreed how often this is so. Cf. S. Brown, 42ff. (a) 15.9 must not be isolated from vv. 7–11. Although there is no reference to Cornelius' faith in ch. 10, it is clear in 15.7. Further, the parallels with 14.9; 16.31 rule out 'hope' for 'believe' in 15.11 (against S. Brown, 41). All this points to the translation 'their faith' in 15.9 (cf. Haenchen, 440, 445). (b) 14.22 is ambiguous, but must be taken in context, and in the light of v. 23 'their faith' must remain a possible translation (cf. v. 21). Bruce, 285 refers to 11.23; 13.43 which would rather point to 'the faith preached'. (c) 16.5 is also ambiguous but the similarity with 14.22 should be noted.

[8] Against S. Brown, 40ff., who thinks there is no continuing faith in Jesus in the language of Acts. He allows 22.19 on p. 41 but by p. 48 ignores it. He treats 6.5; 11.24 as 'charismatic faith', and plays down the meaning of the perfect tenses, treating the perfect participles as meaning 'those in a condition resulting from past belief'. But it is difficult to take this condition as anything other than continuing faith, especially at 16.34; 19.18, and, with the pluperfect indicative, at 14.23. Even if *pistos* in 10.45; 16.1 effectively means 'Christian' it refers to the present not the past, and characterises 'Christian' as 'believing'. He takes no account of *epikaleisthai*.

[9] Cf. *TDNT* VI, 204, 215. The present participle has too many uses for us to be dogmatic in every instance. 10.43 is a general statement in the context of conversion. If 5.14 qualifies 'were added to the Lord' it refers to conversion (Haenchen, 243; S. Brown, 40, n. 144). The alternative is 'believing in the Lord', continuous faith.

[10] The use of *epikaleisthai* derives from the key text in Acts 2.21 (=Joel 3.5). Cf. Rom. 10.12f. There is also the question of 'full of faith' in 6.5; 11.24. S. Brown describes this as 'charismatic faith' (p. 40), but it should be noted that in 11.24 it is linked, not with miracles but with preaching and discernment of God's grace. In 6.8 miracles are linked, not with faith but with power. As 'full' makes clear, what Stephen and Barnabas possessed was not a different sort of faith but an outstanding degree of the common faith.

[11] Cf. P. J. Achtemeier, 'The Lukan Perspective on the Miracles of Jesus', in Talbert, *Perspectives*, 159. At the same time to ask for a sign is a mark of unbelief, cf. 11.29; 1.18–20.

[12] Cf. H. J. Cadbury in *BC* IV, 37; Bruce, 110; Haenchen, 207; Marshall, *Acts*, 92.

[13] Luke 5.17; 6.19; 7.11–17; 8.46 (cf. Mark 5.30); 13.10–13; 14.2–6; 22.51; Acts 5.15; 6.8; 9.32–35; 19.11f. Cf. J. M. Hull, *Hellenistic Magic and the Synoptic Tradition*, London 1974, 87ff. and in reply Achtemeier, op. cit., 161ff.

[14] Cf. Acts 22.3, and above, ch. 2 p. 24.

[15] Cf. Marshall, 652.

[16] Cf. the discussion in Marshall, 304ff.; Fitzmyer, 684ff.

[17] Jeremias' argument (*Parables*, 127) quoted by Fitzmyer, 690 only shows that 'love' in Hebrew, Aramaic and Syriac can *imply* gratitude, not that *agapan* in Luke 7.42, 47 can be *translated* 'feel/show thankfulness'. It is doubtful if H. G. Wood's three examples (*ET*, LXVI, 10.1955, 319f.) are enough to establish an independent Greek usage. Cf. Fitzmyer's reference to Qumran and his further remark (p. 687) that the reference to faith qualifies the woman's attitude to Jesus in terms of its basic orientation to God. Cf. also thanks to Jesus and glory to God at 17.16–18.

[18] The aorist is the minority reading but has good support from B, L and a few other manuscripts, and is now adopted, as the present is regarded as due to the influence of Mark 5.36. The aorist is not finally secure, however, as it may have been influenced by Acts 16.31.

[19] It may be, as Achtemeier has suggested, that Luke sees the man's faith as instrumental to the cure, so that 'believe' is not, as in Mark, just a positive way of saying 'do not be afraid'. Achtemeier, op. cit., 163.

[20] Cf. above ch. 3 p. 37 and p. 191 n. 14.

[21] For a study of salvation in Luke see Marshall, *Historian*, 77ff.; cf. also Fitzmyer, 222f.

[22] Another reason to resist the isolation of certain texts as referring to 'charmismatic faith'; see n. 10.

[23] Cf. Fitzmyer, 9.

[24] *Kai stethi . . . kai anastas este* added to Mark's *egeire eis to meson*.

[25] Acts 3.15; 4.33; 5.32; 10.39, 41; 13.31; cf. Luke 24.48. Cf. Marshall, *Historian*, 42f.

[26] Cf. *TDNT* IV, 492–4, but in view of his vision Stephen is more than 'the confessional witness'.

[27] *TDNT* IV, 503f. 21.13 is probably addressed to disciples (cf. 21.5 with 20.45), but there is nothing to restrict it to the twelve (although Luke may have had the events of Acts in mind); 20.45 suggests the crowd were at least expected to be listening in.

[28] Against S. Brown, 47, they are genuine Christians, otherwise there can be no talk of apostasy. The story of Simon Magus (Acts 8.9–24), which he cites, tells against him, for Simon, a believer, illustrates the corrupting influence of money, and at the end shows evidence of repentance. Cf. Acts 19.18f. for another example of believers who only later finally relinquish their magical leanings. This is not to make their faith only 'exterior' unless the beginning has to be judged by the sequel. For joy as a sign of conversion cf. Acts 8.39; 13.48. It is a mistake to take 'believe' in Luke 8.13 as a reference to conversion. This is covered by 'receive the word'. *Pros kairon* means not, 'only for the present moment' but 'for a limited time'. 8.13 is thus another example of faith after conversion.

[29] Against Conzelmann, 98. Cf. Acts 7.10f., 52; 9.4f.; 8.1; 11.19; 13.50; 20.23; 22.4, 7f.; 26.11, 14f.

[30] Against S. Brown, 14; Fitzmyer, 714. Brown's argument that Luke uses the singular *peirasmos* with a different meaning from the plural (p. 9) cannot be sustained. Cf. Marshall, 326.

[31] S. Brown, 25f., 28.

[32] Cf. *TDNT* IV, 585ff. For the idea of endurance of suffering cf. I Peter 2.20 etc.; for waiting for a delayed parousia, Conzelmann, 103f., 128f.; for

perseverance, S. Brown, 50, though with a different view of other details from that taken here.

[33] For differing views see Conzelmann, 125; Marshall, 752ff. All agree that Mark was at least part of the basis for Luke. It is hard to prove he used any additional connected source.

[34] Conzelmann, 125ff.

[35] Cf. Marshall, 252ff. and, with less emphasis, Fitzmyer, 634f. See the discussion above ch. 2 pp. 19f.

[36] S. Brown, 49.

[37] The strongest argument for a literal meaning of v. 18 is the use of the same OT proverb in Acts 27.34. Cf. especially I Sam. 14.45; I Kings 1.52. While v. 18 cannot have been invented on the basis of 12.7, the earlier passage may have suggested the use of the proverb here. It certainly warns against a literal interpretation. Cf. Marshall, 767ff. That Luke anticipated disciples facing death is also suggested by the passion narrative (below pp. 191ff.).

[38] S. Brown, 118; cf. ch. 3 pp. 41f.

[39] How far back does the exhortation to perseverance refer? It is possible that it includes resistance to the false claims of deceivers in v. 8, who in the name of Christ invite Christians to apostasy. 'Do not go after them' implies, not going out into the desert, but becoming their disciples.

[40] *Merimnais biotikais, merimnoi . . . tou biou*. Cf. also 12.41ff.

[41] For a review of the interpretations of this verse cf. D. R. Catchpole, *NT* 19, 1977, 81ff.; Marshall, 669ff. In spite of the definite article, *ten pistin*, 'faith' here cannot mean 'true Christianity' or 'preaching of the gospel' (Creed, 224; S. Brown, 45, who has not in fact proved that '*pistis* is never used by Luke of the active faith of Christians'; see n. 8). The article might be an Aramaism (Jeremias, *Parables*, 155, n. 13) but as the whole section in Luke from 17.5 has contained references to faith, 17.26ff. deals with the substance of loyal perseverance and 18.1 ('not lose heart') with its opposite, the article could well be anaphoric ('the faith I have been referring to'). Cf. 3.8; Acts 11.18.

[42] Whatever the solution to the problem of *makrothymei*, the idea of delay is clearly conveyed by the general tenor of the paragraph (Marshall, 674).

[43] Or 'suddenly', *en tachei* (Marshall, 675).

[44] The aspect of loyalty is also present in the use of *pistos*, 'faithful' or 'trustworthy' in 12.42; 16.10–12; 19.17, combined with the thought of obedience.

[45] S. Brown, 57–81.

[46] There is a distinction between 'you' (plural, *hymon*) in 22.31 and 'you' (singular, *sou*) in v. 32. This cannot be explained away as the incorporation of earlier tradition, or necessitated only by the prophecy of the denial (S. Brown, 73).

[47] *Epistrepsas* ('turned again', RSV) is the Lucan word for 'be converted'; cf. above, pp. 144f. and *TDNT* VII, 727. For 'sifting' cf. Marshall, 820f.; it must mean 'separate the good from the bad', and the implication is that the disciples will fail the test. For the metaphor cf. 3.17.

[48] Luke has modified Mark 14.30 by changing 'deny me' to 'deny that you know me' (v. 34, adding *me eidenai*), and in v. 57 Peter declares 'I do not

know him'. But v. 61, referring back to v. 34, reads simply 'deny me'. No distinction can be drawn between this and the kind of denial envisaged in 12.9. Mark too illustrates Peter's denying Jesus with 'I do not know this man' (14.71; cf. S. Brown, 69–71).

[49] See p. 124. Cf. also Acts 14.22 (cf. S. Brown, 45, 116, although the faith is not in the kerygma but in the Lord (14.23) and there is nothing to show that the sufferings are only collective). It is ironic that 'outside the christological sphere' Brown admits that Luke depicts the disciples losing faith (p. 72; cf. 12.28; 17.5f.). Faith cannot be so sharply compartmentalized.

[50] See below ch. 8 p. 114.

[51] The details of Luke's understanding of 8.22–25 are far from certain. It is clear that in Matthew the story is to be read as an allegory of the church under threat (cf. Bornkamm, Barth and Held, 52–57). How far is this true of Luke? Does the storm arise only because Jesus is asleep (cf. v. 23)? Is their sense of danger illusory because they would have survived in spite of the storm? Does Luke intend an allegory of Jesus' death and resurrection?

[52] Cf. Marshall, 334; Fitzmyer, 730; S. Brown, 58f. Although only Matthew uses the word 'save' (8.25), it is clear that in all three gospels the disciples' cry that they are 'perishing' implies this.

[53] Cf. Marshall, 643–5.

[54] *Tosauten*, 'so great' (RSV, loosely, 'such').

[55] S. Brown, 39 (italics his), quoting Bultmann in *TDNT* VI, 206; but note Bultmann's next sentence, 'this *pistis* is fundamentally the faith of prayer'. Cf. above, nn. 10 and 22.

7. *Discipleship*

[1] Cf. for what follows K. N. Giles, 'The Church in the Gospel of Luke', *SJT* 34.2, 1981, 121ff.

[2] Luke identifies the apostles with the twelve explicitly at 6.13 and at 9.1, 10, but they are also disciples, 9.12, 16, so that it is not always clear who is in mind. The twelve are introduced at 9.12 (cf. Mark 6.35) presumably because of the twelve baskets, but it is not clear why the apostles are specified at 17.5.

[3] Cf. Giles, art. cit., 130.

[4] Above pp. 24 and 74.

[5] 'The word' is a Marcan phrase (2.2; 4.14ff., 33). Luke takes it over (cf. 1.2), adds 'of God' (8.11), and adds it to Mark at 4.32, 36. Cf. also 10.39; 11.28.

[6] For *katechethes* in this sense in 1.4, cf. Acts 18.25.

[7] Cf. 2.40, 52; 7.35 (cf. Matt. 11.19); 11.31 (=Matt. 12.42); Acts 6.3, 10; 7.10, 22. But Mark 6.2=Matt. 11.19 is represented by Luke 4.22.

[8] Mark 1.39 refers to the whole of Galilee, which Luke alters to Judaea (4.44), probably meaning only 'Jewish territory', Fitzmyer, 557f.; Marshall, 198f.

[9] This is more plausible than Conzelmann's explanation of the lake as a 'dead sea' reserved for manifestations of Jesus' power (Conzelmann, 42). Only once, at 7.1 (cf. Mark 8.5) does Jesus re-visit Capernaum.

[10] *Peirasmois* here cannot mean 'dangers' (S. Brown, 9), nor can 22.28 refer to a period which is only just beginning (Conzelmann, 80f., 83, 199f.).

[11] 23.35 is difficult. 23.27, 48 (note *theoria, theoresantes*) suggest the crowd is sympathetic in v. 35 (cf. G. W. H. Lampe, *Peake's Commentary on the Bible* ed. M. Black and H. H. Rowley, London 1962, 734a). But Ps. 22.8f., 18 LXX (cf. the quotation in v. 34) and the usual meaning of *de kai* (='also') suggest hostility.

[12] Cf. ch. 10 pp. 158f. and p. 208 n. 31.

[13] Cf. e.g. Ellis, 146ff.

[14] Cf. also the use of 'the way' as a designation of Christianity in Acts 9.2; 19.9, 23; 22.4, 14, 22 (cf. 18.25f.).

[15] *Poreuou* in both cases, but Luke regularly avoids Mark's *hypage* and nothing more may be involved here. At 21.8 *me poreuthete opiso auton* may mean 'do not become their disciples' and be equivalent to *me planethete* earlier. But caution must be exercised about regarding *eisodos* (Acts 13.24) and *exodos* (Luke 9.31) too rigidly as the beginning and end of this 'way' (Giles, art. cit., 140).

[16] This and similar sayings, understandably for the time, put the case in terms of the husband leaving his wife. But Luke also thinks of women who have left home (8.2f.); he does not say they are widows.

[17] Cf. *TDNT* IV, 687, 690f., rather than Jeremias, *Theology* I, 224 ('love less'). Contrast 16.13 where 'hate' is defined by the parallel 'despise'.

[18] Strictly, carrying the cross refers to the shame and disgrace of public exposure as a criminal, but everyone knew what it led to.

[19] M. Hengel, *The Charismatic Leader and his Followers*, Edinburgh 1981, 16ff.

[20] For the textual problems of 10.1 (70 or 72?) cf. Marshall, 414f.; Metzger, *Commentary*, 150f.

[21] Luke is not dependent directly on John; cf. Fitzmyer, 560, *PNT*, 114ff.

[22] Note the form of Luke's verb, *esei zogron*: a continuous activity about to begin. Contrast the more remote future of Mark 1.17.

[23] In the light of the context *kyrie* cannot possibly mean 'sir' in 5.8 (as C. F. D. Moule 'The Christology of Acts' in *Studies in Luke–Acts*, ed. L. Keck and J. L. Martyn, Nashville 1966, 160f.) cf. Giles, art. cit., 133f. For kneeling cf. Acts 7.60; 20.36; 21.5; 22.41; for the response more generally in 5.8 cf. Isa 6.5.

8. Imitation?

[1] Conzelmann, esp.149ff. This thesis has been widely discussed (cf. e.g. Fitzmyer I, 18ff., 171ff.; Marshall, *Historian*, 84ff., and the literature in ch. 4, n. 2).

[2] Jervell, 154, points out against M. Dibelius, *Studies in the Acts of the Apostles*, London 1956, 149, that Paul's speeches in the last chapters of Acts contain too much biographical material to be intended simply as patterns for Christians defending themselves against accusation.

[3] 4.38, 'ill with a high fever', literally 'in the grip of a great fever'; Jesus 'rebuked it and it left her', cf. v. 35.

[4] Cf. Acts 1.18, S. Brown, 85f., but there is no warrant for interpreting Acts 1.25, with Johnson, 180ff., as a return to the private ownership of property. Cf. above ch. 3, n. 31.

[5] To turn an innocent bystander who became a victim of police brutality

into a disciple was not necessarily illegitimate. Mark 15.21 suggests that Simon, or at least his sons, became Christian.

[6] Cf. Marshall, 872: to accept one's punishment as justified is an expression of penitence. For *dikaios* cf. 7.29, the people justified God (*edikaiosan*) by repenting and being baptized: they acknowledged God was right.

[7] It is an argument against Luke's dependence on Matthew that he makes nothing of Joseph's wealth (Matt. 27.57).

[8] Luke softens the Marcan picture of the disciples, including Peter (K. N. Giles, *SJT*, 34.2, 1981, 130–3), but this can be exaggerated: he hardly highlights their strengths. It is argued that 'brothers' in 22.32 refers not to the apostles but the wider church, because Peter does not minister to apostles in Acts (*PNT*, 122f.). But (*a*) this would require a plural 'you' in v. 33a, and (*b*) Luke may see fulfilment in 24.34. The rest neither run away nor properly 'follow' (cf. 22.49; 23.26). They stay on only as witnesses. See below and ch. 6, p. 88.

[9] In the light of this it is hard to agree that Luke has softened the portrait of Peter here, even if he has omitted the curses (*PNT*, 112). Luke emphasizes how public the denial is (22.55, *mesos auton*).

[10] Unlike Matt. 27.3–10, Judas does not repent or commit suicide; his death is God's judgment. Cf. Johnson, 180.

[11] Brown, *Birth*, 255–499; *MNT*, 105–77; Fitzmyer, 303–448.

[12] For patterns see charts in Brown, *Birth*, 156; *MNT*, 113. That there are traditional elements in Luke 1–2 is shown by the details common to Matthew, but the use of sources in any fuller sense (as, e.g., Fitzmyer, 309) is more difficult to decide; a case can perhaps be made for parts of some of the canticles; cf. Brown, *Birth*, 244–250. The narrative shows an obvious debt to Old Testament models.

[13] Her prophetic power is shown in discerning the meaning of Mary's pregnancy, and assigning the correct name to her son while Zechariah is still dumb (1.41ff., 60).

[14] For traditional virtues, cf. 1.6f.; 2.25, obedience to the law, 1.59; 2.21–4, 27, 39, the temple, 1.8ff.; 2.22ff., 41ff., expectation, 2.25, 38. See Wilson, *Law*, 20–23. For canticles cf. above ch. 5 p. 63.

[15] Cf. above ch. 1 pp. 14f.; Wilson, *Law*, 106ff.

[16] Against Wilson, *Law*, 104, Luke does not affirm Gentile piety, but those Gentiles who have the best of Jewish piety.

[17] Cf. above ch. 6, pp. 78f.

[18] This is true regardless of whether chs. 1–2 were added after the completion of the rest of Luke; cf. Fitzmyer, 310f.

[19] Cf. Brown, *Birth*, 300f.

[20] Cf. especially for what follows *MNT* 126–34.

[21] *Kecharitomene* means 'one whom God has treated with favour' (cf. Marshall, 65; Fitzmyer, 345f.). 'Full of grace' is a later misinterpretation, cf. *MNT*, 127f.

[22] *MNT*, cf. 117–19; Fitzmyer, 340–42; Brown, *Birth*, 29–32, 312–316.

[23] Luke ascribes praise to Mary but not prophetic inspiration (unless by implication, 1.35, 47). Is this because at Acts 1.14 she is among those who wait for the Spirit?

[24] Here I differ from Brown, *Birth*, 279f.; Fitzmyer, 327; Marshall, 60.

There is a difference between 'how can this possibly happen?' (v. 34) and 'by what sign (*kata ti*) shall I know this?' (v. 18), cf. Gen. 15.7. Otherwise v. 20 is inexplicable. Zechariah's dumbness (v. 22, or deafness vv. 62–64; *kophos* can mean both) of course serves other purposes in the narrative as well, and may have been introduced for the sake of them.

[25] *MNT*, 147–52.

[26] Verse 35a is parenthetical.

[27] Possibly 'fall and rise' refer to the same group (Marshall, 122), but although *anastasis* may mean 'resurrection', 20.18 suggests that falling (*ptosis*) is irremediable; cf. Fitzmyer, 249. Simeon's prophecy refers to the negative impact of Jesus' coming; the positive is expressed in 2.29–32.

[28] Fitzmyer, 429; *MNT*, 155–7, against Marshall, 122f. *Kai sou* (RSV 'also') contrasts with 'Israel' not with 'this child'.

[29] Fitzmyer, 443f.

[30] It is tempting, in spite of Fitzmyer's objections, 441, to see a signal of this interpretation in the three days of 2.46, but Luke uses intervals of three hours, days or months too often to be certain. Cf. J. K. Elliott, *ET*, LXXXVII, 3, 1971, 87–9.

[31] Fitzmyer 722–5 argues vigorously for the translation 'my mother and brothers are the ones who hear and do the will of God', referring back to 8.15 and taking *meter mou kai adelphoi mou* as subject, *houtoi* as resumptive and the rest of the sentence as predicative (cf. *MNT*, 168–70). But the Greek will not bear this. After the previous occurrence in v. 20 the definite article would be expected with *meter* and *adelphoi*, especially with *mou* added. In its absence the nouns must be predicate and *houtoi* with the participial clause the subject. Cf. A. Plummer, *Gospel according to St. Luke*, Edinburgh 1896, 224f.

[32] 'Yes but even more', instead of 'no, rather' for *menoun* (*MNT*, 171f, quoting 1.42) is possible but hardly required by the context.

[33] Assuming the reading *splanchnistheis* at 1.41; with *orgistheis* Luke's omission is more intelligible. Contrast the use of *splanchnistheis* in parables, 10.33; 15.20. Luke's objection is not stylistic.

[34] Luke omits Mark 10.45, and in Acts 8.32f. cites only vv. 7f. of Isa. 53. This leaves only the longer text of Luke 22.19f. and Acts 20.28; neither mentions sin.

[35] Periphrastic future. See BD, 352, MH, III, 89; cf. Luke 12.52 and, for word order, 1.7.

[36] For alternative views cf. Marshall, 269f.; A. J. Mattill, *NT* 17.1, 1975, 40ff.; Fitzmyer, 630f., 641f.

[37] The abrupt introduction of the kings in 2.25 is only intelligible in the light of the authority to be assigned to the apostles in vv. 29f. They are to rule but must model themselves on the king who waits on them at his own table.

[38] Our discussion does not depend on solving the problem whether Luke's passion narrative derives from a special source with borrowings from Mark or from Mark with borrowings from tradition and redaction by Luke. Cf. V. Taylor, *The Passion Narrative of St. Luke*, Cambridge 1972; W. G. Kümmel, *Introduction to the New Testament*, ET London 1965, 93f.

[39] For the text cf. the summary in Marshall, 867f.

[40] Cf. Marshall, 875f.

⁴¹ Cf. V. Taylor, *Gospel according to St. Mark*, London 1953, 597; C. E. B. Cranfield, *Gospel according to St. Mark*, Cambridge 1963, 460; Anderson, 347f.

⁴² I have set out the arguments for what follows more fully in my chapter 'Imitatio Christi and the Lucan Passion Narrative' in Horbury and McNeil, 28–47. For an earlier statement of the case see M. Dibelius, *From Tradition to Gospel*, London 1934, 201; it is easy to overstate it however, and many interpreters have done so.

⁴³ Cf. W. H. C. Frend, *Martyrdom and Persecution in the Early Church*, Oxford 1965, 18ff., 31ff. Pagan literature also offered examples of the suffering of philosophers from Socrates on.

⁴⁴ For IV Maccabees see Charles *A & P*, II, 653–85; for expiatory death note especially IV Macc. 6.28f.; 17.21f.

⁴⁵ See for the parallels Dan. 3.25; III Macc. 5.6ff.; 6.1ff. (Charles *A & P*, I, 169ff.); IV Macc. 17.11–16 (*A & P*, II, 683), *Martyrdom of Isa.* 4.11–5.14 (*A & P*, II, 162), Josephus *AJ* XVII 6.4 (167). *Theoria* is found in III Macc. 5.24. See further 'Imitatio Christi' (n. 42) 30–2.

⁴⁶ Parallels are listed in H. MacLachlan *St. Luke the Man and his Work*, Manchester 1920, 244–56.

⁴⁷ Cf. E. J. Goodspeed, *Problems of New Testament Translation*, Chicago 1945, 90f., G. D. Kilpatrick, *JTS* 43, 1942, 34–6, and against, R. P. C. Hanson, *Hermathena* 60, 1942, 74–8.

⁴⁸ The aorist tense (in a few manuscripts) might suggest the unconscious effect of what he said, but the imperfect is better attested and suggests continued, and therefore deliberate, action.

⁴⁹ *Dikaios* without the definite article is unlikely to be a technical term for the messiah or an allusion to the Servant of Isa. 53, who is only called *dikaios* once, in the LXX of 53.11. See 'Imitatio Christi' (n. 42) 42f.

⁵⁰ How far Luke intends to suggest the eclipse and tearing of the temple curtain also contributed to the centurion's faith is not clear. It would accord with his use of miracle as a basis of faith elsewhere. But he has moved the reference to the curtain to a point before Jesus' death (23.45; cf. Mark 15.38), so that 'what had taken place' (v. 47) must include how Jesus died. Contrast Matt. 27.54.

⁵¹ Cf. A. J. Mattill Jr, *NT*, 17.1, 1975, 15–46.

⁵² Cf. Acts 20.22; 21.11, 14, with Luke 18.31f.; 22.42; Acts 21.36 with Luke 23.18; Acts 23.29; 25.25 with Luke 23.15; Acts 24.5 with Luke 23.2, 5; Acts 25.22 with Luke 23.8.

⁵³ Cf. P. W. Walaskay, *JBL*, 94.1, 1975, 81ff., C. K. Barrett, *Luke the Historian in Recent Study*, London 1961, 63.

⁵⁴ Cf. 'Imitatio Christi' (n. 42) 37–40.

⁵⁵ The background of 22.31f. must be the activity of rival petitioners in the heavenly court. For the judicial procedure cf. I Kings 3.16ff. For Satan as the heavenly accuser cf. Job 1.6–2.10; Zech. 3.1–5. In the case of Simon Jesus has won his case. In 22.41ff. he is still contesting it.

⁵⁶ Cf. Matt. 6.10. *Ginestho* is a 'reverential passive' (cf. ch. 2, n. 14); it implies more than submission, it is a request for God to act.

⁵⁷ *Me eiselthein eis peirasmon* probably means 'not to succumb to temptation' (22.40; cf. v. 46, 11.4); cf. Marshall, 461f.

[58] For *agonia* and *lype* see '*Imitatio Christi*' (n. 42), 39f.

[59] Cf. Fitzmyer, 785.

9. The Pharisaic Mind

[1] For the text and translation see Marshall, 507f., AG, 99.

[2] For the view that Luke is favourable to the Pharisees cf. J. A. Ziesler, *NTS* 25, 1979, 146ff. Cf. also Wilson, *Law*, 111ff.

[3] *TDNT* IX, 11ff.

[4] *TDNT* IX, 38.

[5] Marshall, 496f.; cf. above ch. 2 pp. 19f., 26. It is perhaps another indication of the distance from the details of Jewish teaching that at 4.32 Luke simply describes the authority of Jesus without contrasting it with the scribes (Mark 1.22); cf. Fitzmyer, 544.

[6] The variant reading at 11.53, *nomikoi*, is an assimilation to the earlier references.

[7] This is revealed in the reactions of the commentators: cf. Montefiore, II, 533, 'the charge, so far as we know, lacks historical foundation'; Manson, *Sayings*, 295f., 350, who thinks Sadducees were the original target. Anderson, 285 on Mark 12.40 thinks the charge of devouring widows' houses originally referred to the priestly class.

[8] The meaning of the phrase is uncertain; cf. Marshall, 750. Scribes were not paid for their professional work and lived from the pursuit of a trade and charity. See Jeremias, *Jerusalem*, 111ff. The rulings to this effect suggest that there may have been abuses from time to time, but most of the cases of Pharisaic venality cited on p. 114 turn out to be less explicit than Jeremias claims.

[9] A version of Mark 12.40 appears in some manuscripts of Matthew after 23.12 or 23.14, accusing Pharisees as well as scribes, but not in the best texts. It is a scribal assimilation to Mark, repeating the chorus-like beginning of most of the woes of Matt. 23.

[10] Hill, 313.

[11] Cf. J. W. Bowker, *Jesus and the Pharisees*, Cambridge 1973, 1–52, who argues that the Pharisees with whom Jesus came into conflict were, in effect, an extremist group in the movement.

[12] *Antiquities* XVIII.1.3 (12); on the contrary the Sadducess are 'able to persuade none but the rich', XIII.10.6 (298). The nearest parallels are perhaps *Sotah* 9.15 (Bowker, op. cit., 107; Danby, 305): When R. Eleazar b. Azariah died wealth departed from the Hakamim; and Hillel's ruling by which a loan could be exempted from the law of remission in a sabbatical year, *Shebiith* x.3 (Danby, 51, 795; cf. *TDNT* IX, 30 and nn. 104, 105). But though Luke 16 deals with remission of debts the point is different and the sabbatical year is not mentioned. It is doubtful whether *Ass.Mos* 7.6f. or Ps. Sol. 4.11–13 can refer to the Pharisees; cf. *A & P*, II, 419.

[13] Johnson, 30 n. 1. Not all his examples are persuasive, and to fit the pattern the Pharisees should surely accuse Jesus of secretly lining his pockets. For instances of rabbinical criticisms cf. the references to the 'wounds of the Pharisees' in Bowker, op. cit., 106, 140, 159f.

[14] The evidence of a Jewish threat is to be seen in the reference to synagogues as well as other authorities in 12.11f. 21.12f., which suggest

Jewish initiative, but the lack of specific detail points away from a close encounter of the kind reflected in Matthew.

[15] Ziesler (n. 2) 146.

[16] Johnson, 197f., who cites A. Ehrhardt, *The Acts of the Apostles*, Manchester 1969, 28.

[17] The dramatic aspect of these two sections of Acts should not be missed. Luke likes to show the impotence of the opposition to the Christian preachers, because it is divided and lacks clear purpose. Cf. also Acts 19.23–40.

[18] In 23.6, 'I am a Pharisee', there is no particular significance in the present tense. In these chapters Paul deploys all his connections to his advantage (cf. 22.25ff.). Luke does not imply that Pharisaism, as exemplified by Pharisees in general, is compatible with Christianity.

[19] 22.3; 26.5; the word reflects the 'accurately' (RSV margin) of Luke 1.3.

[20] Cf. Bowker, op. cit., 42. The passion narrative is more credible in this respect than 5.17.

[21] Cf. Fitzmyer, 684ff.; R. E. Brown, *The Gospel according to St. John*, London 1971, I, 449–454.

[22] Mark 2.1; 3.20; 7.17, 24; 9.28, 33; 10.10; Luke 4.38; 5.29; 7.36; 8.41; 10.38; 14.1; 19.5; 22.11; 24.29; note also the hospitality given to Jesus at 24.41f.

[23] It is not necessary to go into all the difficulties of interpreting these two passages to develop the argument set forward here. For the details, cf. Marshall, 568ff., 652ff.

[24] Herod is depicted as less of a threat to Jesus in Luke than the Pharisees. He desires to see Jesus (9.9; 23.8), and although he mocks him he does not condemn him to death (23.11, 15). He is guilty of wickedness, and imprisons and beheads John (3.19f.; 9.9), but does not hunt Jesus down. The Herodians disappear from Luke's account altogether. It is impossible to say for certainty what are the connotations of 'that fox'; cf. Marshall, 571.

[25] Cf. 11.47f.; for the belief that the prophetic vocation included suffering cf. 6.2f.; Acts 7.52; Neh. 9.26.

[26] Marshall, 654.

[27] *Entos hymon* cannot mean 'within you' here. The most likely meaning is 'in your midst', but even 'within your grasp' (Marshall, 655) would support the argument we are advancing. *Estin* must refer to the present not the future. Note also *idou* ('behold'), which points to this, and cf. 11.20.

[28] Cf. Johnson, 116f. It will be seen that I do not accept Ziesler's arguments (n. 2). In addition to the points already made, he does not deal satisfactorily with 11.53f. or 6.14, nor the additions to 5.17, 21. The Lucan modification 'some of the Pharisees' at 6.2 can only be taken as evidence of a softer attitude if the same is allowed of 'some of the Sadducees' at 20.27. Luke does not always use *tines* to mean 'only some' (cf. Acts 6.9; 17.18; 23.9), nor does 19.39 differ from 13.31 (cf. also Mark 2.6, 'some of the scribes', with Luke 5.21!).

[29] 'Justified' (*dedikaiomenos*) in v. 14 picks up *dikaioi* ('righteous') in v. 9.

[30] Against Wilson, *Law*, 35.

[31] Cf. above ch. 3 pp. 39f.

[32] It is conceivable that 'some of' (*tines*) is intended to indicate that

non-Sadducean scribes are meant, but it can as easily mean 'there were some scribes there who sa d'. Cf. 20.27 and n. 28.

[33] The connection between the God of the patriarchs and the resurrection of Jesus is explicitly made in Acts 3.13, 5.30. Luke 20.41–4 does not follow vv. 39f. by coincidence. Luke omits Mark 12.28ff., not only because it is covered by the parallel in 10.25ff., but perhaps also because in Mark the scribe praises Jesus' reply and is said to be not far from the kingdom. It is possible that Luke 20.39 reflects Mark 12.28 and 32, but the tone is different as v. 40 shows. Note Luke's 'for' for Mark's 'and'.

[34] Cf. above ch. 2 pp. 23f. and ch. 3 pp. 36f.

[35] Cf. below ch. 10 pp. 161ff.

[36] Cf. *TDNT* VII, 743.

[37] Verses 2f. cannot be addressed to the Pharisees (*TDNT* III, 705), nor are they about disciples proclaiming the messianic secret (Ellis, 173) for they differ at crucial points from Matt. 10.26f. See Marshall, 509ff. The beginning of v. 4 indicates a change of subject, not of audience.

[38] So also *TDNT* VIII, 567 n. 45. Marshall, 512 objects that Mark 8.15 does not connect hypocrisy and leaven; but Luke does, either by using Mark 8.15 or a saying very similar. 'Which is hypocrisy' reads as an explanatory insertion.

10. Luke's Structure

[1] There is general agreement on major divisions at 4.14 and 9.51, but uncertainty about where to divide ch. 19, how to subdivide the major sections and what to identify as the themes which might account for the resulting plan.

[2] E.g. Bailey; C. F. Evans, 'The Central Section of St. Luke's Gospel' in Nineham, *Studies*, pp. 37ff.; M. D. Goulder, *The Evangelists' Calendar*, London 1978; C. H. Talbert, *Literary Patterns, Theological Themes and the Genre of Luke-Acts*, Missoula 1974.

[3] 12.40, *ginesthe hetoimoi*; 12.43 *poiounta houtos*; 12.47 *hetoimasas e poiesas*. For a similar case where two key verbs are combined see the discussion of 9.25 above ch. 3 p. 40.

[4] Luke switches attention from the desecration of the temple (Mark 13.14) to the destruction of the city (Luke 21.20ff.); neither this nor rumours of wars however are for him the beginning of the final events (Mark 13.8; cf. Luke 21.10f.24).

[5] Cf. ch. 9, n. 33.

[6] For *pisteuein*, *pistis* and *pistos* see 7.9, 50; 8.12f., 25, 48, 50; 16.10–12; 17.5f., 19; 18.8, 42; 19.7; for *soteria* and *sozein* 7.50; 8.12, 36, 48, 50; 17.19; 18.26, 42; 19, 9f. *Soter* and *soterion* occur only in the infancy narratives and 3.6.

[7] Fitzmyer, 684ff.; Marshall, 304ff.

[8] Above, ch. 6, pp. 78f.

[9] E.g. hearing and doing in 8.4–21.

[10] E.g. B. H. Streeter, *The Four Gospels*, London 1924, 172ff.; Ellis 146ff.; Fitzmyer, 89–97.

[11] See above ch. 7 p. 95.

[12] Ch.6 pp. 79f.

[13] Cf. e.g. Marshall, 396f.

[14] Peter at 9.20, as elsewhere, is the spokesman for the group.

[15] Note too the frequency of words suggestive of discipleship, 'follow' (*akolouthein*), vv. 11, 23, 49; 'be with' (*syneinai*), v. 18; 'taking along' (*paralabon*), vv. 10, 28; and 'come after', v. 23. For 9.37–43 see also ch. 6, pp. 79f. above.

[16] Esp. 9.57ff; but as in these verses discipleship is interpreted as mission, 10.1–24 can also be included.

[17] For what follows compare G. Sellin, 'Komposition, Quellen und Funktion des lukanischen Reiseberichts', *NT*, XX, 2, 1978, 100ff., who adopts similar methods with somewhat different results. Not all his syntactical criteria for dividing the text are strong enough to be decisive, and even on his analysis the general sense sometimes overrides them (p. 108).

[18] Luke also extends the period of time in which the clashes occur; they are not the result of an 'off day' (6.6, 'another sabbath', cf. Mark 3.1).

[19] The precise text and meaning of *tines ton archonton (ton) Pharisaion* is unclear. Cf. Marshall, 578.

[20] Cf. above ch. 9 p. 134.

[21] *Syneporeuonto* suggests more than the RSV's 'accompanied'; cf. ch. 7 p. 97.

[22] Cf. above ch. 3 pp. 36ff.

[23] Note that Matt. 5.32 which is the nearest parallel to Luke 16.18 is part of a series of illustrations of the principle that the law is imperishable stated at Matt. 5.18, to which Luke 16.17 forms a broad parallel. Cf. Sellin, art. cit., 130, Wilson, *Law*, 51.

[24] Cf. 13.24, and for a discussion of alternative views, Wilson, *Law*, 45–51.

[25] For the translation of 20.20 see ch. 9 p. 140.

[26] Cf. above ch. 9, n. 33.

[27] There is perhaps a ray of hope at 21.24. Luke apparently does not believe that the rejection of Jerusalem is final.

[28] Because, writing after the fall of Jerusalem in AD 70, Luke regards the destruction of the temple as the judgment of God (as, earlier, in Jeremiah and Ezekiel), he does not see any future for it as 'a house of prayer for all nations' (19.46; cf. Mark 11.17).

[29] 23.27, 48. The exceptions are 23.13 with 18, and possibly 23.35, if 'watching' as well as 'mocked' is a reflection of Ps. 22.7.

[30] Marshall, 648, with hesitation breaks at 17.11; Achtemeier takes 17.1–19 together (Talbert, *Perspectives*, 160).

[31] If *dia meson* means 'through', the territories are in the wrong order (south to north); if it means 'between', the border runs north–south instead of east–west. Cf. Sellin, art. cit., 117.

[32] Above p. 87.

[33] The messianic secret for Luke is the necessity of Jesus' passion; cf. 24.25–7.

[34] Cf. ch. 6 p. 87; ch. 9 p. 135.

[35] Cf. ch. 3 pp. 36f.

[36] See above n. 6.

[37] Cf. Achtemeier in Talbert, *Perspectives*, 160.

[38] Cf. ch. 6 pp. 90f.

[39] Above p. 154.

[40] It is difficult to see any other purpose in 'for you say that I cast out demons by Beezebul', which is absent from Matt. 12.26.

[41] For the meaning of 'generation', see above chapter 3, n. 9. Here however there is also a chronological distinction. These people differ both in time and character from their ancestors.

[42] Note the repetition of *poneros* ('evil', v. 29, 'not sound', v. 34), *poneria* ('wickedness') v. 39; and *en soi* ('in you') v. 35, *to esothen hymon* ('inside you ...') v. 39, *holon* ('whole') vv. 34, 36, *panta* ('everything') v. 41.

[43] Cf. above ch. 9 pp. 141f.

[44] *Lego de hymin tois philois mou*, 'I tell you who are my friends' (not RSV), marks a new beginning in topic rather than audience; cf. v. 8. There is no parallel in Matt. 10.28. 'Friends' perhaps contrasts with those who have become infected by hypocrisy and are unfaithful.

[45] For the interpretation of 12.49f. cf. Marshall, 545ff.

[46] It is difficult to think that 'narrow' has much force in v. 24, and tempting to believe that it is an element in the source that Luke has neglected to edit out. The stress in the parable is on entering before the door shuts.

[47] Cf. 12.57 'what is right', 13.27 'workers of iniquity' (*to dikaion ... tes adikias*).

[48] If the reference to the birds of heaven in 13.19 is a reference to the coming of the Gentiles (cf. Ezek.17.23; 31.6; Dan. 4.12, 21f.), then it anticipates v. 29. But it may just be a picturesque description of the size of the tree (cf. Ps. 104.12) as there is no similar point in the twin parable.

[49] Cf. above ch. 9, p. 135.

[50] It is difficult to decide whether *aphietai* in 13.35 is a futuristic (prophetic) present (cf. MH, III, 63), or a genuine present reflecting the fact obtaining as Luke wrote. Verse 35b must refer to the parousia, not to the entry into Jerusalem in 19.38, and rather supports the latter view of *aphietai*. Cf. 21.24; Marshall, 576f.

[51] Here I differ from the emphasis of Maddox, *Purpose*, 17, 54, although he comes nearer to my position later, 113, 139. The interpretation of chs 12–13 are crucial here. The crowds cannot simply be identified as the Jews of the past.

11. Conclusions

[1] Cf. K. Grayston, 'New Testament Moral Codes and Situation Ethics', *Church Quarterly*, 3.3, Jan. 1971, 181–188.

[2] E.g. G. Theissen, *The First Followers of Jesus*, London 1978; H. C. Kee, *Christian Origins in Sociolgical Perspective*, London 1980.

[3] Above, p. 52. Also Dupont, *Béatitudes*, III, 89ff.; J. Drury, *Tradition and Design in Luke's Gospel*, London 1976, e.g. 19, 146.

[4] Above, pp. 84, 124, 196 (n. 33).

[5] Above, p. 60.

[6] S. G. F. Brandon, *Jesus and the Zealots*, Manchester 1967, and, against, M. Hengel, *Was Jesus a Revolutionist?*, Philadephia 1971; J. P. M. Sweet,

'The Zealots and Jesus', in E. Bammel and C. F. D. Moule, *Jesus and the Politics of his Day*, Cambridge 1984, 1ff.

[7] Above p. 48.

[8] Cf. M. Hengel, *Victory over Violence*, London 1975, 41ff.

[9] Above p. 157.

[10] He can allude to the legend of Philemon and Baucis of Acts 14.11ff. but treats the Athenian philosophers with contempt, 17.18–21.

Bibliographical Details

Bibliographical details are generally given in the notes when a work is first mentioned. Details of more frequently cited works are listed here. They are cited in the notes by author's surname only unless otherwise stated.

✓ H. Anderson, *The Gospel of Mark*, London 1976

K. E. Bailey, *Poet and Peasant. A Literary Cultural Approach to the Parables in Luke*, Michigan 1976

G. Bornkamm, G. Barth, H. Held, *Tradition and Interpretation in Matthew*, London 1963

· R. E. Brown, *The Birth of the Messiah*, London 1977 (cited as *Birth*)

S. Brown, *Apostasy and Perseverance in the Theology of Luke*, Rome 1969 (cited as S. Brown)

✓ F. F. Bruce, *The Acts of the Apostles: the Greek text with Introduction and Commentary*, Chicago and Toronto 1952.

H. J. Cadbury, *The Making of Luke-Acts*, New York 1927, London 1958

✓ H. Conzelmann, *The Theology of St. Luke*, London 1961

J. M. Creed, *The Gospel According to St. Luke*, London 1930

G. Dalman, *The Words of Jesus*, Edinburgh 1909

H. Danby, *The Mishnah*, Oxford 1933

H-J. Degenhardt, *Lukas Evangelist der Armen*, Stuttgart 1965

J. D. M. Derrett, *Studies in the New Testament I*, Leiden 1977

J. Dupont, *Les Béatitudes*, I Bruges-Louvain 1954, II–III Paris 1969, 1973 (cited as *Béatitudes*)

E. E. Ellis, *The Gospel of Luke*, London 1966

J. A. Fitzmyer, *Essays on the Semitic Background of the New Testament*, London 1971 (cited as *Essays*)

J. A. Fitzmyer, *The Gospel According to St. Luke*, 2 vols, New York 1981, 1985 (cited simply as Fitzmyer)

F. Godet, *A Commentary on the Gospel of St. Luke*, Edinburgh, 5th ed. 1976

W. Grundmann, *Das Evangelium nach Lukas*, Berlin 1964

E. Haenchen, *The Acts of the Apostles*, Oxford 1971

D. R. H. Hare, *The Theme of Jewish Persecution of Christians in the Gospel According to St. Matthew*, Cambridge 1967

O. F. Harris, *Prayer in Luke-Acts: A Study in the Theology of Luke*, Ann Arbor 1966

D. Hill, *The Gospel of Matthew*, London 1972

W. Horbury, B. McNeil, *Suffering and Martyrdom in the New Testament*, Cambridge 1981

J. Jeremias, *Jerusalem in the Time of Jesus*, London 1969 (cited as *Jerusalem*)

J. Jeremias, *The Lord's Prayer*, Philadelphia 3rd ed. 1969 (cited as *Prayer*)

J. Jeremias, *New Testament Theology, I The Proclamation of Jesus*, London 1971 (cited as *Theology*)

J. Jeremias, *The Parables of Jesus*, London rev. ed. 1963 (cited as *Parables*)

J. Jervell, *Luke and the People of God*, Minneapolis 1972

L. T. Johnson, *The Literary Function of Possessions in Luke-Acts*, Missoula 1977

A. R. C. Leaney, *A Commentary on the Gospel According to St. Luke*, London 2nd ed. 1966

R. Maddox, *The Purpose of Luke-Acts*, Edinburgh 1982 (cited as *Purpose*)

T. W. Manson, *The Sayings of Jesus*, London 1937, 1949 (cited as *Sayings*)

I. H. Marshall, *The Acts of the Apostles*, Leicester 1980 (cited as *Acts*)

I. H. Marshall, *The Gospel of Luke, A Commentary on the Greek Text*, Exeter 1978 (cited simply as Marshall)

I. H. Marshall, *Luke: Historian and Theologian*, Exeter rev. ed. 1979 (cited as *Historian*)

D. L. Mealand, *Poverty and Expectation in the Gospels*, London 1980

B. M. Metzger, *A Textual Commentary on the Greek New Testament*, London, New York 1971 (cited as *Commentary*)

C. G. Montefiore, *The Synoptic Gospels*, London 2nd ed. 1927

D. E. Nineham, *Studies in the Gospels*, Oxford 1955 (cited as *Studies*)

C. H. Talbert, *Perspectives on Luke-Acts*, Danville, Va. and Edinburgh 1978 (cited as *Perspectives*)

G. H. P. Thompson, *The Gospel According to St. Luke*, Oxford 1972

S. G. Wilson, *Luke and the Law*, Cambridge 1983 (cited as *Law*)

M. Zerwick, M. Grosvenor, *A Grammatical Analysis of the Greek NT*, Rome 1974, 1979 (cited as *Analysis*)

Index of authors cited in the notes

Page references are followed by note numbers in brackets.

Achtimeiter, P.J., 197(11,13), 198(19), 208(30), 109(37)
Anderson, H., 204(41), 205(7)

Bailey, K.E., 188(20), 191(10), 207(2)
Balz, H., 195(9)
Bammel, E. and Moule, C.F.D., 210(6)
Barrett, C.K., 187(3), 204(53)
Beck, B.E., 187(9), 204(42)
Bornkamm, G., Barth, G., and Held, H., 189(9), 200(51)
Bowker, J.W., 205(11,12,13), 206(20)
Brandon, S.G.F., 209(6)
Brown, R.E., 194(13), 195(20), 202(11,12,19,22,24), 206(21)
Brown, S., 196(1), 197(4,7,8,9), 198(28,30,31), 199(32,36,38,41,45,46), 200(48,49,52,55), 201(4)
Bruce, F.F., 188(21), 197(7,12)
Büchsel, F., 190(19)
Bultmann, R., 187(4), 189(11), 195(14), 200(55)

Cadbury, H.J., 194(19), 197(12)
Catchpole, D.R., 199(41)
Charles, R.H., 204(44,45)
Conzelmann, H., 193(2), 194(8), 198(29,32), 199(33,34), 200(9,10), 201(1)
Cranfield, C.E.B., 204(41)
Creed, J.M., 190(20), 191(15), 199(41)

Dalman, G., 189(6)

Danby, H., 205(12)
Degenhardt, H-J., 190(1)
Derrett, J.D.M., 190(5,9), 191(22)
Dibelius, M., 187(4), 195(14), 201(2), 204(42)
Drury, J., 187(5), 209(3)
Dupont, J., 189(2,4), 190(1), 193(6), 194(9,15,16), 209(3)

Ehrhardt, A., 206(16)
Elliott, J.K., 203(30)
Ellis, E.E., 190(6), 193(2), 201(13), 207(37;10)
Evans, C.F., 187(6), 207(2)

Farmer, W.R., 187(3)
Farrer, A.M., 187(3)
Fitzmyer, J.A., 187(3,9), 188(18,19), 189(1,2,3,4,7,8,9), 190(55), 191(20), 192(36), 193(44), 195(4,20), 197(16), 198(17,21,23,30), 199(35), 200(52;8), 201(21;1), 202(11,12,18,21,22,24), 203(27,28,29,30,31,36), 205(59;5), 206(21), 207(7,10)
Frend, W.H.C., 204(43)

Giles, K.N., 200(1,3), 201(15), 202(8)
Godet, F., 190(20)
Goodspeed, E.J., 204(47)
Goulder, M.D., 187(5), 207(2)
Grayston, K., 209(1)
Grundmann, W., 191(23)

Haenchen, E.,   188(21),
    197(6,7,9,12)
Hanson, R.P.C.,   204(47)
Hare, D.R.H.,   189(7)
Harris, O.F.,   196(25,26,27,28,35)
Hengel, M.,   201(19), 209(6),
    210(8)
Hill, D.,   191(20), 205(10)
Horbury, W., and McNeil, B.,
    195(12), 204(42)
Hull, J.M.,   197(13)

Jeremias, J.,   188(18), 190(3,7),
    191(11,20,21,22), 193(5), 194(20),
    196(27,31,33,35,38), 198(17),
    199(41), 201(17), 205(8)
Jervell, J.,   201(2)
Johnson, L.T.,   190(1), 192(29),
    194(12), 201(4), 202(10),205(13),
    206(16,28)
Jülicher, A.,   195(14)

Karris, R.J.,   190(1), 194(19)
Kee, H.C.,   209(2)
Kilpatrick, G.D.,   204(47)
Kosmala, H.,   190(6)
Kümmel, W.G.,   187(2,3,9),
    193(2), 203(38)

Lampe, G.W.H.,   201(11)
Leaney, A.R.C.,   191(9)

MacLachlan, H.,   204(46)
Maddox, R.,   187(9), 193(2,3),
    209(51)
Manson, T.W.,   194(13), 205(7)
Marshall, I.H.,   188(20),
    189(24;1,5,7,10,13,16,17,24),
    190(18;2,3,6,8),
    191(12,13,19,20,21),
    192(23,26,30,31,32,33,35,36),
    193(38,39,42,43,44,45;4),
    194(14,23), 195(4,8),
    196(30,31,32,33,34,35),
    197(12,15,16), 198(21,25,30),
    199(35,37,41,42,43,47),
    200(52,53;8), 201(1,20),
    202(6,21,24),
    203(27,28,36,39,40), 204(57),

205(1,8), 206(23,24,26,27),
    207(38;7), 208(13,19,30),
    209(45,50)
Mattill, A.J.,   203(36), 204(51)
Mealand, D.L.,   190(1),
    194(12,17)
Metzger, B.M.,   193(4), 201(20)
Montefiore, C.G.,   205(7)
Morgenthaler, R.,   188(10)
Moule, C.F.D.,   187(3), 194(11),
    201(23)
Murray, J.,   187(1)

Neirynck, F.,   193(2)
Nineham, D.E.   187(3,6), 207(2)

Perrin, N.,   187(4)
Plummer, A.,   203(31)

Rohde, J.,   187(4)

Sellin, G.,   189(13), 208(17,23,31)
Soulen, R.N.,   195(14)
Spicq, C.,   189(17)
Streeter, B.H.,   187(2), 207(10)
Styler, G.M.,   187(3)
Sweet, J.P.M.,   209(6)

Talbert, C.H.,   196(25), 197(11),
    207(2)
Taylor, V.,   187(3,4), 203(38),
    204(41)
Theissen, G.,   209(2)
Thompson, G.H.P.,   190(20)
Trites, A.A.,   196(25)
Tuckett, C.M.,   187(3)
Turner, N.,   191(15)

Walaskay, P.W.,   204(53)
Walls, A.F.,   195(19)
Wanke, G.,   195(10)
Wilson, S.G.,   187(9), 188(21,23),
    189(15), 193(2), 202(14,15,16),
    205(2), 206(30), 208(23,24)
Wood, H.G.,   198(17)

Zerwick, M. and Grosvenor, M.,
    191(15)
Ziesler, J.A.,   205(2), 206(15,28)

Scripture Index

Page numbers in italics refer to scriptural references in the endnotes. More than one reference on a page is indicated by a figure in brackets after the page number

Genesis
6.5–8, 11f.	41
15.7	*203*
17.17	113
18.12	113
19.12ff.	41

Exodus
2.22	*190*
3.11	113
20.12	98
22.25–27	19

Leviticus
12.8	49
14.1ff.	75
17 and 18	14
19.18	21, 22

Deuteronomy
5.9f.	98
6.4	*192*
6.4f.	21(2), 22
7.9f.	98
20.5–7	*191*
21.17	31, *191*
24.10–13	19

Judges
6.15	113

I Samuel
2.1ff.	49
2.1–10	63
14.45	*199*

II Samuel
5.8	*191*

I Kings
1.52	*199*
3.16ff.	*204*
8.31ff.	195
19.19–21	102
21.27ff.	*195*

II Kings
22.18f.	*195*

Nehemiah
8.10–12	*191*
9.26	*206*

Job
1.6–2.10	*204*
8.1–8	195

Psalms
14.1	*191*
22.7	*208*
22.8f.	*201*
22.18	*201*
31.6	120, 122
31.18	122
53.1	*191*
94.8	*191*
104.12	*209*
110	140
110.1	157

Isaiah
2.12ff.	*195*
6.5	*201*
53.7f.	*203*
53.12	*188*
61.1ff.	48, 50

Ezekiel
14.17	114
17.23	*209*
28	*195*
31.6	*209*
34.16	163
36.23	*196*

Daniel
3.25	*204*
4.12	*209*
4.21f.	*209*
6.4f.	124

Joel
3.5	*197*

Zechariah
3.1–5	*204*

Malachi
1.2f.	98

Tobit
12.8–10	*194*

Wisdom
1–5	121(2), 122

Wisdom (cont.)

1.16–3.9	121
2.18	122
3.2f.	122
4.16ff.	122

II Maccabees

6.12–7.42	121
9	*195*

Matthew

3.7–10	43
5.10–12	100
5.11f.	85
5.12	20
5.18	*208*
5.21ff.	15
5.32	*208*
5.38–42	17
5.38–48	17
5.39–41	19
5.39–42	18
5.42	18
5.43–48	18
5.44	18, 100
5.45	18
5.46f.	18
5.47	*188*
5.48	17, 18
6	31
6.1–18	*194*
6.9	69
6.10	*204*
6.11	*196*
6.12	12, *196*
6.24	25, *190*
6.31	32
6.31–33	69
6.32f.	32
6.33	32(2)
7.1f.	18
7.7–11	69
7.12	18
7.13f., 22f.	167
7.16–18	*189*
8.10	149
8.21f.	99
8.25	*200*(2)
10.9f.	44, *193*
10.24f.	117
10.26f.	*207*
10.28	*209*

10.39	41
11.19	*200*(2)
12.22–45	164
12.24	141, 165
12.26	*209*
12.42	*200*
13.33	142
13.52	95
15.5	129
15.14	117
15.21f., 35	159
16.6–12	142
17.20	90
18.6f.	159
19.21	37
21.45	133
22.1–14	34
22.5	35
22.34f.	133
22.35	129
22.36	24
22.37–39	22
22.40	22
22.41	133
23	142, 164
23.2ff.	133
23.6	25
23.6f.	129
23.12	*205*
23.14	*205*
23.23	26
23.25	129
23.25f.	39
23.26	39
24.1ff.	41
24.38	41
26.6–13	75
27.3–10	*202*
27.54	204
27.57	3, *202*
27.62	133

Mark

1.15	*195*
1.16–20	102
1.17	*201*
1.22	*205*
1.27	*189*
1.39	*200*
1.40–45	75
1.41	*203*
1.45	106

2.1	95, *206*
2.1–12	72, 78
2.1–3.6	127, 152
2.2	*200*
2.3f.	78
2.6	127, *206*
2.12	59(2), 62, 106
2.13	95
2.13–17	50
2.14	*192*
2.15	107
2.16	147, *195*
2.17	11
2.18	50, 127, 128,
	147, *195*
2.18–22	50
2.24	127
2.25, 27	137
2.28	137
3.1	*208*
3.2	127
3.3	66
3.6	128
3.7	94
3.14	94
3.20	*206*
3.20f.	116
3.22	141
3.22–30	164
3.31–35	116
3.33–35	116
4.8	83
4.10	94
4.14ff.	*200*
4.14–20	42
4.17	83, 84
4.19	42, 84, 97
4.33	*200*
4.34	93
4.40	90
4.41	59
4.43	*187*
5.15	58, 74
5.17	58
5.18	74
5.20	58, *195*
5.21	96
5.21–43	72
5.23	78
5.25–34	76
5.30	*197*
5.31	102

5.34	73	10.23	37	14.53–72	109
5.36	*198*	10.29	101	14.54	109
6.1	150	10.29f.	37	14.65	120
6.2	*200*	10.33f.	133	14.66	109
6.6	72	10.42	101	14.71	*200*(2)
6.6f.	150	10.43–48	101	15.15	120
6.8f.	43	10.45	*203*	15.16–20	120
6.17–29	150	10.46	96	15.21	107, *202*
6.32f.	96	10.46–52	73, 77	15.34	119
6.34	117	10.49	77	15.38	*204*
6.35	*200*	10.52	73, 97	15.39	62, 120, 122
6.45–8.22	150	11.9	62		
6.45–8.26	149, 150	11.11–14	148	*Luke*	
6.46	150	11.15–17	43	1–2	109, 110, 112,
7.6–13	129	11.17	*208*		146, *202*(2)
7.11	129	11.18	148	1.1	2, 143
7.17	*206*	11.19–26	148	1.1–4	82, 105, 179
7.17ff.	93	11.22f.	90	1.2	96, *200*
7.24	*206*	11.27	148	1.3	*206*
8.5	*200*	12.13	133	1.4	95, *200*
8.11	95	12.18	129	1.5	49
8.11–13	164	12.25	47	1.5f.	11
8.15	142(2), *207*	12.28	*207*	1.6	97, 110, 111
8.21	95	12.28ff.	*207*	1.6f.	*202*
8.31	133, *187*	12.28–34	21	1.7	*203*
8.34f.	40	12.28–35	147	1.7f.	49
8.35	101, 173	12.30f.	22(2)	1.8ff.	*202*
8.35f.	40	12.31	22	1.13	110, 111
9.11–13	79	12.32	*207*	1.14	68
9.14	96	12.34	24	1.15	110
9.14–21	117	12.35	157	1.16	*196*
9.14–29	73, 79	12.37f.	94	1.17	65
9.21–24	79	12.38f.	140	1.18	114, *203*
9.22	117	12.39f.	129	1.18–20	*197*
9.28	*206*	12.40	68, 129, *205*(2)	1.20	89, 114, *203*
9.28f.	79	12.41	43	1.22	*203*
9.30–32	79	12.41–44	43	1.24	68
9.33	95, 150, *206*	13	85, 147	1.26ff.	11
9.33ff.	66	13.1	148	1.28	113
9.35	94	13.8	*207*	1.30	113, *189*
9.38	97, 151	13.9	100	1.31	114
9.40	151	13.12	85, 100	1.32f.	113, 117
9.42–50	101	13.13	86	1.34	113, *203*
9.47	151	13.14	85, *207*	1.35	113, 117, *202*
10.1–12	101	13.15f.	41	1.36	114
10.2–12	129	13.33–37	86	1.37	114
10.10	*206*	14.3	134	1.38	95, 113
10.16	161	14.3–9	75	1.39	*194*
10.17	21, 36, 37,	14.27–31	108	1.39–45	112
	147	14.30	*199*	1.41	63, 110
10.21	37, 98, 117	14.34	119	1.41ff.	*202*
10.22	37	14.50	88, 108	1.44	63

Luke (cont.)

1.45	89, 113
1.46ff.	49, 62, 63, 110
1.47	*202*
1.48	63
1.48f.	64, 113
1.50	18, 58, 111
1.51	66
1.51–53	114
1.52f.	64
1.53	49, 64
1.54	18
1.54f.	64, 167
1.58	18, 63
1.59	*202*
1.60	*202*
1.62–64	*203*
1.63	56
1.65	58
1.65f.	58
1.67	64(2), 110(2)
1.67ff.	110
1.68ff.	63
1.68–75	64
1.72	18
1.72f.	167
1.76	63, 110
1.77	181
1.78	18, 62
1.80	110
2	67
2.7	56
2.10	62
2.11	117
2.12	114
2.13	63
2.13f.	64
2.14	63
2.17	110
2.17f.	82
2.18	56, 114
2.18f.	56
2.19	66, 114, 115, *194*
2.20	62, 110(2), *195*
2.21	114
2.21–24	*202*
2.22ff.	*202*
2.24	49

2.25	11, 107, 110, 111, *202*(3)
2.25–27	110
2.25–28	62
2.25–38	138
2.25	11, 111
2.27	*202*
2.28ff.	76
2.29ff.	63
2.29–32	64, *203*
2.33	56
2.34	66
2.34f.	114
2.34ff.	*195*
2.35	114, *203*
2.35f.	66
2.36	110
2.37	11, 110, 111
2.38	110(2), *202*
2.39	*202*
2.40	*200*
2.41ff.	*202*
2.42	68
2.42–51	116
2.46	*203*
2.46f.	62
2.47	115
2.47f.	55
2.48–51	114, 115
2.49	115
2.50	115
2.51	99, 114, 115
2.52	*189, 200*
3.1	68
3.1f.	105
3.3	95, 136
3.6	*207*
3.7–9	43
3.8	12, 43, 62, 85, *199*
3.10–14	13, 43
3.12	13
3.15	147
3.18	*194*
3.19f.	150, *206*
3.21	67
3.21f.	117
4	16
4.1–13	117, 125
4.14	*207*

4.15	95
4.16ff.	48, 181, *195*
4.16–30	152
4.18	181, *194*
4.20	82
4.21	65, 181
4.22	55, 82, *200*
4.23ff.	68
4.28	57
4.31–5.16	152
4.32	55, 95, *200*, *205*
4.33	106
4.35	*201*
4.36	56(2), *189*, *200*
4.38	102, *201*, *206*
4.39	106
4.43	95
4.44	*200*
5.1	56, 95, 103
5.1ff.	113
5.1–11	72, 88, 102(2), 104, 108(2)
5.3	49, 102
5.5	103, 113
5.8	59(2), 103(2), *201*(2)
5.8ff.	*188*
5.9	59, 103
5.10	103(2)
5.11	49, 50, 99, 103, 107, *192*
5.12	95
5.12ff.	48
5.12–16	75
5.13	117
5.15	*195*
5.15f.	106
5.16	67
5.17	95, 128, 129(2), 139, 152, *197*, *206*(2)
5.17ff.	48
5.17–26	72
5.17–6.11	127
5.18f.	78
5.19	82
5.20	78
5.20ff.	*188*

5.21 129, 136(2), 206(2)
5.22 66
5.24 97
5.24ff. 76
5.25 62, 82, 106
5.25f. 62(2)
5.26 58, 59
5.27 95, 98, 113
5.27f. 106
5.27–32 50
5.28 49, 50, 99, 192
5.29 50, 107, 206
5.29ff. 188
5.29–32 107
5.30 13, 50, 63, 128, 129, 136, 139(3), 147, 195
5.30–32 63
5.32 11(2), 138
5.33 50, 67, 128, 134, 137, 139, 147
5.33f. 137
5.33ff. 139
5.33–35 68
5.33–39 50
5.34 63, 129, 195(2)
5.35 110
5.40 147
5.41 62
5.43 147
5.44, 47 19
5.50 78
6.1–5 137
6.1–11 137, 153
6.2 206
6.2f. 206
6.6 68, 106, 208
6.6–11 137, 140
6.7 139(2)
6.8 66, 82
6.9 40, 78
6.11 128, 134, 139
6.12 67, 194
6.12–19 16
6.12–7.1 152
6.13 94, 151, 200
6.13f. 102
6.14 206
6.15 176

6.17 17, 49, 94
6.17f. 98, 195
6.17ff. 94
6.17ff. 94
6.17–19 82
6.19 17, 197
6.20 17, 49, 50
6.20f. 49
6.20ff. 48(2)
6.20–23 17, 62
6.20–26 20
6.20–49 16
6.22 20, 49
6.22 100
6.22f. 85, 123, 189
6.23 20(2), 21, 63, 65
6.24 17, 31, 53, 189
6.24–26 17(2)
6.25 189(2)
6.26 52, 189(3)
6.27 17, 18(2), 20, 118, 181, 189
6.27f. 18, 19, 100
6.27ff. 27, 49
6.27–29 123
6.27–36 17
6.27–38 17(2), 18
6.28 19, 20, 68
6.29 19(2), 20, 129
6.29f. 18
6.30 19
6.31 18, 19(2), 23(2), 123
6.31–35 34, 196
6.32 18, 118
6.32f. 18
6.32–34 181, 188, 190
6.32–35 19
6.33 19
6.33–35 20
6.34 18, 52
6.34f. 19, 189
6.35 18(2), 19(3), 20(2), 23(2), 34(2), 48, 53, 181
6.35f. 53, 123
6.36 17, 18(2), 19, 34
6.36ff. 61

6.37 18, 26
6.37f. 18, 19(2), 20
6.38 19(2), 54
6.39 18, 117, 118(2), 189
6.39f. 17
6.39–45 17, 189
6.40 117, 118(3)
6.41 118
6.41f. 117
6.42 143
6.43f. 85, 189
6.43ff. 12
6.43–45 118
6.43–46 195
6.45 21, 66, 189
6.46 93
6.46–49 17, 21
6.47 189
6.47ff. 95
6.47–49 57
7–8 91
7.1 17(2), 94, 200
7.1ff. 111
7.1–10 73, 78, 149
7.1–8.56 148
7.4 59, 79
7.5 18, 25
7.6 59
7.7 79
7.9 91, 96(2), 149, 207
7.11 96(3), 106
7.11ff. 48
7.11–17 82, 149, 197
7.12 117
7.13 117
7.16 59, 62
7.21 96
7.22 48, 49, 53, 164, 194, 195
7.22f. 149
7.23 149
7.29 60, 149, 202
7.29f. 156
7.30 24, 56, 72, 128, 129, 136, 139
7.31 66
7.31–35 76, 149
7.32ff. 136
7.33 13

Luke (cont.)

7.34	11, 13(2), 50, 63(2), 134
7.34f.	63
7.35	60, 149, 200
7.36	128, *206*
7.36ff.	81, 128, 134, *188*(2)
7.36–50	26, 75
7.37	76
7.39	136, 137
7.40	134
7.41	*188*
7.41f.	26
7.42	18, *198*
7.47	11, 12, 18, 26, 75, 76, 138, *198*
7.48	76(3)
7.49	66, 136
7.50	76, 148, 149, 207(2)
8	39
8.1	96
8.1–3	96, 101
8.2f.	49, 50, 51, 74, 106, 107, *201*
8.4ff.	149, 158
8.4–21	*207*
8.7	84
8.8	57, 62, 83
8.9	94
8.9f.	93
8.9ff.	95
8.11	83, *200*
8.11f.	167
8.11–15	42, 83, 118
8.12	42, 57, 66, 72, 83, *207*
8.12f.	148, *207*
8.13	42, 62, 64, 83, 89, *198*
8.14	42, 52, 84, 87, 97(2)
8.14–21	93
8.15	42, 66, 84, 86, *203*
8.18	57
8.19–21	116
8.20	*203*
8.21	57(2), 95, 99, 116

8.22	68
8.22–25	*200*(2)
8.23	148, *200*(2)
8.24	59, 68
8.25	56, 68, 69, 90, 149, *207*
8.26ff.	106, 149
8.26–39	74
8.35	74, 95, 101
8.35	58
8.36	74, 148(2), *207*
8.37	58, 59, *195*
8.38	74, 97
8.39	58, 62, 83(2), 101, 110, 181, *195*
8.40–42	78
8.40	96
8.40–56	72
8.41	37, 140, *206*
8.42	117
8.43ff.	106
8.43–48	76
8.45	102
8.46	*197*
8.47	77(2), 82, 83(3), 110
8.48	77, 97, *207*(2)
8.49–56	78
8.50	58, 148, *207*(2)
8.51	103
8.56	56
9.1	149, 51, *200*
9.1ff.	43, 44(2)
9.1–6	103
9.1–50	149
9.4	43
9.4f.	100
9.7f.	150
9.9	151, *206*(2)
9.10	103, 151, *200*, *208*
9.11	96(2), 117, *208*
9.12	151, *200*(2)
9.13	151
9.16	*200*
9.18	78, 96, 150, *208*
9.18–21	88

9.18	67
9.19	150
9.20	151, *208*
9.21	56
9.22	139, *187*
9.23	97, 100(5), 173, *208*(2)
9.23ff.	94, 96, 98
9.23–25	40(2)
9.23–27, 57–62	98
9.24	78, 101, 173
9.24f.	100
9.25	40, *192*, *207*
9.26	100, 101, 117, 173, *193*
9.27	48
9.28	67, *208*
9.28ff.	93, 103
9.31	79, 95, 115, *201*
9.33	102
9.34	58
9.35	57, 117
9.37	96
9.37–43	73, 79, 117, *208*
9.38	117
9.40	68
9.41	79, 81
9.42	117
9.43	56, 79, 94
9.43ff.	56
9.43–45	150
9.44	79
9.44f.	79, 115
9.46	94, 95
9.46f.	66
9.46–48	61
9.48	113, 151
9.48f.	151
9.49	97, 151(2), *208*
9.49f.	151
9.50	101, 151, 152
9.51	95, 115, 150(2), 156, *207*
9.52	96
9.52f.	23
9.52ff.	44
9.53	95, 150
9.54	23

9.57	97	10.30	14, 68	11.29ff.	93, 116,
9.57f.	98	10.31	111		163, 167
9.57ff.	96, *208*	10.33	*203*	11.29–32	114
9.57–62	98	10.34f.	111	11.30–32	117
9.58	50, 100	10.37	18, 21,	11.31	*200*
9.59	98, 101, 113		22(2), 23(2)	11.33–36	164
9.59f.	98	10.38	96, *206*	11.34	*209*(2)
9.60	101(2), 104,	10.38ff.	57	11.34–36	165
	115	10.38–41	24	11.35	*209*
9.61f.	98, 99	10.39	24, 56, 74,	11.36	58, *209*
9.62	102		95, *200*	11.37	128, 134,
10.1	*201*	10.40	24		147, 165
10.1ff.	43, 44(2)	10.41	106	11.37f.	39, *192*
10.1–16	102	10.41f.	*189*	11.37ff.	39, 165
10.1–24	*208*	10.43	26	11.37–52	165
10.2	111	10.46	62	11.37–54	164
10.2ff.	51	10.52	62	11.38ff.	142(3),
10.3–11	100	11	142		166
10.4	43, 44, 97,	11.1	67(2), 117	11.38–41	137, 165
	111(2)	11.1ff.	68, 104,	11.38–44	139, 165
10.7	20, *192*		118	11.38–52	127
10.9	68	11.2	68, *193*	11.39	13, 130, 153,
10.12	*193*	11.2ff.	110		*192*, *209*(2)
10.14	*193*	11.2–4	67, 68	11.39ff.	11
10.15	60	11.3	69, 100, 173,	11.39–41	39, 134,
10.16	57(2)		*196*		166, *192*
10.17	91	11.4	12, 68, 174,	11.40	40(2), *191*
10.17ff.	65		*188*, *204*	11.41	39, 40(2),
10.17–20	73	11.5–13	69		*192*(2), *209*
10.18	64	11.13	*190*, *196*	11.42	13, 14, 18,
10.20	61, 64, 91	11.14	56, 147		26, 40, 129, 137, *192*
10.20–23	104	11.14ff.	163	11.43	18, 24, 136,
10.21	60, 64(3),	11.14–36	164, 165		140, 153
	67, 69, 147	11.14–13.35	168	11.44	137, 166
10.21–23	69	11.15f.	141,	11.45	129(2),
10.21–24	64		164(2), 165		139(2), 165
10.22	111(2), 117	11.16	147	11.45f.	24, 129
10.23	102	11.17	66	11.46–52	139
10.23f.	62, 72, 93,	11.18	62, 164	11.47f.	165, *206*
	135	11.20	65, *194*(2),	11.49	95, 165
10.24	152, *195*		*206*	11.50f.	165
10.24f.	118	11.23	62, 97	11.52	24, 129
10.25	22, 37, 38,	11.24–26	164	11.53	129, 139(2),
	48, 129, 139, 140	11.27	64, 80, 156,		*205*
10.25ff.	27, *207*		*191*	11.53f.	55, 127,
10.25–29	180	11.27f.	116, 163,		128, 134, 139, 140,
10.25–37	21		164(2)		142(3), 165, 166,
10.26ff.	14	11.28	57, 95, 99,		167, *206*
10.27	18, 21, 22,		116, *200*	11.54	39, 152, 153
	26(2), 66	11.29	114, 147,	12	33, *190*
10.28	21, 22(2), 23		158, 164(2), 165,	12–13	*209*
10.29	*189*		*197*, *209*	12.1	39, 82, 128,

Luke (cont.)		12.35ff.	94, 166	13.27	*209*
	137, 140, 141,	12.35–40	42, 166	13.28f.	48, 167
	142(4), 147(2),	12.35–48	61	13.29	*209*
	165(3), 168	12.37	118	13.31	96, 128, 134,
12.1–34	166	12.39f.	*193*		135, 139, 168,
12.2	165	12.40	*207*		*206*
12.2f.	66, 114, 137,	12.41	94, 102, 154,	13.31–35	168(2)
	142, 165, *207*		166	13.32	97, 135
12.4	*207*	12.41f.	*194*	13.33	95, 97
12.4ff.	139, 142	12.41ff.	*199*	13.34f.	157, 158
12.4–7	58	12.41–46	42	13.35	*209*
12.4–9	85	12.42	*199*	13.48	62
12.4–12	109, 142,	12.42–46	166	13.52	62, 64
	165, 166	12.43	*207*	14.1	34, 37, 38,
12.5	68, *194*	12.45	13, 50		128, 134(2), 139,
12.7	58, *199*	12.46	*193*, *194*		152, 153, 154, *206*
12.8	*209*	12.47	147, *207*	14.1ff.	128
12.8f.	83(2)	12.47f.	57, 166	14.1–6	82
12.9	*200*(2)	12.49f.	166, *209*	14.1–24	34, 153
12.10	15	12.49–53	166	14.1–17.10	163
12.11f.	*205*	12.51–53	166	14.2	106
12.12	166	12.52	167, *203*	14.2–6	134, 137(2),
12.13	80, 147, 165	12.52f.	99		140(2), 152,
12.13f.	31	12.54	166(2)		153, *197*
12.13–21	143, 166, *191*	12.54–56	57	14.2–24	60
12.13–34	31(2), 42	12.54–13.9	93	14.3	24, 129
12.14	*191*	12.56	143, 167	14.7ff.	174
12.15	13, 31, 38,	12.57	*209*	14.7–10	60(2), 61
	41	13.1–3	68	14.7	174
12.16f.	33	13.1–5	*194*	14.7–11	35, 143,
12.16–20	32	13.4	12, *188*		152
12.16–21	166	13.6–9	167	14.11	59, 60, 61(2),
12.18	*191*	13.10	167(2)		155, 162, 174
12.19	50, 69, *191*	13.10ff.	134	14.12	34
12.20	40, *190*, *193*	13.10–13	*197*	14.12ff.	38, 53
12.20f.	46, 48	13.13	62, 106	14.12–14	34(2), 35,
12.21	32, 33(2), 38	13.13ff.	62		60(2)
12.22ff.	*194*	13.14	140	14.13	34, 35, *191*
12.22–32	69	13.15	140	14.13f.	50
12.22–34	32, 143,	13.16	53, 168	14.14	34(4), 35, 48,
	166, *191*	13.17	62, 140		52, *193*
12.28	90, *200*	13.18	167	14.15	35, 48, 63, 80,
12.29	32(2), 36, 42	13.18–21	167		153, *191*
12.29–31	44, 69	13.19	*209*	14.15ff.	65
12.30	32	13.21	141, 142	14.15–24	34(2)
12.31	32(4), *192*	13.22	95, 96, 150,	14.16	*191*
12.31f.	38		167, 168, *194*	14.16ff.	53(2)
12.32	33, 48, 58	13.23	167	14.16–24	60
12.33	33, 49, *191*	13.23–30	93, 168	14.20	36, 99
12.33f.	38	13.24	*208*, *209*	14.21	35(2), 36,
12.34	33, 42, 52,	13.24–30	167		50, *191*
	66	13.26f.	64	14.22	36

14.23	35(2), 36, *192*	15.29f.	154	16.22	46, 48, 50, *190*
14.24	35, *191, 192*	15.30	13, 184	16.23–26	*194*
14.25	36, 96, 153, 158	15.31	62	16.24	18
		15.32	28, 41, 154(2)	16.25	31, 53, 68, 69, *191*
14.25ff.	52, 94, 96	16	5, 33–34, *205*		
14.25–33	38	16.1	28, 30, 154(2), *190*	16.26	48
14.25–35	98, 107, 153(2)	16.1ff.	38, 154	16.29	57, 154
		16.1–9	30	16.29–31	136
14.26	98, 100, 115	16.1–13	28, 51, 143, 155	16.30	154
14.26f.	173			16.31	154, 155
14.26ff.	98	16.1–19.27	148	16.34	181
14.26–32	36	16.4	29, *190*	16.39	62
14.27	97, 99, 100, 174, *197*	16.5	*188*	17	5
		16.6	154	17.1	158
14.28ff.	109	16.7	*188*	17.1f.	101
14.28–32	101	16.8	28, 29, 30, 40, *190, 191*	17.1–4	155, 159
14.33	36(3), 42, 51, 52, 99, 154			17.1–10	158, 162, 163
		16.8ff.	49		
14.34	101	16.8–13	28, 30, *190*	17.1–19	*108*
14.35	57, 154(2)			17.1–19.27	158
15.1	13, 56, 154	16.9	29(2), 30, 33, 46, 48, *190, 191*	17.2	101, 163
15.1f.	63, 136			17.3	142
15.1ff.	*188*	16.9–13	*191*	17.5	162, *200*
15.2	38, 63, 128, 134, 139, 153, 154(2)	16.10	29, 30	17.5f.	90, 91, 113, *200, 207*
		16.10–12	30, 61, *199, 207*		
15.3	62			17.5ff.	162
15.3–7	163	16.11	29, *190*(2)	17.5–10	162
15.5	154	16.11f.	30	17.6	90, 91, 162
15.6	40, 41, 63(2), 154(2)	16.12	29, *190*	17.7ff.	61, 94
		16.13	18, 25, 30, 33, 36, 137, 154, *190*(2), *201*	17.7–10	113, 162
15.7	11, 28, 138, 154(2)			17.9	*189*
				17.10	65, *188*
15.8	154	16.14	8, 38, 52, 57, 66, 129, 130(3), 134, 136, 137(2), 140, 153(2), 154, 155, 166	17.11	95, 96, 150, 158(2), 159, 163, 180, *208*
15.9	40, 41, 63(2), 154(3)				
15.10	28, 63, 154(2)				
15.11ff.	41, 65	16.14f.	127, 162	17.11–19	75
15.13	13, 28, 41	16.14–18	28, 155	17.11–18.8	159, 160
15.17	28, 154	16.14–31	143, 163	17.11–19.27	163
15.18	13, 28, 154	16.15	11, 60(2), 66, 122, 136(2), 137, 142, 143, 153, *189*	17.11–21.38	162
15.18f.	59			17.12ff.	162
15.20	*203*			17.12–19	73, 159
15.21	13, 28, 59, 154	16.16	163	17.13	18
		16.16f.	155(2), 158	17.15	62
15.22f.	63	16.17	155, *208*	17.15ff.	62, 65
15.23	154(2)	16.18	13, 38, 101, 129, 155, 184, *208*	17.16	75
15.23ff.	63			17.16ff.	106
15.24	28, 41, 154	16.19	*191*	17.16–18	*198*
15.25	63, 154(2)	16.19ff.	33, 38, 137	17.17ff.	75
15.25ff.	154			17.18	62, 75, 91, 110, 160
15.29	28	16.19–31	30		

Luke (cont.)
17.19   159, 162, *207*(2)
17.20   134, 135,
      139, 159(5), 160(2),
               162, 163
17.20f.   160, 162
17.20ff.   87, 160
17.20–37   86
17.20–18.8   160
17.21   159, *194*(2)
17.22   160
17.22f.   87
17.22ff.   135, 160
17.22–37   41
17.22–18.8   159
17.24ff.   *193*
17.25   160
17.26ff.   87, *199*
17.27f.   41, 42, 50
17.28   52
17.31f.   41, 101
17.32   41
17.33   41(2), *86*(2),
                   100
17.34   48, *194*
17.34f.   41
18.1   68, 87, *199*
18.1–8   87, 125,
      141, 162, *196*
18.2   58
18.3   87
18.4   58
18.5   87
18.6   *190*
18.7   160
18.7f.   68, 87
18.8   87(3), *193*,
                  207
18.9   37(3), 60,
   122, 136(2), 141,
           162, *206*
18.9f.   38
18.9ff.   11, 67, 155,
                  188
18.9–13   61
18.9–14   162
18.9–34   161
18.10   159
18.10ff.   37, 136
18.11   13, 64, 184
18.11f.   140, 153
18.11ff.   128

18.12   137
18.13   13
18.13f.   68
18.14   59, 60(2),
   61, 110, 136, 143,
           162, *206*
18.15   37, 101, 159,
                161(2)
18.15f.   98, 141
18.15ff.   141
18.16   98
18.16f.   60, 162
18.17   48
18.18   21, 36, 37,
   38, 48, 80, 140, 147,
      161, *191*, 199(2)
18.18ff.   38, 40, 52,
                   53
18.18–30   36, 38
18.20   13, 14, 184
18.22   38(2), 98(2),
               99, 117
18.22–25   49
18.23   37, 52
18.24   38, 40, 98,
                  162
18.24f.   37, 48
18.24–27   37, 38,
                  161
18.24–30   37
18.26   37, 38, 207
18.27   113, *192*
18.28   37, 49, 99,
             102, 161
18.28–30   37,
           38(2), 99
18.29   37, 101, 162,
               192(2)
18.29f.   38
18.30   38, 48, *192*
18.31   96
18.31f.   *204*
18.31ff.   95
18.31–34   38, 88,
   115, 158, 160, 161
18.34f.   87
18.35   97, 158, 161
18.35ff.   106
18.35–43   73, 77,
             82, 159
18.35–19.27 159, 160
18.36   96

18.38f.   18
18.42   159, *207*(2)
18.43   62(3)
19   207
19.1–10   40, 159,
                  163
19.1   158
19.1ff.   *188*
19.2   160
19.5   *206*
19.6f.   63
19.7   134, 160, 207
19.8   13
19.9   159
19.9f.   40, 104, *207*
19.10   163
19.11   95, 147, 150,
   158, 159(3), 160(3),
                  161
19.11f.   162
19.11ff.   46, 160
19.11–27   36, 160
19.12   160
19.12ff.   61
19.14   160
19.14f.   162
19.15   *194*
19.17   94, 160, *199*
19.26   191
19.27   160, 162
19.28   95, 96, 150,
   156, 158, 161(2), 163
19.28–46   157
19.28–21.38   156,
      158, 160, 163
19.30   167
19.37   62(3), 63, 96
19.37f.   88
19.38   162, *209*
19.39   80, 128, 156,
   158, 159, 160, 161,
                  206
19.39f.   63
19.39ff.   138
19.41ff.   169
19.41–44   57, 158
19.42   57
19.45   148
19.45f.   43
19.45–21.4   157
19.45–21.38   128,
      133, 147, 156

19.46	*208*	21.12	100	22.37	12, *188*
19.47	139, 158(2)	21.12f.	*205*	22.39	96, 119, 124
19.47f.	82, 148,	21.12–19	85	22.39–46	119, 124,
	156	21.13	83(2), *198*		125
19.48	56, 148	21.15	85, 95	22.40	68, 119, 174,
20	21	21.16	85, 100(2)		*204*
20.1	139, 148, 158	21.16f.	99	22.40ff.	89, 121
20.1–8	156	21.18	85(2), 86	22.41	67
20.2	156	21.19	85, 86(4), 89	22.41ff.	67, 124,
20.5	72, 90	21.20	62		*204*
20.9	156	21.20ff.	*207*	22.42	69, 113, 121,
20.9–19	156	21.22	157, *194*		*204*
20.15ff.	157	21.24	*207, 208,*	22.43	121
20.17f.	114		*209*	22.43f.	119, 124
20.18	*203*	21.25–36	*193*	22.44	121, 124
20.19	57, 139, 156	21.31	42, 162	22.45	125
20.20	11, 66, 122,	21.34	13, 42, 52,	22.46	68, 119, 174,
	133, 140, 142, 156,		66, 84, 142		*204*
	166, *208*	21.34–36	42, 86,	22.47f.	109
20.20–26	156		157	22.49	*202*
20.21	97	21.36	87	22.49f.	125
20.23	140, 156	21.37	148	22.50	106
20.26	55	21.37f.	148	22.51	119, 121,
20.27	129, *206,*	21.38	56		*197*
	207	21.45	42	22.52	14, 124
20.27–40	157	22.2	57, 139	22.53	88, 121
20.34–38	47(2),	22.3	121	22.54	108
	193	22.3–5	106	22.54–62	108(2)
20.35	47, 48	22.8	103	22.55	*202*
20.36	34, 53, 68,	22.10	97	22.56	97, 108
	157	22.11	*206*	22.57	*199*
20.37	132	22.14	97	22.58	108
20.38	47, *193*	22.18	*193*	22.59	97, 108
20.39	140, *207*	22.19f.	*203*	22.61	109, *200*(2)
20.39f.	140	22.24–27	61	22.62	89
20.40	140	22.25	*203*	22.63ff.	109
20.41–44	156, *207*	22.27	118	22.63–65	120, 121
20.43	94	22.28	96, 97, *200*	22.66	109, 139
20.45	56, *198*	22.29f.	48, *203*	22.67	89, 90
20.45ff.	94	22.31	121, *199*	22.67f.	119
20.45–47	140, 143	22.31f.	124, 125,	22.67–71	119
20.46	142, 153		*204*	22.69	46, 123
20.46f.	11, 140	22.32	67, 87,	23.2	119, *204*
20.47	68, 129, 153,		88(3), 89, 102, 109,	23.2f.	119
	192		*196, 199, 202*	23.3	125
21	175, 177	22.33	97, 108, *202*	23.4	119
21.1–4	43	22.33f.	108(2)	23.5	119, *204*
21.5	68, 148, *198*	22.34	*199, 200*(2)	23.6f.	25
21.5–36	157	22.35f.	51	23.7	*194*
21.8	*199, 201*	22.35ff.	44	23.8	151, *204, 206*
21.9	58, 86	22.35–38	44	23.9	129
21.10f.	*207*	22.36	176, *193*	23.10	139

Luke (cont.)

23.11	120, 121, 206
23.13	37, *208*
23.14	119(3)
23.14f.	107
23.15	119, *204*, 206
23.18	*204*, *208*
23.18f.	175
23.19	14, 124
23.22	107, 119
23.23	25
23.24	181
23.24f.	124
23.25	14, 120, 124
23.26	97, 99, 107, 202
23.27	96, 158, *201*, 208
23.27–31	121
23.28–31	119, 157
23.32	14
23.34	12, 67, 68, 69, 119, 121, 122, 123(2), *188*, 201
23.35	37, 47, 107, 119, 122, *201*(2), 208
23.35–39	121
23.37	47, 78, 107
23.37f.	119
23.39	47, 78, 107
23.39–41	14
23.39–43	107, 119
23.40	58, 107
23.41	107(2), 119(2), 122, 123
23.42	47, 107
23.42f.	121
23.43	47(2), 97, 122
23.44ff.	121
23.45	*204*
23.46	47, 67, 69, 119, 123
23.47	62, 119, 120, 122, *204*
23.48	121, 122, 158, *201*, 208
23.49	88(2), 96
23.50	108, 122
23.50–53	107

24.7	*188*
24.11	88
24.13–32	88
24.15f.	56
24.19	82, 114
24.20	37
24.21	88
24.21	107
24.22	56 (2)
24.25	56, 66, 89(2)
24.25f.	115
24.25–27	*208*
24.26	46, 107, 124, 132
24.29	*192, 206*
24.32	97
24.34	89, 202
24.35	97
24.36ff.	*194*
24.37	57
24.39	132
24.41	56, 62, 63, 88
24.41f.	*106*
24.44ff.	89
24.44–49	88
24.46	132
24.47	181, *188*
24.48	88, *198*
24.52f.	62

John

12.1–8	75
18.3	133
21.1–11	103

Acts

1.1	2
1.11	*193*
1.14	112, 115, 202
1.15	102
1.16ff.	109
1.18	20, *201*
1.21f.	16, 82, 96
1.22	96
1.25	*201*
2.5, 38	111
2.7, 12f.	56
2.11	64
2.14	82, 102

2.17	64
2.17–21	110
2.21	72, *197*
2.22	81
2.22–36	113
2.23	12, *188*
2.32	47
2.33	*195*
2.34	140, 157
2.36	46
2.37	102
2.37f.	*197*
2.38	181, *188*(2)
2.40f.	*197*
2.42ff.	51
2.44	71, *197*
2.44f.	*193*
2.44–47	82
2.47	*189*
3.1ff.	103
3.6	49(2)
3.8–10	83
3.13	*207*
3.14f.	12
3.15	*198*
3.16	65, 73, 74(2), *194*
3.17	37, 158
3.19	*188*(2), *196*
3.21	117
3.22f.	57
3.30f.	46
4.1	128, 131
4.4	*197*
4.7	82
4.9	74
4.10	74, 82
4.12	74
4.13	82, 83, 97
4.13ff.	103
4.16	82
4.19f.	142
4.20	*195*
4.29	83
4.31	83
4.32ff.	51, *193*
4.33	*198*
4.34f.	*193, 194*
4.36f.	51, 107
4.48	*196*
5.1–11	107
5.3	12–13

5.4	178, *193*	9.21	72	13.38f.	*197*
5.9	12–13	9.25f.	94	13.43	113, *197*
5.14	72, *197*(2)	9.27f.	82	13.44	*195*
5.15	*197*	9.32–35	*197*	13.46	82
5.17	128, 131	9.35	*196*	13.48	*196, 197,*
5.29	102	9.36–43	107		*198*
5.30	*207*	9.38	94	13.50	*198*
5.30ff.	47	9.39	107	14.1	*196*
5.31	181, *188*(2)	9.42	72, 82, *196,*	14.3	82(2), 83, 113
5.32	90, *198*		*197*	14.7f.	73
5.34	129, 131	10	111, *197*	14.8–10	73
5.34ff.	128	10.1ff.	180	14.4	73, *197*(2)
5.35	142	10.2	58	14.11ff.	*210*
5.36ff.	175	10.4	11	14.14ff.	15
5.39	132	10.22	58	14.15	60, *194, 196*
6.1ff.	94	10.26	15, 60	14.15–18	179
6.1–6	24	10.31	11	14.17	32
6.3	*200*	10.34f.	111	14.21	*197*
6.5	*197*(2)	10.35	58	14.22	48, *197*(2),
6.7	72	10.36ff.	51		*200*
6.8	82, *197*(2)	10.38	95	14.23	*197*(3), *200*
6.9	*206*	10.39	*198*	14.27	71
6.10	*200*	10.39f.	88	15	14, 111
7.6	190	10.41	*198*	15.3	71
7.10	*200*	10.43	72, 181, *188,*	15.4	133
7.10f.	*198*		*197*(3)	15.5	72, 133
7.22	*200*	10.44	*195*	15.6ff.	110
7.51–53	12	10.45	72, *197*	15.7	*194, 196, 197*(2)
7.52	*198, 206*	10.46	64	15.7–11	*197*
7.55	64	11.5–12	64	15.9	*197*(2)
7.55–60	123	11.17	*196, 197*	15.10	133
7.56	46	11.18	11, 111, *199*	15.11	113, *197*(2)
7.60	12, *201*	11.19	*198*	15.19	*196*
8.1	*198*	11.19ff.	82	15.19–21	133
8.4	102	11.19–21	102	15.20	14, 184
8.4ff.	82	11.21	*196*(2), *197*	15.28	133
8.5ff.	82	11.23	113, *197*	15.29	14
8.6	72, *195*	11.24	*197*(3)	16.1	72, *197*
8.9–24	*198*	11.27ff.	51, 178	16.5	*197*
8.12	*197*	11.29f.	185	16.14f.	107
8.12f.	*196*	12.1ff.	108	16.15	72, *192*
8.13	72	12.14	63	16.17f.	*194*
8.14ff.	103	12.21–23	60	16.31	73, 78, *197*(3),
8.22	*188*	13.1–3	110		*198*
8.32f.	*203*	13.7	*195*	16.34	*197*(2)
8.39	*198*	13.8	72	17.12	*196*
9.1	94	13.12	72, *196*	17.18	47, *206*
9.2	*201*	13.16, 26	58	17.18–21	*210*
9.4f.	*198*	13.24	*201*	17.22	82
9.10	94	13.27	158	17.22ff.	15
9.14	72	13.31	16, 96, *198*	17.22–31	179
9.19	94	13.38	181, *188*	17.28	179

Luke (cont.)					
17.30	11	22.4f.	132	26.20	*196*
17.31	*193*	22.7f.	*198*	26.22	83
17.34	*196*	22.7ff.	132	26.22f.	82
18.8	*196, 197*(2)	22.14	*201*	26.23	*194*
18.25	*200*	22.15	82, *195*	26.26	81, 82
18.25f.	*201*	22.16	72, *188*	27.21	82
18.27	72, 113	22.18	83	27.30f.	78
19.2, 4	*196*	22.19	72, *197*	27.34	*199*
19.6	64	22.20	82, 83	27.35	82
19.8	82	22.22	*201*	28.27	*196*
19.9	*201*	22.25ff.	*206*	28.28	57
19.11f.	*194, 197*	22.41	*201*	26.31	82
19.11–20	73	23	140		
19.17	81	23.1	132	*Romans*	
19.18	72, *197*	23.6	47, 128,	8.15	69
19.18f.	83, *198*		132(2), *206*	10.12f	*197*
19.23	*201*	23.6–9	131	13.1ff.	177
19.23–40	*206*	23.7	132	13.11	177
20.17ff.	105	23.8	129		
20.21	*197*(2)	23.9	128, 132(2),	*I Corinthians*	
20.22	*204*		136, *206*	1.26–29	49
20.23	*198*	23.11	82, 83	3.15	*192*
20.24	113, *194*	23.27	95	5.6–8	141
20.25–28	106	23.29	*204*	7.29ff.	177
20.28	142, *203*	24.5	*204*		
20.31ff.	106	24.15	47, *193*,	*Galatians*	
20.32	113, *197*		*194*	4.6	69
20.33	15	24.24	72, *197*	5.9	141
20.33–35	44	25.22	*204*	5.19–21	9
20.35	53, *193*	25.25	*204*	5.22f.	9
20.36	*201*	26.5	132, *206*		
21.5	*201*	26.5f.	128	*I Thessalonians*	
21.11, 14	*204*	26.6f.	180	4.13ff.	177
21.20, 25	72	26.7ff.	128		
21.26	*192*	26.9–11	132	*I Peter*	
21.29	14	26.11	*198*	2.19f.	124
21.36	*204*	26.14f.	*198*	2.20	*198*
22.3	24, 132, *197, 206*	26.16	82		
22.4	*198, 201*	26.18	71, 181, *188*,	*Revelation*	
			196, 197	14.6	*194*

Subject Index

Transliterated Greek words are printed in italics. Parables are listed under that heading. Multiple references on a page are indicated by a figure in brackets after the page number.

Acts of the Apostles, 6–7
adikia/adikos, 28, 29
adultery, 13
agape/agapan, 8,11,25(2), 198 n.17
agathopoiein, 19
aletheia, 9
aleuangelizesthai, 194 n.23
allotrio, 190 n.8
almsgiving, 33, 38, 39–40, 45
   reward of, 52–4
amemptos, 9
amomos, 9
anaideia, 196, n.35
anomos/anomia, 12
apatheia, 11
apechete, 31
apelabes, 31
aphistantai, 84
apostles, 16, 94, 96,151
   as witnesses, 82, 96
   see also disciples
Apostolic Fathers, 171
asceticism, 50–1
   John the Baptist and, 134
asotos, 41
Augustine of Hippo, 15

beatitudes, 49–50
blepon, 101
Brandon, S.G.F., 175
Brown, Schuyler, 87–8
Bultmann, Rudolf, 1

canticles, 63, 65, 110, 112, 181
centurion at Calvary, 120, 122–3

charete, 21
charis, 20
cleanliness, ritual and inward
   39–40
cleansing of the temple, 43
Clogg, F.B., 1, 8
'communism', 51, 193 n.46
conversion
   faith and, 71–2, 81
Conzelmann, H., 46, 105
Cornelius, 110–111
crowds, the, 96

Dead Sea Scrolls, 1, 63, 171, 190
   n.6
Decalogue, 14–15
Degenhardt, H-J., 51
diakonia, diakonein trapezais, 24
dialogizesthai/dialogismos, 195 n.21
diaskorpizein, 28
Didache, 171
dikaios, 111, 120, 121, 122(3), 140,
   202 n.6
dikaiosyne, 9
diogmos, 84
diokein, 20
disciples, 16, 150–2
   in Acts, 51
   faith of, 88
   mission, 43–4, 101–4; *see also*
      apostles
   response to Jesus, 57
   the seventy, 102
   teaching addressed to, 30, 32,
      37–8, 41–2, 93–5, 163, 179

discipleship, 93–104
  asceticism and, 50–1
  conditions of, 40, 98–102
  cost of, 36, 96, 101, 109
  humility, 61
  poverty and, 49–52
  prayer and, 69–70
  repentance and, 11–12
  sedentary and itinerant, 95–8

edoxazen, 122
ekdikesis, 87
ekpeirazon, 24
eleos/eleein, 9, 18, 22
en meso, 82
enemies, 19–20, 181, 184
enkrateia, 8
entos hymon, 206 n.27
epibalon, 101
epieikeia, 8
epikaleisthai, 72
epiousios, 196 n.34
episteuse/spisteusan, 71
epistophe, 71
epistrepsas, 199 n.47
eschatology, 157
  ethics and, 171
esothe, 74
Essenes, 171
ethetesan, 56
euangelizesthai, 194 n.23
eulabeia, 10
euthetos, 102
euthys, 9

faith, 33, 71–92, 103
  conversion and 71–2, 81
  fear and, 58
  healing and, 72–81
  hearing and, 71–2, 89
  persistence in; see perseverance
  salvation and, 148–9, 162
  witness to, 81–3
family ties, 36, 38, 45, 98–9, 115,
  116
fasting, 195 n.18
fear, 57–9
forgiveness, 76

Gentiles, 25, 111–12, 171, 180
  see also Cornelius
gluttony and drunkenness, 13

'golden rule', 23

hagios, 9
hamartia, 12
healing, 72–81
Herod Antipas, 135 ?
hodos, 97
Holy Spirit, 64, 69
humility, 59–61, 70, 79, 174
hygies, 74
hymeis, 151
hypocrisy, 137, 140, 141–3, 165–6
hypomone, 8, 85

iasthai, 80
inwardness, 65–7, 70

Jeremias, J., 69
Jerusalem Council, 14, 133
Jesus
  death, 117, 119–121
  as example, 116–19
  innocence, 123–4
  as messiah, 117, 119
  response to, 55–70
  temptation of, 117
Jewish-Christian relationships, 20
John, gospel of, 171
Joseph of Arimathea, 3, 107–8
joy, 21, 61–5, 174
judgment, 114–15
  day of, 46
justice, 13, 26, 178

kakourgoi, 14
kalos poiein, 18
kardia, 65
kataromenous, 20
kathos ... homoios, 19
kecharitomene, 202 n.21
kingdom of God, 46–8, 162
krisis, 26
ktesesthe, 86

lawyers, 23–4
  see also scribes
Lord's Prayer, 68, 173
Lot's wife, 41, 101
love, 16–27, 53, 175
  in action, 18–19, 22
  of God and neighbour, 22, 26,
    138

God as model, 19
non-reciprocal, 19
see also agape
Luke, gospel of, 2, 4–6, 170
conformist?, 175–8
contemporary significance,
182–6
distinctiveness?, 178–82
ethics, 8–11
Gentile setting, 20
moralization?, 172–5
sociological background, 171–2
structure, 145–69
lype, 125

makrothymia, 8
Mark, gospel of, 3
Luke and, 5–6, 147–52
martyrdom, 120–1, 123–4, 173–4
Mary, mother of Jesus, 109–110,
112–16
Mary and Martha, 24
Matthew, gospel of, 171
me eisenkes, 196, n.33
misein, 20
misthos, 20

nomikos, 129
nomodidaskalos, 129

obedience, 22, 70, 93, 103, 113
oikia, 192 n.30
Old Testament
background to the gospel, 5,
22, 30, 49, 58, 60, 63, 97, 110,
112, 113, 146
continuity with, 168, 180
Hebrew terms, 9, 10
ontos, 122
opheilein, 12
oral tradition, 3–4

parabasis, 12
parables:, 93–4
battle, 101
blind leading blind, 118
disobedient servant/faithful
stewardship, 42, 57
good Samaritan, 21–4, 138
great feast, 34–5, 60, 99, 153,
154
leaven, 167

mustard seed, 167, 168
Pharisee and tax collector, 59,
60, 67, 141, 143, 162
places at table, 60–1, 152–3, 174
pounds, 46, 159, 160
prodigal son/two brothers,
40–1,59, 65, 154
rich fool, 32, 166
rich man and Lazarus, 30–1, 49,
154
sower, 42, 72, 83–5, 86, 149
tower, 101
two houses, 57
unjust steward, 28–30, 154
vineyard, 156
widow, 87
paradoxa, 59
paraklesin, parakaleitai, 31
paraptoma,12
parresia, 82
Pastoral Epistles, 171
Paul, St
ethical teaching, 8–9, 15
at Miletus, 105–6
peirasmois, 200 n.10
peirasmos, 42, 84, 174
pepisteukotes, 72
persecution, 85–6, 99–100, 123
perseverence, faith and 77–8,
83–9, 87, 91–2, 125
Peter, St
call, 102–4, 108
denial, 108–9
Pharisaism/Pharisees, 12, 38–9,
60–1, 127–44 passim, 152–8
passim, 169
eating with, 60, 96, 128, 134,
152–3
'leaven of', 141–3
perushim, 130
and wealth, 129–30, 137
pisteuein/pistis/pistos, 71, 72, 87,
207 n.6
pleonexia, 8
poiein, 22
polla, 43
ponerous, 19
poor; *see* almsgiving; poverty
poreuesthai/poreuomenoi, 84, 97
porneia, 8, 14
possessions, 19, 99
renunciation of, 51–2

see also wealth
poverty, 48–53, 178, 183, 185
praise, 61–5
prayer, 67–70, 104
  example of Jesus, 117, 118, 119, 124–25
praytes, 8
preparedness, 41–2, 48, 166
priorities, 137
prosechete, 142
'Proto-Luke', 3
Proverbs, book of, 15

'Q', 3, 43(2), 78

rapacity, 13
repentance, 11–12, 57, 60, 93, 109, 136, 138, 155, 163–4, 168–9, 178
resurrection of the dead, 34, 47–8, 132(2), 140, 157
reward as motive, 20, 23, 52
robbery, 14

Sadducees, 131–3, 171
salvation, 148–9
  healing and, 81
Satan, 124–5
Schweitzer, Albert, 1
scribes, 23–4, 128–9, 139–40, 158, 164–5
selt-denial, 100–101
self-righteousness, 136–7, 184
'sense of God', 55–70, 180–1, 186
'sermon on the plain', 16–21, 34, 48, 94(2), 105, 123, 129, 138, 175, 181
sesoken/sesotai, 73, 74, 75–8
sexual morality, 184
Simon Magus, 198 n.28

sin, 12
skandalizein, 84
skirtan/skirtesate, 21, 63
sophronein, 10
soter/soterion, 207 n.6
sothenai, 73
sozein, 74–80 passim
Stephen the martyr, 123
symphyeisai, 84
synoptic gospels, 3

ta idia, 37
tapeinophrosyne, 8, 11
tax-collectors, 13
testimony, 81–3
thambos, 103
thanksgiving, 62, 64–5, 75–6
Theophrastus, 15
theoria, 121
thlipsis, 84
tithing, 26
touto, 22

wealth, 21, 28–54 passim, 137, 143, 155
  generosity, 54, 107; *see also* almsgiving
  Pharisees and, 129–30, 137
  see also possessions
Weiss, Johannes, 1
widow's mites, 43
Wisdom literature, 95, 121–2
Wisdom of ben-Sira, 15
witness, 81–3
wonder, 55–6, 59

Zacchaeus, 40, 51, 180
Zealots, 171, 175–6
Zechariah, 114
zemiotheis, 40